FIGHTING MEN
OF
LONDON

FIGHTING MEN
OF
LONDON
VOICES FROM INSIDE THE ROPES

ALEX DALEY

First published by Pitch Publishing, 2014

Pitch Publishing
A2 Yeoman Gate
Yeoman Way
Durrington
BN13 3QZ
www.pitchpublishing.co.uk

© Alex Daley, 2014

All rights reserved. No part of this book may be reproduced, sold
or utilised in any form or transmitted in any form or by any means,
electronic or mechanical, including photocopying, recording or
by any information storage and retrieval system, without prior
permission in writing from the Publisher.

A CIP catalogue record is available for this book
from the British Library.

ISBN 978 1-90962-665-2

Typesetting and origination by Pitch Publishing
Printed in Gutenberg Press Ltd

ON THE BILL

FOREWORD BY COLIN HART

WHEN I was a lad growing up in east London just after the Second World War, you could watch boxing every night of the week. In those days there were more than 3,000 boxers licensed by the British Boxing Board of Control.

With so many fighters looking for work it wasn't difficult for regular shows to be held at Leyton Baths, West Ham Baths, Hoxton Baths, Poplar Baths, Manor Place Baths, Lime Grove, York Hall, Seymour Hall, Mile End Arena and many other popular venues on both sides of the Thames.

And it wasn't uncommon in the 1940s and 50s for some fighters to perform four or even five times a month. Many were exploited by ruthless promoters who paid them a pittance for risking their lives.

With ringside seats costing just a few shillings many of the youngsters starting out on their careers were paid no more than a fiver a fight. And the facilities they had to put up with in the majority of arenas were spartan to say the least. For example, at the Mile End Arena there wasn't even a tap for the boys to have a wash when they got back to the dressing room.

Alex Daley, who has a deep love of boxing, wrote a riveting book about his grandfather, Nipper Pat Daly, and has followed it up with *Fighting Men of London*. He wanted to put on record what it was like for the fighters of 60 and 70 years ago; men who despite the hardships they faced and the little money they earned always gave London fans value for money.

Daley, because he has such a feel for the sport, has produced seven fascinating interviews that make for a most enjoyable read. Sammy McCarthy, Teddy Lewis, Albert Carroll, Jack Streek, Jock Taylor, Ted Berry and Sid Nathan were a great credit to boxing. The stories they told Alex Daley are not only entertaining, I also found them educational.

Colin Hart was boxing correspondent of The Sun *for 31 years. He left the staff on reaching retirement age 14 years ago and since then has written a regular boxing column for the paper. He broadcasts regularly on TV and radio. He was inducted into the International Boxing Hall of Fame (IBHOF) at Canastota, USA in 2013.*

ACKNOWLEDGEMENTS

FIRST and foremost, I would like to thank the seven ex-boxers who gave freely of their time to share their thoughts, feelings, reminiscences and philosophies with me. Without them there'd be no book.

I am also grateful to Colin Hart for writing his excellent foreword, to my friend Miles Templeton and boxing memorabilia collector Larry Braysher for generously supplying photos, programmes and other material, to *Boxing News* editor Tris Dixon for allowing me access to the *Boxing News* archive and to the London Ex-Boxers Association (in particular Stephen Powell) for making introductions to five of the boxers possible.

I would also like to thank Derek O'Dell, who introduced me to Jack Streek, and Mary Taylor (Nink) for introducing me to her wonderful father, Jock Taylor, through whom this book began. My thanks also to Mary's sister June for providing added insight into Jock's life after boxing.

Photo credits: The photograph of Ted Berry with Reggie, Ronnie and Charlie Kray is reproduced courtesy of John Griffiths with permission from Rita Smith. The photo of Ted Berry and others at the Old Horns pub is courtesy of John Griffiths. The photo of Sid Nathan refereeing a boxing match is copyright Derek Rowe and reproduced with his permission. Other photos are courtesy of the boxers themselves, the *Boxing News* archive, the Larry Braysher collection and the author's collection.

Every effort has been made to contact all copyright holders. The publishers will be glad to rectify in future editions any errors or omissions brought to their attention.

INTRODUCTION

*F*IGHTING *Men of London* started life one autumn day in 2011 – quite by chance. I had just spent an absorbing few hours talking boxing with Jock Taylor, one of Britain's leading light-heavyweights of the late 1940s, after discovering we lived in the same town; and our chat planted the seed of an idea.

After my first book, *Nipper: the Amazing Story of Boxing's Wonderboy*, I wanted to wait a few years before I even thought of starting another, but my conversation with Jock made me rethink my plans, as a realisation dawned on me...

British boxers of the 1940s and 50s with strong recollections of their fighting days were still around, but the details of their career and life experiences would, before long, be lost for ever. The job of recording their recollections could not wait five or ten years. If I wanted to preserve some of their stories (and I *did*), I needed to act now.

Thus began my quest to track down pro boxers of the 40s and 50s, with Jock as my first subject. Six other interviewees with interesting stories to tell were enlisted, the common theme being their connection to London boxing.

But why London? And why the men of the 40s and 50s?

Well, London in those days was the epicentre of British boxing. Innumerable top fighters came from other parts of the country, but London was where they flocked to get ahead, for it housed the nation's leading managers, promoters and gyms. The places to get noticed and the people who pulled the strings were London-based on the whole.

The 1940s and 50s was a fantastic time to be a British boxer or boxing fan, and London was about the best place to experience this special era. Britain's working classes have long forgotten the love affair they had with boxing, both on the paid and unpaid side of the sport.

Yes, London – and Britain – were boxing-mad, and packed-out shows gave fight addicts their fix in a variety of permutations, ranging from the smoke-filled small hall (the grass roots of boxing) to the grandiose outdoor stadium. On almost any given night boxing took place somewhere, and there were then thousands of Brits trading leather for money (though they may have worked as labourers or market porters during the day).

The status of the British professional boxer then was much higher than it is now. Like today's Premier League footballers, British champion boxers were household names and schoolboy idols. And there were just eight British weight classes then (there are now 15), which made competition in each division all the more intense.

Globally, aside from disputes over vacated titles, boxing in the 40s and 50s had only one champion at each weight – that's just eight universally recognised world champions. By contrast, today world boxing has 17 weights with four bona fide titles up for grabs at each one. This means four men at 17 weights can all share the glory of being champions of the world; potentially that's 68 concurrent world champions, instead of eight. Given these facts, it's difficult to dispute that boxing titles were more meaningful years ago.

The stories in this book track the development of British boxing on several levels. The 1930s saw the sport reach its peak in popularity, both in the number of shows and the number of active pro fighters. There was an inevitable downturn during the Second World War when many boxers were called up. But a post-war boom brought the number of shows and active pros close to pre-war levels. Then, with little warning, a 33 per cent live entertainment tax introduced by the Tory government of 1952 put countless small-time promoters out of business – a blow from which British boxing never fully recovered.

Then there were social and technological changes. The poor and the hungry have always flourished in professional rings. In pre-war London this meant a generation of young Jewish men, but in the late 40s and 50s they were replaced by fighters from the Caribbean and West Africa, who arrived in Britain in growing numbers. The rise of TV and cinema as rivals to live entertainment, improvements in living standards and eventually the disappearance of boxing from schools would finish the fight game as a sport of the British masses. Afterwards the country's once thriving fight industry lived on, but on a smaller scale and with narrower appeal.

I hope this information will set the scene for the boxing milieu of the men in this book. Before I finish I will briefly outline my intentions and methodology in writing it.

My aim was to understand what led the fighting men of this golden era to lace on gloves for a living. I wanted to find out what the fight game was really like then, to know about their backgrounds – where they came from, where their journeys in life had taken them – and to learn their thoughts, feelings and philosophies on boxing and life.

Theirs was a London far removed from the modern metropolis; a London of ration books, pea-soup fog and old-fashioned values; a site of much adversity where community spirit pulled people through. It was a simpler yet tougher time and the prize ring offered a route out of poverty. For countless working-class lads with a flair for fighting it was well worth the risks of this uncertain and unforgiving trade.

Memories are unique by their very nature, and the men in this book recall their lives and ring careers in different ways. Some will remember scant detail of their fights but will recall sparring sessions with big-name fighters or the atmosphere of a gym or fight hall vividly. Others will recall near every blow of a key fight but the venues they fought at meant little to them and the aesthetics of an arena, the sounds of its crowds and such ephemeral detail, have long faded from memory. For this reason each piece is structured around that boxer's recollections and seeks to tell his story from the angle he remembers it.

I have endeavoured, where possible, to capture the idiosyncrasies of each man's speech, so not every quoted sentence follows the rules of grammar. In the interests of clarity, I have made small edits to some of the dialogue, but only where necessary.

Ultimately I hope this book will – to some degree – preserve an aspect of London culture and boxing history that is not well known or understood today.

Alex Daley
March 2014

Weight Classes in British Professional Boxing Pre-1967

Flyweight	8st and under
Bantamweight	8st 6lb and under
Featherweight	9st and under
Lightweight	9st 9lb and under
Welterweight	10st 7lb and under
Middleweight	11st 6lb and under
Cruiserweight (or light-heavyweight)	12st 7lb and under
Heavyweight	Unlimited

SID NATHAN
(ALDGATE)
1939–40

IT is 23 March 1939 and we are at the Prince of Wales Baths in London's Kentish Town. People file in through the arched doorways of this ornate redbrick and terracotta edifice and make their way into the main hall. At other times their visit would entail a wash, for these are the days when many London homes lack bathrooms. Tonight, though, is fight night.

Wooden boards have been laid across the water and the usually damp, steamy atmosphere has been replaced by the aroma of tobacco smoke, resin and embrocation. Fight fans sit on chairs around a temporary ring while others lean over balconies for a bird's-eye view. Dusk has fallen and chandeliers light up the room. People chatter loudly, bookmakers yell odds and pocket money, while journalists leaf through notebooks and discuss the imminent fights.

Madison Square Garden this is not, but in rings like this one champions are made.

Out of sight and away from the hubbub, 16-year-old flyweight Sid Nathan sits tentatively in a shabby dressing room, waiting to be called out for his first professional contest. Around him are managers, peripheral characters and other boxers, including the man he is about to fight, Mike Constantino of Soho.

'Are we on yet, Alf?' Sid asks his manager.

'Not long now, son,' he replies.

Naturally, Sid is a little nervous but this tension serves to sharpen his senses and makes him more eager to show the crowd how well he can box.

He would not be sitting here, contemplating the task before him, if his stablemate Billy Nolan of Stepney had not withdrawn from this very contest with injured ribs. Nor would he be travelling the scheduled distance of eight rounds for the first time in his life.

Suddenly the door swings open and a whip (ring usher) marches in and points at Sid and his opponent. 'You're up next, boys,' he says. 'Give us a good scrap!'

% % %

Fast-forward 73 years to 2012 and I have the privilege of reliving this moment with Sid, who is now one of Britain's last surviving pre-war pro boxers. He has also been an internationally renowned referee and is still an avid follower of boxing. I interview him on three occasions at his home in Boreham Wood where sadly, due to the death of his wife a few years ago, he now lives alone.

Arriving at his flat, I discover that boxing is still a big part of his life. He has stacks of DVDs of fights that he refereed and around his sitting room are mementos of his time as a third man, as well as photos of himself with famous fighters such as Herol Graham and David Haye. On my second visit, just after the Haye–Chisora press conference fiasco in Germany, I notice the photo of Haye has been moved behind some others. 'I've moved it there until he redeems himself,' Sid says half-seriously. 'But I don't know how he's gonna redeem himself after that disgraceful shemozzle!'

Sid keenly follows current boxing but is saddened by the lack of press coverage the sport receives today. Our third interview is the day after Tyson Fury's clash with Martin Rogan, and although Sid doesn't feel Fury has what it takes to reach the top, he is still eager to know the result, which to his annoyance is missing from his morning paper. He is probably the only follower of Haye and Fury who saw such old-time stars as Ted Kid Lewis, Nel Tarleton, Dick Corbett, Dave Crowley, Harry Mizler and Eric Boon box, and once shared a fight bill with Jack Kid Berg.

Today former fighters approach Sid and proudly remind him that he refereed one of their fights. He is recognised regularly as 'That boxing ref who used to be on the telly' and is delighted when people tell him he looks the same as he did 30 years ago – and they're right. There is a timeless quality to Sid. Admittedly, while he was refereeing, his horn-rimmed glasses and thinning hair made him look slightly older than his years. But now, in his 90s, the reverse is certainly true. His mental and physical vitality are nothing short of amazing.

Though short and slim in stature, Sid oozes confidence and personality. He is charming, quick-witted, enthusiastic and ever eager to ensure a guest of his is made to feel welcome. The phrase old-fashioned gentleman was coined for men like Sid.

His voice is strong and clear and his speech is precise and carefully modulated – you have to listen closely to detect his East End roots. But he is an East End man without question, and his boyhood there along with his boxing experiences have made him the astute and resilient person he is today.

A Jewish Tradition

To understand Sid's early life and his entry into professional boxing, we must first understand the milieu in which he lived and how he got there. Today there are few Jewish boxers in the world, let alone in England. But in the first half of the 20th century England (and London particularly) had an abundance of Jewish fighters, promoters, managers and trainers. Boxing was as important to Jewish people as Jewish people were to boxing.

There were 26 Jewish world champions between 1910 and 1940, and many of them – such as Benny Leonard, Barney Ross and Max Baer – were global stars. London had two Jewish world champions of its own in Ted Kid Lewis and Jack Kid Berg, plus a host of British champions of Jewish identity. Men such as Young Joseph, Mike Honeyman and Matt Wells before the Great War, were succeeded by 20s and 30s champions such as Jack Bloomfield, Harry Mason, Johnny Brown, Al Foreman and Harry Mizler. Some wore the Star of David on their shorts or dressing gowns, which as well as presenting a statement of faith, secured the loyalties of thousands of Jewish fight fans.

The main reason for such a strong Jewish presence in boxing is clear. For young men with few means of elevating themselves it was a possible route to wealth, fame and a better life; a way to escape the poverty that was endemic to the East End at that time and the hardship that had befallen their parents and grandparents.

Sid Nathan's grandparents, like the forebears of many other Anglo-Jewish boxers, were part of a late 19th-century and early 20th-century wave of immigration. Between 1880 and 1914 nearly three million Jews fled persecution and the threat of violence from the pogroms (anti-Jewish riots) in Eastern Europe. Most went to America, but 150,000 sailed to Britain. Upon arrival many headed for London's East End, which already had established Jewish communities and was a place they could worship in the accustomed manner, buy kosher food and converse in languages they understood. But living conditions were crowded and squalid and job opportunities limited, and what's more the existing Jewish fraternity was not wholly welcoming to the new arrivals.

Early on in my first interview with Sid, I ask him about his forebears, but I discover that the details of his ancestors' arrival in London have been lost with the passage of time. He tells me that both his parents were born in England and that his grandparents emigrated there from either Russia or Poland, but that is all he knows of the subject. With this information, I trawl through some archival records and find, to my delight, that I am able to fill in some of the blanks.

The original family name was Natalski (later spelt Natalsky) and Sid's paternal grandfather, Nathan Natalski, a boot-maker by trade, arrived in London from Russia with his wife, Leah (also known as Rachel), and their young daughter Esther some time between 1879 and 1882. By 1891 Sid's grandparents were living at 4 New Church Street in Bethnal Green and had four further children to look after. The youngest was Sid's father, Jacob (soon to be changed to the more English-sounding Jack), who was born on 2 May that year.

Within a decade, two more children had been born but sadly Nathan Natalski died in 1900, aged 42, leaving his widow, Leah, and their eldest daughters as breadwinners. By 1901 the family had moved to 184 Old Montague Street in Whitechapel and Leah's son-in-law Joe Cohen – a boot-maker like Leah's late husband – was living with the family, most probably to augment the household income and save them the hardship and indignity of the workhouse.

But Sid's father, Jack, was soon old enough to help financially and found work as a machinist in one of the East End's many clothing factories. Aptly dubbed 'sweatshops', these were cramped, dingy places where the workers toiled for long hours at appallingly low pay. At the time of the 1911 census, 20-year-old Jack was working in such a place while living with his family at 12 Lily House in Brick Lane. His gruelling day job, however, would probably have prepared him well for another tough vocation that, by then, was helping him earn a few extra 'bob'.

Alongside his factory work, Jack was boxing professionally under the nom de plume of Jack Arbour. 'He used the name Arbour so that his mother didn't know that he was boxing as a professional. He chose Arbour because around that time he lived in Arbour Square, in the East End, which was very well known,' Sid tells me.

The details of Jack's ring career are difficult to piece together all these years later, especially given he may have used multiple pseudonyms. Jack Arbour (Bethnal Green) can be credited with numerous bouts between 1908 and 1911, while a certain Jack Nathan (Aldgate), who was fighting at the same time, seems highly likely to be the same man.

One certainty is that Jack had his most memorable fight at the Judean Club in Princes Square (off Cable Street) on 27 August

1911. Part boxing hall, part gymnasium, part social club, the Judean was a nursery for Jewish boxing talent until it was destroyed by Zeppelin bombs during the First World War. Jack's opponent that day was a lad named Gershon Mendeloff, who was boxing under the pseudonym Kid Lewis. Ted Kid Lewis, as he was later widely known, was destined to win the world welterweight crown and make history as one of Britain's greatest ever fighters. But in 1911 he was just an up-and-coming preliminary boy.

The official verdict shows he beat Jack Arbour on a third-round disqualification, but Sid heard a different story of the fight from his father. 'My father told me that he put Lewis down with a perfect body punch,' Sid recalls. 'He said, "That punch was a perfect punch to the solar plexus, put him down, and they disqualified me." Kid Lewis pleaded for a foul and got away with it, and my father was disqualified.' There were no hard feelings between Lewis and Sid's father, however, whatever the merit of the decision, as the pair were pals.

'I can't tell you how many fights my father had because he never divulged how many,' says Sid, 'but he always said to me, "You were a better boxer than I ever was", which I felt was a great compliment for a father to pay his son.'

An Aldgate Upbringing

In 1915 Jack Natalski (or Jack Nathan as he was now widely known) married Golda Silver in the City of London. Their first child, Louis, was born in 1919, and Sid (whose birth name was Samuel) followed on 1 September 1922.

The family lived in Buckle Street, off Leman Street, in Aldgate, a stone's throw from the well-known Gardiner's Corner, a junction dubbed 'the gateway of the East End' for it connects the five main thoroughfares of east London. In Sid's day it was a bustling working-class area and a hub of East End life, packed with pubs, coffee stands, all-night cafes and, of course, jellied eel stalls.

'Tubby Isaacs ran the jellied eel stall at the corner of Goldstone Street,' remembers Sid, referring to one of the East End's best-known characters of those days. 'Everybody knew of Tubby Isaacs.'

Sid explains to me that jellied eels are not kosher and therefore should not be eaten by those who observe Jewish dietary laws. But ironically Tubby Isaacs's stall was pitched in front of the Beth Din, the office that handles the affairs of kosher foods, and directly beneath a large sign bearing its name. 'Tubby Isaac's stall is under the Beth Din' thus became a local Jewish joke uttered tongue in cheek.

Initially Sid attended Buckle Street Infant School and then, when he reached the requisite age, the Jewish Free School on Bell Lane. 'There were a couple of masters there who were very tough guys as far as I was concerned. They were a little bit brutal in their work. I won't explain any more,' says Sid, ominously. 'They were hard taskmasters.'

But apart from some tough schooling, Sid has fond memories of his childhood. 'From what I remember of it, before that dirty dog Mosely came along – and he started making speeches on different street corners to try to turn people's minds to race hatred – before that time, I thought the East End was a lovely place to live,' he says poignantly, referring of course to the fascist Oswald Mosely. 'Everybody in my street knew each other – they were a mixed people, Jewish and non-Jewish – and when a funeral took place *everybody* came out for the funeral.

'I was called in regularly to a friend's house, who was council no doubt, but he was non-Jewish, he was a gentile – Johnny Herring. I was taken in regularly by the Herring family and supplied with a slice of bread with drippings spread on it, which was of course not kosher and therefore I wasn't supposed to have it. But I knew no different and I appreciated what I was given.

'It was a wonderful place to be,' he adds, 'because we knew no different. We only knew of poverty. We didn't know anything about having money given to you free, *ad lib*, like the government is giving now.'

Boxing Barmy

It is difficult to convey to the modern reader just how popular boxing was in Britain in the 1920s and 30s, for today it is a fringe sport by comparison. Back then regular fight shows were held all over the country and the boxers often fought several times a month, some even several times a week. London was the hub of this boxing industry and a place to where aspiring boxers flocked in their droves. Fight shows could be seen across the city, with some venues putting on two or three bills a week.

Pro boxing had a following akin to professional football today and the fighters, in terms of status though not salary, were the Premier League footballers of their day. Every London district had its own ring idols, their successes and reverses fervently cheered and bewailed by their devotees. Their exploits provided reams of newspaper fodder and every national paper had its own dedicated boxing columnist.

As chance would have it, just two streets away from Sid's Buckle Street home stood Premierland (pronounced 'Pree-mier-land'), one of Britain's leading fight halls of the 1920s. I ask Sid whether he went to boxing shows with his father during this exciting period. 'I was taken to the odd one or two,' he says, 'but I wasn't taken much. Maybe he thought it wasn't the atmosphere for a young boy to be in.

'The only one I *can* remember,' he adds, 'is when he took me to see Kid Lewis at the Premierland, and I saw him box Joe Rolfe, who was quite a well-known boxer in those days. I remember seeing Lewis defeat Joe Rolfe and, at ringside where we were, Kid Lewis leaned over the ropes, took me under the armpits – I was only a little toddler – and picked me up to show me off. I don't know *why*, but I suppose it was because my father was a friend of his. As I got older I realised how important that was, that he did that for me.'

As a boy Sid's father showed him some of the rudiments of boxing, particularly how to deliver a decent left lead. But his fistic education really began at age nine or ten, when he joined the Jewish Lads' Brigade, a youth organisation similar in purpose to the Boys' Brigade, with an emphasis on morality and physical fitness.

'I had a uniform, a haversack, a belt and a hat to wear, like one of those hats that they wore in the air force on the side of the head,'

Sid recalls. 'And I belonged to Underwood Street Company. We all had different branches, but everybody assembled at Camperdown House.'

Camperdown House, in Aldgate's quaintly named Half Moon Passage, was the organisation's headquarters. There the lads had the use of a large assembly hall, two smaller halls, two gyms, a common room, games and sitting rooms and several bathrooms. The last of these were especially welcomed by East End youngsters, most of whom did not have bathrooms at home. Activities on offer included gymnastics, physical training, handball, badminton, a social union, dances, occasional amateur concerts and, of course, boxing.

The boxing instructor was a Sergeant-Major Butterwasser. 'Quite a peculiar name,' says Sid with a smile, 'and later on he changed his name to Butterworth. But he used to take us in the boxing class and he made it that interesting that I wanted to learn more.'

The Camperdown House boxing classes produced several future professionals – men such as European lightweight champion Al Phillips, Harry Lazar and the brothers Johnny and Alec Lyons. With its regimented structure and emphasis on clean living, the Jewish Lads' Brigade was an ideal environment for a budding boxer. Between the ages of ten and 15, Sid did plenty of sparring there, mainly against older boys, but he was not rushed in to actual bouts.

'I never had an amateur career as such,' he explains. 'I was only asked to box on one show, and that took place in the main hall at Camperdown House, and they said that I would be boxing Harry Lazar. Well I knew of Harry Lazar and didn't like him very much, because he was, I suppose, that popular but he was a bit cocky with it. And they put me in against him, untrained as I was, even though I had been doing a bit of sparring in the main hall.

'But there was an audience and there were three judges appointed. It went the full three rounds and I got the verdict. I believe I got it because – apart from our boxing ability, because we both had boxing ability – I had him in trouble at one time, he leaned over the ropes and I refused to punch at that point. I stepped back and waited for him to stand up and box again.'

Harry Lazar (pronounced Lazer), a future star professional, was already causing a stir as an amateur, so his loss to the unknown Sid Nathan was quite an upset. Some time later, after Lazar had turned professional, he invited Sid to spar with him at the gymnasium where he trained.

'I think the idea was to get me to go in that ring and box my head off,' Sid chuckles. 'And he taught me what good boxing was all about! We had three rounds of boxing but I feel that, if there'd been anybody to judge it, he would have got the verdict. So he more or less gained revenge for his defeat in the amateurs. But his manager liked the fact that I was able to take a punch, give a punch, make a few moves that made Harry miss, and with that he asked me if I would like to box as a pro.'

The manager was Alf Jacobs, a bookmaker who had turned to boxing management and possessed an impressive stable of fighters. 'Although I felt that I hadn't had the experience,' Sid says, 'he nevertheless went to see my dad and said to my dad that I'd be good as a professional. Initially my parents disagreed totally with me boxing as a professional, but eventually they succumbed and I signed a contract for five years.'

Sid began to train at Jacobs's gym, a ramshackle place above a disused stable in Mile End, which adjoined the La Boheme dance hall. The trainer and masseur was a man named Fred Ordway. 'A good old boy was Fred. A very nice man, but he was a nervous type of man,' says Sid. 'Always had a cigarette sticking out the corner of his mouth. When I had my training sessions he'd massage me from head to foot. He'd even massage my toes!'

After leaving school at the standard age of 14, Sid had initially worked as a messenger boy at the BBC, a job he had acquired through a cousin who worked for the broadcaster as a typist. 'It was amazing that I was able to work there,' he declares, 'because it wasn't known for Jewish people to work at the BBC. "*You worked at the BBC!*" It was unusual. I sometimes wish I'd stayed there. It would have been a job for life.'

But he left the BBC for a position at the law firm H.H. Wells & Sons, whose offices were at 17 Paternoster Row, hard by St Paul's Cathedral, in the heart of the City. 'I was doing County Court work,' he says. 'I was taking cases that they gave me, which were for people who owed money for goods received, and I used to have to go to court and issue a summons against them. It was quite an important role.'

As incongruous as a role in a solicitors' office may seem next to a prize-fighting career, Sid managed to combine them. After finishing work at 5.30pm each day he boarded a bus bound for Mile End, sweated and swapped blows for a couple of hours at Alf Jacobs's gym, then headed home for supper and bed in readiness for another day's legal work.

'I trained every day,' says Sid, 'I don't remember ever leaving a day out. I spent a lot of time keeping fit. That's how I got my six-pack in that photograph,' he laughs, nodding towards a photo resting on his mantelpiece of his younger self in a fighting stance, taken in 1939. 'For an eight-stone-three boy, I had a good six-pack.'

Stablemates

Despite Sid's inexperience, training and sparring with Alf Jacobs's other fighters soon sharpened his boxing skills and helped prepare him for his first professional fight. He has fond and lucid memories of his stable mates, some of whom were among the best men in the country at their respective weights. His eyes twinkle and he smiles warmly as he turns his mind back 73 years and tells me about them.

*Les Johnson (Finsbury Park)

'I learnt a lot from Les Johnson,' he says. 'I used to spar with him regularly, and we had some real tussles between us. He once hit me with a punch and I thought the world had come to an end! I could feel myself sway forward and I could feel him put his hands up against me to stop me from falling. He said to me, "You all right, Sid?" I said, "I'm all right now. Now you've stopped me falling!"

Les Johnson was a cousin of British champions Dick and Harry Corbett, but paradoxically as a child he hated fighting and at all costs avoided physical confrontation. After leaving school he boxed as an amateur at the Mildmay Club in Newington Green but only did so half-heartedly and with no ambitions of turning pro.

That all changed quite by chance when his sister went to a dance and met the Southern Area flyweight champion Dave Keller, pride of Billingsgate, who invited Les to spar with him. Les took up the offer and despite taking a pasting from Keller, he did sufficiently well to prompt Alf Jacobs (who managed Keller at the time) to sign him as a professional.

Les decided his birth name, Leslie John Spence, did not befit a prize fighter, so after a period of training he turned pro under the nom de plume of Les Johnson. Born in Hoxton on Boxing Day 1911, he made his pro debut at 26, an age by which, in those days, many fighters were finished.

Boxing out of Finsbury Park, he stopped the talented Pat Warburton twice, drew with the world-class Joe Curran and on 27 November 1938 KO'd his sister's old dancing partner Dave Keller, who was still Southern Area flyweight champion, in a non-title affair. Les later challenged unsuccessfully for the Southern Area bantamweight title and in 1949, at the age of 37, caused a sensation by beating the number three flyweight contender Dickie O'Sullivan (a great uncle of the snooker player Ronnie O'Sullivan).

'He was a nice bloke,' says Sid of Les Johnson. 'He was about 28 at the time; a bit of a late starter. He was only a little fella; he was even shorter than me – and I'm not tall. But sparring with him did me a lot of good and he was very good to me.'

*Al Marson (Canning Town)

'I went in the ring with Al Marson just to speed around him,' recalls Sid, 'make him move more quickly. It was at the manager's request. Make like I'm boxing but making sure that we didn't exchange punches. Otherwise I wouldn't have lasted more than half a minute because he could have knocked me out with one punch. But he was a good boxer – had a very good left hand. Nice tall guy – nice fella. Marson rarely ever lost a fight.'

Al Marson, like Les Johnson, was a latecomer to professional boxing. He had taken up amateur boxing after struggling against a smaller boy in a schoolyard fight and joined the Benjamin Franklin Club where the coach was the experienced Harry Brooks. Al won a London Federation of Boys' Clubs' 10st title and as a senior was a member of Limehouse and Poplar ABC. Then he lost interest in boxing and instead started weightlifting to develop his physique. But the allure of the ring proved irresistible.

He would watch brothers Bill and Tommy Partridge sparring in the gym, observing that Tommy always struggled against Bill, who was a decent pro heavyweight. So Al offered to spar with Bill instead and as their workouts became a regular fixture, Al's gym-mates urged him to turn professional. He signed a contract with Alf Jacobs and had his first paid fight in 1938. His progress was steady and in the 1940s he battled his way up the rankings to become number one light-heavyweight contender to champion Freddie Mills (more on Al Marson in the section of this book on Jock Taylor of Sidcup).

*Harry Lazar (Aldgate)

'I kept away from him,' Sid says of Harry Lazar. 'I never really, honestly, liked him at all, because he was a bit of a flash guy and I wasn't like that. But he was brilliant. He *was brilliant*. I used to admire him. I used to watch him and say, "I wish I could box like him."

'He was brilliant at what he did – that I will always remember. And whenever I talk to anybody about boxing, *I* talk about Harry Lazar as being a good, good fighter and a brilliant boxer.

'He was improving so much that he was beating everybody that came his way, and he was getting heavier as well, so there was never any chance of us boxing each other again. But I knew Lazar was gonna lose sometime because he just wouldn't train. I saw him lose contests that normally, if he'd have been trained and fit, he'd have made a mess of whoever it was.'

Harry Lazar (real name Lazarus) was born five days after Sid on 6 September 1922, into a poor and crowded Aldgate household that eventually comprised eight boys and five girls. His grandfather

Harry Solomons was a bare-knuckle champion of England and his father was a bookmaker, so entry into the fight game was a natural move for Harry.

Boxing almost exclusively at the Devonshire Club and the Mile End Arena, Lazar won his first 26 pro fights. In his prime a lightweight, then later, when slightly over the hill, a welterweight, he won 84, lost 25 and drew six of 115 fights. In a 12-year career he beat champions and leading men such as Johnny McGrory, Dave Crowley (twice), Harry Mizler, Tommy Hyams, Dave Finn and Henry Hall but never fought for a title.

His kid brother Lew Lazar, though less gifted than Harry, was perhaps more committed, winning the Southern Area middleweight title and challenging for British and European crowns. Another Lazar brother, Joe, earned a formidable reputation as an unlicensed bare-knuckle fighter, but was unable to get a licence to box legitimately due to his prison record. While yet another brother, Mark Lazarus, found fame as a professional footballer.

'I remember him fighting Harry Kid Silver,' says Sid enthusiastically as he recalls one of his keenest memories of Harry Lazar in the ring. 'Lazar beat him on points: wonderful, wonderful contest. The whole East End was alert to Lazar boxing Harry Kid Silver. That's how well known they were, and that's how boxing was recognised, in those days, as a sport.'

Harry Lazar, who dazzled British fight fans but failed to reach the heights his exceptional talent should have taken him to, died in 1985.

Pro Debut

Sid's first paid fight arrived unexpectedly when Alf Jacobs entered him as a substitute in place of Billy Nolan (Stepney), who had withdrawn from a contest with injured ribs. It was a tall order for a lad with only one amateur fight to his name, especially since the scheduled distance was eight rounds. But there was no mollycoddling of debutants in those days. The venue, as stated in this story's opening, was Kentish Town's Prince of Wales Baths. The date: 23 March 1939.

'My opponent was Mike Constantino of Soho,' remembers Sid, 'and he'd had a lot of fights. He wasn't any good, but he was a trial horse. If you got past him you could be sure the manager would accept you. If you didn't get past him, no one would want you.

'Harry Lazar had knocked him out in two rounds. I saw it myself. That was at the Mile End Arena, and when it came for me to box Mike Constantino in my first fight, I thought, "I know, if I can put one on his chin, I'll knock him out like Lazar did." But he was wily; he knew the game, and I couldn't knock him out, and I didn't even know how to knock a man out.

'But I out-boxed him, took him the full distance and won the verdict on points. And they said it was a brilliant fight. The MC announced to the whole audience – and it was a full house – that this was my first professional contest, and the reception I received was absolutely outstanding.'

Thrilled by his victory and the rapturous reception, Sid was even more delighted when he leafed through the sports pages of the next day's papers and read several glowing reviews. 'The brightest spot of the evening,' reported *The Mid-Day Standard*, 'was the debut of Sid Nathan, a 16-year-old youth taking part in his first professional contest. He displayed great boxing ability and fine generalship to out-point a stronger and hard-hitting opponent. His performance stamped him as a boxer of definite promise.'

Boxing (forerunner of *Boxing News*) meanwhile called Sid's fight with Constantino 'the pièce de résistance of the evening. Nathan showed most promising form, and his neat footwork and good left were generally too much for the more rugged style of Constantino.'

A prominent presence at boxing halls in those days were the bookmakers and gamblers who crowded round the ringside, brazenly ignoring signs that warned 'Betting Strictly Prohibited'. I ask Sid what he remembers of these characters, whether he was conscious, while boxing, of the bets being placed outside the ring, and whether they featured in his debut.

'You could hear what was going on ringside,' he tells me. 'Especially as things got whipped up a bit, among the fighters, then you would hear it even more because they would bang on ringside.

There were no satchels or anything like that, such as they'd have with stands at the greyhounds or horse racing. It was just a question of taking money by hand, remembering who it was they'd betted with, and whatever money they got, they stashed in their pockets.

'But I could hear them say, "I'll bet two to one" or "I'll bet five to two" or whatever. I don't know how they betted in my first fight when I went in as a substitute. I may well have been betted against – probably I was. If you came in as a substitute they didn't reckon you had much chance.'

So Sid's emphatic debut win would have surprised the betting boys. And they were reacquainted with him when he won his next three fights in quick succession, proving he could hit when he knocked out Richmond's Al Ross in two rounds and forced Poplar's Ginger Softley (a brother of the well-known lightweight Johnny Softley) to retire at the end of the first. But his next opponent, Len Garrett (Blackfriars), proved a tougher proposition. 'I remember distinctly, he was a *hard* boy, a good fighter,' says Sid, who ground out a points win over six tough rounds. 'When we came out of the ring he said to me, "Sid, how many fights have you had?" I said, "This was my fourth fight." "Hmm," he said, "you're *good*. You're very good." I thanked him very much and said thanks for a good bout, and we left it at that. I never met him again.'

The Devonshire Club

Sid's second fight, versus Al Ross, was at a venue that holds a special place in British ring history, and one that few people alive today can honestly say they saw first-hand.

The Devonshire Sporting Club – more commonly called the Devonshire Club, the Devonshire or simply the Dev – was originally dreamt up by Joe Morris, a manager of such fistic stars as Teddy Baldock and Dick Corbett. Morris had the chance to buy the lease of an old church in Devonshire Street, Hackney, which he proposed to convert into a dance hall and boxing arena. He recruited a syndicate of three others into his scheme, including Ridley Road fishmonger Jack Solomons, a man destined to make an indelible mark as a boxing promoter.

The venue opened its doors to boxing on 21 October 1934 but initially its shows were unsuccessful. There was strong competition from other halls, such as the Whitechapel Pavilion and the Blackfriars Ring, and it was difficult to lure fans away from these tried and tested fight centres. Doubtful of the Devonshire Club's future, Joe Morris and the other two partners sold their shares to Solomons, whose gut instinct told him it was only a matter of time before the Dev became a paying proposition.

His hunch proved accurate and soon the Devonshire's weekly Friday night and Sunday morning boxing shows were sell-outs. Fans loved the atmosphere of a hall in which those sat on the balcony could practically shake hands with the boxers in the ring. The Dev held only 1,500 and the entrance fees were so low that even the fighters topping the bills received relatively paltry purses. But it proved a cradle for up-and-coming talent and men of the renown of Eric Boon, Dick Corbett, Al Phillips, Harry Lazar, Alby Day, Tiny Bostock and Harry Kid Silver boxed there. The Devonshire quickly became east London's leading small-hall venue.

With the threat of bombing looming and with more and more boxers being called up to serve, many London fight halls closed during the Second World War, but the Devonshire continued its regular shows. By then, due to a fall-out with the British Boxing Board of Control (BBB of C), Solomons was promoting without a licence, and some of the boxers, seconds, managers and referees who worked for him were suspended for continuing to do so. But a Nazi bomb obliterated the Devonshire Club in 1940, and its last show took place in May that year.

So what does Sid, who is no doubt one of the last men alive who boxed there, remember of this long-extinct fight hall?

'The Devonshire Club was a sort of round house,' he says. 'The building itself was built in a circular fashion but inside it was more or less square up top: it had balconies which went from one end of the room to the wall. You could see the ring in the centre when you went in and on the ring ropes, all round, they had advertising for the following week's boxing.

'It was all printed out on large posters that covered the three ring ropes – 'cause there used to be three ropes, now they have four – pinned to them. And of course I got a kick out of it, because I saw my name on the bill. At the very bottom, mind, because I was very new to the game, but it gave me a kick to see my name up on the bill. You could more or less say like in lights.'

I ask if the posters stayed on the ropes while the fights were on, and Sid explains, 'Oh no, they were all taken off.

'The MC was a very rotund man whose name was Buster Cohen,' Sid continues. 'He could quieten an audience that was having a riot, but he knew *how* to do it. "Gentlemen, please!" and everybody would pay attention. When they say MC, it's Master of Ceremonies, and that's what he was – he was master of the situation. He had that air of superiority that people took notice of. He was the MC for whatever fights I had there and he was very impressive.

'The boxers came out of a door, which led to the dressing rooms upstairs, and walked to the ringside, with no blare of music or anything like that. We just got in the ring, then he announced who the fighters were and so on.'

'Did the boxers enter the ring at the same time?' I enquire, wondering if the importance placed nowadays on entering the ring after your opponent was an issue back in the 1930s.

'Yes, same time. Didn't matter,' replies Sid. 'I don't think they were that fussy in those days about who appeared first, whether he be champion or challenger. Anyway, championship fights rarely took place there, that I remember.'

Next I ask about the Dev's dressing rooms, those transitory, limbo-like places where a boxer sits inertly just before bursting into adrenaline-fuelled action. 'They were poor; very poor, unpainted and dishevelled,' Sid tells me. 'You'd find anywhere to sit down – whether it be a bench or a chair, didn't matter. It wasn't a very pleasant place to be.

'And *the gloves* left a lot to be desired,' he adds. '*Dread*ful. The gloves must have been used from time immemorial. They were six-ounce gloves and they'd become that thin, or that worn, that it was as though you were boxing with skin gloves. There didn't seem to be any padding in them and when you hit a man with a punch – with a good solid punch – you *hurt* him. Today they're puffed up with a good sponge interior and so the punches are not quite the same as they were in those days.

'If you lost a fight at the Devonshire Club you got one pound, and if you won it you got one pound five shillings. That was the standard fee. But of course men who boxed for longer fights than six rounds received, I think, a pound a round. If they had a ten-round fight they got ten pound, which was wonderful, considering ringside seats were only three and sixpence: three shillings and sixpence!'

Back to Sid's boxing career, and the Devonshire was the venue for his next contest after his win over Len Garrett. On 9 June 1939 he took on Tommy Atkins (Southall) but suffered his first career setback.

'He was a short guy,' remembers Sid, 'and he would come forward with his head down, and I was doing the right thing by throwing uppercuts. I was catching him with the uppercuts but I was hitting him on the forehead – he must have had a terrible headache after that fight! But I hurt my hands so badly, every time I threw a punch it hurt.

'My manager, Alf, said I could retire if I wanted. He said, "You'd beat this boy seven days a week, so you can retire." But I didn't want to, just in case I might get the verdict. But it went to the end of the contest and he got the verdict. I knew I hadn't done enough because I was holding back – I couldn't punch any more. I had to just defend myself.' Afterwards Sid's hands were so sore that he was referred to a West End osteopath for a short course of treatment, paid for by the BBB of C.

'I couldn't even pick up a pen, my hands were so sore,' says Sid. 'This osteopath was a tall gentleman who was blind. He was the first British officer to be blinded in the First World War. He used to put my hands in water and used electrical currents, and he said to me, "You've got the worst case of bruising I've ever known without a bone being broken." But he done my hands a lot of good. He made them feel better and I think, because of it, they got stronger and I punched harder.'

The Atkins defeat was especially disappointing given the circumstances. But after his treatment and a two-and-a-half-months' rest, Sid's injured fists were ready to go to work again. Five days before his 17th birthday he stopped Len Mills (Dagenham) in four rounds at the Mile End Arena. This he followed with a contest against a familiar face in fellow Aldgate fighter Sammy Lang.

'Sammy was a boy who I knew pretty well,' says Sid. 'I saw him have a terrific fight with a boy by the name of Mickey Jones from Southend, who was being lauded as an up-and-coming boy. And Lang gave him a hell of a fight, had him in trouble several times, but in the end Sammy tired very badly, because he didn't train. He was a taxi driver and he didn't train so he lost that fight. I think he was stopped. He boxed to be able to get a few extra pounds to take home – or gamble – which he did a lot of.'

So Sid's contest with Lang was, on paper, a tough test. It was at the Devonshire Club, where Sid had lost last time out, in no small part due to his damaged fists. This time, therefore, a sterling performance was needed; but the fight finished prematurely with a surprise in the second round.

'I caught him with a good left hand,' remembers Sid, 'it was a really solid left-hand punch – *bang!* – and it caught him smack on the nose. He went down from the punch and stayed down for the count. He wouldn't get back up. And later on, when I got to know him better, I asked him why he did that. He said, "Well, you damaged my nose, you hurt it badly, so I went down and took the count." It isn't as though I knocked him out. That proves what a good solid punch the straight left is.'[1]

The disappointment of the Tommy Atkins defeat was now all but forgotten. Sid entered his next fight justifiably brimming with confidence. After all, he had won all his fights so far in

---

1 'Straight left' is a chiefly British term that refers to a straight punch delivered with the lead arm from the orthodox stance. Until the late 20th century the term straight left was more commonly used in Britain than 'left jab', which seems to originate from America. Today the term straight left has fallen out of popular use and the punch is usually referred to as left jab (or jab). In keeping with the era, the term straight left appears frequently in this book.

emphatic fashion and his only loss had been due to injured hands. Johnny Gould was the opponent and the venue the now familiar Devonshire Club. Sid remembers this one with frustration:

> I got stopped in two rounds, and it was because I was so inexperienced. I got caught with a good punch that put me down. It dazed me, but I got up at the count of eight or nine, which I knew I could do, and as I came to I thought, 'I can't let him get away with this, I've gotta go in and show him that he can't hit me and not get hit back.' So I went into him, I hurt him, then I led with a long left but it was out of distance.
>
> He went back on his heels and then counter-punched me with a beautiful punch – same punch as before – I went down very heavily, and with that I tried to make my way up. But as I was getting up, the referee, who was Jack Hart, stopped the fight. So I got stopped in the second round – I can't believe it, even to this day.

I ask if Jack Hart was right to stop the fight.

'Well, I felt that he wasn't justified in stopping it when he did,' says Sid. 'He could have given me another few moments to see whether I'd recovered from the punch that put me down. Instead of that I was stopped before I was able to get going again.

'I always felt that if I took a punch, even in training, I'd shake it off and I'd be able to go on. So I was a little hurt to think that I lost the bout, and I called out to Jack over the ring ropes, "Why did you stop it?" He waved me off as if to say, "Hop it – it's none of your business. I stopped it, that's all there is to it."'

Though unhappy with the decision that day, Sid would come to hold Jack Hart in extremely high regard, and found him a guiding influence in the early days of his own refereeing career. When asked about Hart's capabilities as a third man, Sid describes him as 'a referee as good as one can be'.

'I always had a lot of respect for him, both as a referee and as a man,' Sid told *Boxing News* in 1975. 'He would always look in command of a contest, and yet one wasn't really aware he was there until something untoward occurred, and he was needed. Then he'd be there, to take whatever action was necessary.'

Hart had been a good-class boxer until an eye injury curtailed his career. He began refereeing in the 1920s, at the legendary Premierland, and carried on as Britain's leading third man well into the 1960s.

Holborn Stadium

The defeat to Gould would be Sid's last. He won all his remaining fights, including one that he considers his finest victory, when he out-pointed Teddy Catlin (Luton) at the Stadium Club, Holborn, where Catlin was undefeated.

The Stadium Club holds a special place in Britain's ring history, but like the Devonshire it was destroyed by a Nazi bomb. In 1895 (then called the Holborn Hall) it was the site of a battle between Frank 'Paddy' Slavin and Frank Craig, in 1919 Georges Carpentier's one-round demolition of Joe Beckett happened there, and in 1929 it was the site of 16-year-old wonderboy Nipper Pat Daly's clash with British featherweight champion Johnny Cuthbert.

In the 1930s many more of Britain's top names – men of the calibre of Jack Petersen, Tommy Farr, Benny Lynch and Harry Mizler – boxed there. Yet sadly, in February 1941, the Stadium was obliterated by the Luftwaffe and the wreckage later hit by a second bomb.

When I ask Sid to tell me about the Stadium Club, he recalls the place vividly and with great enthusiasm.

'A lot of good professionals boxed at the Stadium,' he says. 'I remember seeing Harry Mizler box there – brilliantly. It was more or less like a gentlemen's club. It was situated in Holborn, Kingsway, right opposite the Holborn Empire, where all the famous music hall actors and actresses appeared.

'Inside it was very old-fashioned. The interior looked rather – I can't say dull; it looked brownish; I got a brownish impression, and that stays with me today. It had a tone about it that suggested it was not a rough house, such as the Devonshire would be or the Mile End Arena. It *looked* refined.

'It had balconies and people sat downstairs and upstairs. Gentlemen used to have meals at ringside, which I never understood because there *was blood* unfortunately, and it would happen that blood would splash onto their food! But no one ever seemed to mind.'

Discussing the patrons of the Stadium Club, Sid says, 'They were a different sort of spectator, and if they weren't any different, they behaved differently when they were there. It wasn't the spit and gob type; it was a more gentlemanly outlook. They were very well conducted, because they would clap after a round was over, and also they prescribed to nobbings.

'If they thought the contest was good enough, they would throw money into the ring. There weren't always nobbings because not all the fights were up to their liking, but if there was to be any nobbings it would be better class than elsewhere. They wanted to see good sporting contests that went the full distance, and if they were contented with what they saw they would contribute to the boxers' purses.'

Mile End Arena

Having spoken to Sid about the Holborn Stadium and the Devonshire Club, our discussion turns to that other well-known London arena of that era, the Mile End Arena, where Sid boxed three times in 1939.

Built behind Mile End Tube station inside corrugated iron and crumbling walls, the Arena epitomised the makeshift boxing venue. Though some fighters and fans may have found charm in this ramshackle, rough-and-ready setting, Sid was not among them.

'When you were boxing at the Mile End Arena you were boxing at the lowest possible place. It was like a cattle market,' he laughs. 'That's how it seemed to me. Pretty sparse, open air, just bare seats or stalls. But there was no finesse about it – it just looked like a cattle market, which I suppose in a sense it was – that's all we were considered, as cattle. I didn't think much of it at all.'

Sharing the Bill with Kid Berg

Sid's fourth contest of 1940, a sixth-round stoppage of Danny McShea (East Ham) at the Devonshire Club, was on a show he recalls with some excitement, for topping the bill was the legendary Jack Kid Berg.

I ask Sid if Berg was a boyhood hero of his, as I'm sure he was for many East End lads, but he answers obliquely before recalling sharing the bill with Berg.

'He was considered a hero,' declares Sid, 'because he had had some fantastic fights in America and won the light-welterweight championship of the world – that was the American version, but over here we didn't recognise that weight division. So they didn't consider him over here to be a world champion. But they did in America because they allowed light-welter – 10 stone.

'Anyway, he fought a fella named Harry Davis, from Bethnal Green – he was a good fighter, and they had a *good* fight. It was a return, and I was on that bill. I was very proud to be on it. Harry Davis did very, very well against Berg, but Berg was already finished by then, though Berg more or less overwhelmed him with his speed.

'They called him the "Whitechapel Whirlwind" and there was a very good reason for it. Because he moved very quickly – arms all over the place. His arms were never out of action. And Harry was a good boxer and he fully justified the liking that people had for him. He was a gentleman both inside and outside the ring. As for Berg, he was a bit of a rough diamond.'

Though, as Sid notes, Berg was well past his prime, he beat Davis on both occasions, which was impressive for a man who had been in many hard fights and was nearing retirement.

※ ※ ※

In 1940 Sid notched up eight consecutive wins in the space of six months. On 3 June that year he was back at the Holborn Stadium – in an eight-rounder against the Welshman Idris Pickens, who was part of a well-known fighting family. Sid, by this time, had expunged the memory of his two 1939 defeats, and was brimming with confidence. The reputation of the Pickens boxing family did not concern him at all.

'I didn't think he had a chance against me,' Sid recalls, 'I was boxing that well. I can't even remember him hitting me – I was always too fast and too sharp for him. I finished the eight rounds without any cuts or bruises, so I felt I'd done well.'

Things were rapidly falling into place for this fistic hopeful. Press reports show he was improving markedly with every contest and, incidentally, gaining weight as well. 'My first fight, I think I was 8st 3lb,' Sid recalls. 'And I grew a little, from training particularly, and I remember having my last contest at 9st. So I'd grown into a featherweight.' It is odd, then, to relate that after his win over Idris Pickens, aged still only 17, Sid's promising ring career came to a close. Intrigued, I ask him the reason.

'I was walking out with a young lady,' he smiles, 'who eventually became my wife. She said to me, "I don't like boxing", and I believe it was because her parents didn't like her going out with a boxer, because we were supposed to be a rough and ready sort, which I wasn't. I said, "Fine. You don't like boxing, I won't box any more. That's it." Then eventually we got married and we stayed married for 66 years. *Wonderful* marriage.'

Though Sid looks back on the curtailment of his ring career with a hint of regret, he believes that his late wife, Lilian, whom he met at a Camperdown House Sunday night dance in his mid-teens, may have saved him from long-term damage. For the sport was poorly regulated in those days, and though hardly an overworked fighter by 1930s and 40s standards, it's a fact that Sid's 16 pro fights took place in a period of under 15 months. Had he gone on fighting at such a rate for a further five or ten years, one wonders if his mental faculties would be as sharp as they are today.

Ring Reflections

I'm curious to know what type of boxer Sid was, whether he had any pet punches or adopted a particular strategy in the ring. How did the young fighting version of Sid Nathan compare with the no-nonsense referee British fight fans and TV audiences of the late 20th century became acquainted with?

'I never went into a fight believing that I was going to hurt a man,' he says. 'I boxed with a good left hand. I didn't want to fight. I did *have* to fight because there were some boxers that wouldn't let you box – they made you fight. But my intention was never to hurt anybody. I wanted to box, out-point a man and get a verdict, but not to injure in any way.

'I was quite satisfied with my boxing career because I really had a good record: 14 wins out of 16 fights was very good. I think today they'd be boxing for an area title. And I had good press reports all the way. They were good write-ups. I shall be very sorry when I'm dead or when these are faded and I can't read them any more,' he adds with a touch of dry wit as he pats his career scrapbook.

Exploitation

My research into the British fight scene of the 1920s and 30s, particularly for my first book, *Nipper: the Amazing Story of Boxing's Wonderboy*, revealed numerous instances of boxers who were recklessly mismanaged, often conceding age, weight and experience to opponents and fighting with startling regularity.

Although the reconstitution of the BBB of C in 1929 eventually led to better conditions for boxers, improvements were slow to arrive. During the 1930s a British boxers' union was formed in a bid to combat exploitation by promoters and managers.

I ask Sid whether he feels the exploitation of boxers was still taking place when he was boxing, and he says, 'Oh absolutely. I remember a taxi cab drawing up and out of that cab came six black guys, and they were all managed by the same man. I don't suppose they were managed by him – he probably promised them some money if they came with him and put the gloves on, and they'd get a few pounds, and he would certainly earn out of it. When I say managed, it would take more than somebody that he'd picked up from the street before he would manage them.

'I remember a particular fighter named Jimmy Norton from Gold Coast. Black. What a nice fella he was. I used to spar with him in the gym and I also sparred with him in a so-called six-round contest under a tent, on a boxing booth. Well, he boxed at the Devonshire, several times, and I think he also boxed at the Stadium Club, Holborn. But he was fighting good fighters and for the amount of boxing that he had done, which I don't think was a terribly large amount, he was in with too good men. With too good fighters.

'And he was a nice fella. What a nice man. I hate to think what happened to him.'

I ask if Sid recalls the name of the manager from the taxi. 'Yes, that was Jack Burns,' he says. 'He carried black fighters around with him. He was known for always having boxers with him to appear on a show that men may have pulled out of, and he always had a substitute to put in, which was a promoter's dream.

'Well, they [the boxers] wanted the money and so he put them in. It served both of them; it wasn't just for his benefit. But there was no such thing as records in those days, not as such [to highlight how recently a boxer had fought or whether he had recently suffered a knockout and should therefore be rested].'

London Ablaze

When war was declared, in September 1939, Sid had just turned 17, was six fights into a professional boxing career and living with his parents at 44 Ickburgh Road, Upper Clapton. His ring career and weekday work at H.H. Wells & Sons solicitors continued, and though the threat of aerial bombing loomed ominously in the background, life in London ticked by as usual at first.

That all changed in the summer of 1940 when Hitler's bombing campaign, intended to pave the way for an invasion of Britain, got under way. Initially the targets were British ships, ports, airfields, aircraft factories and radar stations, but in the autumn the attacks took a terrifying twist.

From 7 September 1940 the daily bombing of civilian areas started, and London was the chief target. Hitler's thinking was that by targeting the people of Britain, he could scare them into surrendering. Initially the attacks were restricted to daylight hours, but after a few weeks, to disrupt sleeping patterns and increase the fear factor, they started bombing at night.

'They were bombing continuously,' Sid says gravely. 'Day after day, night after night. It was a terrible time. They put me on the top of the building in Paternoster Row, where I worked. I was up on the rooftop with someone else waiting for incendiary bombs to drop. And if they fell on your building, you had to try and extinguish them before they actually caused a fire.'

Incendiary bombs (or firebombs) are designed to damage a target through fire rather than from the effects of a blast. In a built-up urban area such as inner London they can prove devastating, as the fires often spread to adjacent buildings which would be unaffected by conventional bombs.

'We could see fires in the distance,' Sid continues, 'and it was London that was burning. I could see all the flames of fires that had been started by incendiary bombs about half a mile away. But it looked terrible, it looked like everywhere was on fire. It was a horrible, horrible sight and a horrible feeling to experience. I was terrified. I really mean it. I was never that scared to enter the ring, but I was certainly terrified when I thought any moment there could be a plane coming over and dropping incendiary bombs where I was.' I point out to Sid that he would have a good case for suing an employer that put him at such risk nowadays. 'Well, people must have been doing it all over London,' he replies in a matter-of-fact tone. 'It's what everybody was doing – their duty.'

The bombing of London, of course, ravaged residential areas as much as industrial ones, and in the autumn of 1940 the Blitz struck terrifyingly close to home for Sid. When a bomb fell on a pub on Ickburgh Road, his family's rented home and many other houses on the street were severely damaged and rendered uninhabitable. When the bomb fell, Sid and his family were huddled together in an air raid shelter, as he recalls:

> The shelter was on the opposite side of the road to the pub, down below stairs. When the bomb hit the pub it destroyed it and killed many people. A man that was walking by the stone

SID NATHAN (ALDGATE) 1939-40

steps to go down to the shelter was blown into the shelter by the explosion of the pub. With that, it broke his leg, and we picked him up, did what we could for him and laid him on one of the benches that were in the shelter. We attended to his wounds as best we knew how, until the medics came with ambulances that were coming to see about the people who were injured or killed in the public house.

After losing their home, Sid and his family moved to 139 Princes Avenue in West Watford, close to Watford FC's Vicarage Road ground, which in those days doubled as a greyhound track. From here, in theory, Sid was further removed from the horror of the bombings; but his job in the City still placed him at the centre of the chaos.

On the night of 29–30 December 1940, the area from Islington to the edge of St Paul's churchyard was subjected to a terrifying air assault. In what was later dubbed the Second Great Fire of London, due to the fact it was more destructive than the Great Fire of 1666, incendiary bombs started over 1,500 fires, many of them converging to form three huge blazes.

On the instructions of Prime Minister Winston Churchill a large contingent of firemen fought to keep the flames from St Paul's Cathedral, and while they succeeded in saving the famous landmark, much of what surrounded it was destroyed. Paternoster Row, the street where Sid's employer was based and also the hub of the London publishing trade, was seen first hand by Sid after the smoke had cleared.

'That was terrible,' he recalls. 'I went there more or less to see what was happening to my job. But when I got there, I saw everything was down. Everything along the Paternoster Row was wiped out. It was just rubble and blocks of space where there'd been buildings, and these buildings were God knows how old.

'To look and see the whole row – Paternoster Row – had been bombed out, it was devastating. It was awful to see. And I was rather concerned about the housekeeper and her husband, who were living in that block. I never found out what happened to them but I think they must have gone to the shelters before the bombing started. I hope so, but I don't even know to this day. I mean, you ask around. Who was there to ask? If you asked people, they were just glad to be away from it all themselves.'

One night of bombing had wiped Paternoster Row off the map. Today in its place stands Paternoster Square, home of the London Stock Exchange. I wonder how many 21st-century City traders are aware of the site's interesting past.

Marriage and Military Service

In 1942 Sid married his childhood sweetheart, Lilian, at a synagogue in Hackney, but both were well aware that their connubial happiness could be disrupted at any time. Sid was resigned to the likelihood he would be called up to serve and admits it was not a prospect he relished.

'I knew that I'd have to go eventually,' he tells me, 'and I made up my mind that I'd do my duty but I wouldn't wanna go into battle or anything like that. Hated the thought. Because I thought battles should be fought with the fists and not with guns. That was my way of thinking.'

As fate would have it, Sid was called into the RAF later that year but would ultimately serve on the ground staff at a bomber base in East Fife. For three months he studied assiduously to learn Morse code and qualified as a wireless operator but to his frustration he found this was a skill he was not required to use.

His job, upon instruction, was to switch on an illuminated arrow that guided planes returning to base to the aerodrome. 'All I had to use were my eyes to light the arrow,' he recalls. 'I was in the middle of a bloody field, in a small stone building, where I used to sleep and cook my meals. That was a bad time. It made me ill. Not that I wasn't strong physically, I was. But it was upsetting my inner mind.'

The monotony and isolation, coupled with months spent tediously learning Morse code, left Sid, who is a gregarious man, in a bad state psychologically, and he was placed in Gleneagles Hospital for a few weeks under observation. It was with some surprise that he was suddenly called before a group of officers and discharged.

'I was in front of three or four officers, who I think might have been psychiatrists. They asked me how many fights I'd had, how many I lost, "How many times did you get knocked out?" and "Did you take punches to the head?" All those sort of things. And they decided that I should go home. They sent me home with another couple of blokes who seemed quite all right, but they must have also suffered something. My discharge certificate said I was unfit for further service but fit for work in civilian life.'

As unpleasant as Sid's wartime experience was, his brother Louis, who served in the King's Royal Rifles army regiment, had a far more harrowing time. After being captured at Dunkirk, he spent five years in a prisoner-of-war camp.

'He was lucky to come out of it alive,' Sid recalls wistfully. 'He was a tailor so he knew how to make suits look good on the German officers. And they said to him, "You're Jewish, *aren't* you?" He said, "No, I'm not." He couldn't say yes, because he thought he'd be taken away and put in a gas chamber. But they looked after him because he made all their clothes.'

Back to Boxing

After the war, Sid found work at a plastic and bakelite moulding company in Edmonton but despite his absence from the ring his interest in boxing never waned. He continued to train at various gyms and sparred with some of the top men of the 1940s, including Claude Dennington and Alf Danahar, of whom Sid says, 'He was heavier than me but I think I held my own with him – I was just that little bit faster.'

At one point Sid was on the verge of a ring comeback and had actually signed a three-year contract with up-and-coming manager-promoter Jarvis Astaire, who was impressed by Sid's form in the gym.

Ultimately, though, Sid stuck to his original plan. He made no post-war comeback and fortunately future star promoter Astaire did not try to hold him to the contract.

But Sid did have a couple of unofficial bouts on travelling boxing booths (an aspect of boxing history discussed in more detail in the section on Teddy Lewis of Dagenham). As mentioned earlier, the first of these was against Jimmy Norton (Gold Coast), a staged fight (or 'gee' fight) in which the boxers pull their punches and add theatrical touches for the benefit of the crowd.

As a newcomer to booth fighting, however, Sid was not used to pulling his punches and hit with greater force than was needed. 'After the fight was over,' he recalls, 'his manager, who ran the booth, came to me and he said, "You didn't have to throw punches the way you did – look what you've done to his eye! He won't be able to box for me now." Apparently I'd brought his eye up.'

Sid's other booth fight took place when he was in his late 20s. He asked if he could box on a booth that was pitched at the rear of the Simpsons clothing factory in Stoke Newington, as he says 'not for glory but so as to get a few pounds'. This one was not a gee fight but a genuine bout.

'They billed me as being the champion of Stoke Newington,' chuckles Sid. *Champion of Stoke Newington*! They might just as well have said I was champion of my own household. Anyway, I boxed a boy by the name of Les Haycox. He was known, because he used to box on some of the bills at Mile End Arena and the Devonshire. We had a good fight – I can't remember how many rounds it was now – probably it was six. And we went round with the hat, as you did after the fights to boost up the money you got. I was considered to be the winner and I got three pounds for it.'

After that, aside from a stint as a coach at Harrow Amateur Boxing Club, Sid's involvement with boxing seemed to be over. That is until a fortuitous event in 1957.

The Third Man

A chance encounter and a facetious remark at a fight show at Caledonian Road Baths, Islington, one evening in 1957 gave Sid the impetus to become a referee. As he recalls, 'Bill Williams was the top referee of the night, and considered to be one of *the* top referees. I watched him referee the last fight of the evening,

SID NATHAN (ALDGATE) 1939–40

and he gave a verdict which I thought no way is that the right verdict.

'So I went up to him and I said, "Bill, I saw that fight just now that you refereed. I didn't agree with your verdict. Thought the other man won it." He said, "Well, if you feel that way about it, why don't you become a referee yourself?" tongue in cheek. So I said, "It's not a bad idea. I'm gonna apply to the Board, see if I can get a referee's licence."'

True to his word, Sid wrote to the BBB of C but received a reply stating that they did not need further referees at that time. If he wrote again in six months, said the letter, the Board would re-consider; but Sid did not want to wait six months. 'I wrote again,' he recalls, 'and I said "I'm not happy with the thought that I can't referee, or that I can't get an interview to get a licence, so I'm applying again." And then they wrote back to me again and said they wanted me to go to the Board's offices for an interview.

'So I went up there and I saw a lot of expert referees, so-called, sitting round a large table in the office, and they asked me many questions. I had this interview, and I then received a letter from them to say that if I attend Shoreditch Town Hall on so and so date, I would be asked to conduct a fight – or a contest they called it, never called it a fight – and I would conduct this contest in the ring, but the actual referee would sit ringside and give his verdict against whatever I gave. His would over-rule mine.

'So I attended and I went into the ring and conducted two fights, and I stopped both of them, quite justifiably. When I came out of the ring, the referee who was watching from ringside said to me, "Sid, you're gonna get your licence. You don't have to wait for me to have a meeting. I'm deciding now that you can have your licence." I thought, "fantastic!"'

Sid duly received his licence and took charge of his first bout in May 1958: a welterweight clash between Mike Robbins (Camberwell) and Buster Gaffney (Croydon), which he stopped in favour of Robbins in the fourth round. *Boxing News* noted, 'Trainee referee Sid Nathan acted correctly when stopping the uneven exchanges.'

'I started off as a trainee referee, then I got a B licence,' Sid recalls. 'But my B licence lasted so long, I thought they had something against me. But they didn't, it's just that they kept me hanging on. They kept me, I think, 11 years as a B-licence holder and I was refereeing, in some cases, better fights than I should do as an ordinary B-licence holder. I made many applications, but they kept refusing. But Jack Hart saw me one day and he said to me, "You'll get your A licence, Sid. Don't worry about that. You'll get it, but it'll take a little bit of time." I said, "Well, it's taken 11 years already." And then, sure enough, I did get my upgrading. So maybe he had something to do with it.

'So I was now an A-licence holder, but within two years, which was really unheard of, I got my Star licence, which meant that I could referee anywhere in the world, as long as the Boxing Board approved the fight I was being sent to handle. So that was pretty good. And from there I went on for the next 30 years refereeing all over Britain, all over Europe. I was made an international judge by the World Boxing Council, which was the highest council you could get in boxing.'

Sid's style of handling bouts earned him a reputation second to none in British boxing. There was an easy flow to his work and an understated mastery in the way he controlled a contest without intruding on it. 'I believe in making asides to boxers during the course of a round,' he told *Boxing News* in 1975, 'and not stopping the action for minor infringements. That breaks up the boxers' rhythm and mars the fight.'

'It was important to get the decision right,' Sid tells me, 'because a boxer never forgets a fight he loses but feels he should have won. It stays with him for the rest of his life.' But not everyone recognised Sid's diligence or agreed with all his decisions. Leading promoter and manager Mickey Duff, for one.

'I refereed several of his boxers, who didn't get the verdicts and he said to me one time – I shan't mention what he said,' Sid chuckles. 'It was unrepeatable.' Sid's response to Duff's criticism, though, typifies his composed, straightforward manner. 'I said, "Well, if they'd have won the fights, they'd have got the verdict,

Mickey. But they didn't win, they lost." As far as I was concerned, they lost on points. That's it.'

As cool-headed as Sid usually was, there were limits to his patience. At a referee conference in Birmingham in 1985, when Sid was 63, he lost his cool with the BBB of C's then-deputy general secretary, Simon Block, whom some newspapers claimed he punched in the mouth. I ask Sid about the alleged incident and he assures me these reports are 'absolute rubbish'. However, an incident did occur after Mr Block refused to repay Sid's rail fare.

'He'd given a couple of the others their money back,' explains Sid. 'I said, "What about me?" And he said, "No." I don't know why, I couldn't tell you now. But he said something to me about *you people*, and I took that to mean you Jew people. I took it very badly. I had some papers in my hand, and I hit him across the mouth with the papers; smacked him across the mouth. I didn't hit him with my fist. And that was it.

'When I saw him later he said something about not reporting it. I said, "Well, I'd be pleased if you didn't, it was just a misunderstanding." But he did report it and I had to go before the Board and tell them what had happened.'

As a consequence, the Board suspended Sid for three months and he missed a couple of big fights he was due to referee. To be clear, Sid had completely misinterpreted Mr Block's remark and today the two are on genial terms. 'I thought he said something far worse than he did, and I took great offence by it, but it's absolutely in the past,' Sid declares.

There were no hard feelings between them, and there were no hard feelings between Sid and the Board either. He was soon back refereeing top-level fights and when, under BBB of C rules, he was obliged to retire after turning 65, they thoughtfully allowed him to continue for a further ten months to complete his annual licence.

To write about the 1,246 fights Sid refereed would require several large volumes. Among the stars he officiated over were Ken Buchanan, Alan Minter, John Conteh, John H. Stracey, Nigel Benn, Frank Bruno, Herol Graham, Charlie Magri and Dave Boy Green. While it is hard to pick out highlights from such a dizzying number of contests, there are several fights and several fighters that spring readily to mind.

For instance, Sid names John Conteh as one of the finest boxers he refereed and Charlie Magri as the man whose fights he most enjoyed officiating. One special memory is of refereeing three Muhammad Ali exhibition bouts at the Royal Albert Hall, and then being recognised by the world's most famous sportsman some years later in Las Vegas.

In terms of the contests themselves, Conteh's May 1973 clash with Chris Finnegan for the British, Commonwealth and European light-heavyweight titles is a favourite. 'That was a great fight,' Sid enthuses. 'I gave the verdict to Conteh and he well deserved it in my opinion. But a lot of people said they didn't think he'd won it, they thought that Finnegan had won it, but no he didn't. Conteh won it, no doubt.'

Then there is fellow East-Ender John H. Stracey's June 1976 WBC welterweight title battle with Carlos Palomino. Not an enjoyable night for Stracey, who lost his world title, but a fantastic night's action for fight fans. In the twelfth Sid compassionately stopped the contest after Stracey had been floored twice.

'John fought a brilliant fight,' Sid recalls, 'but Palomino was just a bit too good for him. When he got up off the floor I put my arms round him and said, "John, I've stopped the fight because I think you've had enough. You've fought like a champion, you've lost it like a champion, and that's the most you can do. You boxed brilliantly but you weren't quite good enough for this guy." And I took him back to his corner and he was grateful, he didn't argue about it.'

Having played an active part in boxing from the 1930s through to the 1990s, Sid is well placed to compare the old-timers with the modern-day men. On this subject he is objective and unsentimental and does not definitively rate one era above the other.

'It's difficult to say how they compare,' he tells me after some consideration. 'For a start they had more fights than today, which must make a difference to a boxer's knowledge of boxing. But I think they're more polished today with better feeding and better training facilities. Scientifically they were better then. Scientifically I mean in the sense that they were taught differently. Generally speaking I think they had more to lose in those days,' he concludes in reference to the 1930s. 'They really depended on boxing for a living.'

Sid's final role in boxing was perhaps his most prestigious. After he was obliged to retire from refereeing at 65 he continued to work as a judge for the World Boxing Council, adjudicating from ringside at world title fights across the globe. This role took him to Caesars Palace in Las Vegas and Madison Square Garden in New York as well as rings in France, Italy, Spain, Holland, Croatia and Puerto Rico.

A frequent companion on these jaunts was that other eminent British referee, the late Harry Gibbs, whom Sid recalls fondly. 'I remember we chatted to Jose Sulaiman, the president of the World Boxing Council, and he told us, "I reckon you two to be the best international judges that one can get." Which was quite an honour.'

Today Sid's passion for boxing still burns brightly. I talk to him on the phone just after the London 2012 Olympics and he turns our discussion to the Games. He is especially enthusiastic about the British gold medallist Anthony Joshua's victory in the super-heavyweight final, which he scored, unofficially, from his armchair at home. 'If this boy only took up boxing four years ago,' he advises me, 'my goodness, he's certainly a prospect!'

Once a month Sid attends an ex-boxers' association meeting where he chats with other fighters from days gone by. 'You can bet that nine-tenths of them are those that I refereed,' he says. 'And there are those there, obviously, who I had given decisions against. But those that I did, they make a joke of it. They say to me, "Oh, you weren't wearing your glasses that day, Sid" or something similar. But they don't mean anything by it. In fact, I know that I'm loved and cared for by them. They're very kind to me.'

Sid has lived an interesting and varied life, which has been testing at times. But through it all, from childhood to old age, boxing has been a steadfast companion.

To end this story, it seems fitting to reiterate something Sid told the late veteran boxing journalist Ron Olver back in 1988:

> Boxing has been my life. I was just a kid from the East End, but boxing has enabled me to travel the world, and meet some wonderful people, experiences that money can't buy. I've been fortunate and I appreciate it very much, and everyone who has helped me along the way.

TED BERRY
(BETHNAL GREEN)
1948–49

MY NEXT interview takes me into the heart of London's East End, to an area that has been the lifeblood of London boxing more than any other. The district of Bethnal Green has changed unrecognisably since its fistic heyday and most of its native Cockney inhabitants have long since left. The once bustling pie and mash shops have given way to restaurants for Asian cuisine, and the hawkers and barrow boys have all gone west. But one lifelong resident, who has watched this transformation, will almost certainly never leave. For this area – and more particularly the street he lives on – are part of who he is.

For Ted Berry, Canrobert Street is a place of bittersweet memories, where the past and present meet. He witnessed the Second World War here – a time of fear and anxiety for most East End adults but a period of excitement for street-hardened youngsters such as he was then. It was on this street that his first boxing coach lived and it was to here that he returned after each of his ring victories. Yet it was from here that he got involved with the infamous Kray twins and it was close by this street that the most tragic event of his life occurred one evening in 1964. He has lived with the consequences ever since.

%%%

I had read scraps of information about Ted Berry, both in the context of professional boxing and his connection with Ronnie and Reggie Kray. But none of the accounts published on him have told his story with any real depth or clarity. There are many pieces missing from this intriguing puzzle.

The last couple of decades have seen a slew of books published about the Krays and Ted Berry's name crops up occasionally. His brother, Checker, is said to have been a good friend of the twins, while he and Ted, it has been written, worked for them in some capacity.

Most astonishing of all, however, is the claim made in several books that Ronnie Kray shot Ted, leading to the amputation of his right leg. When interviewed by Ron Olver of *Boxing News* in 1986, Ted said of the shooting, 'To this day I have no idea why this happened, who did it, or what I have done to deserve it. It was a dastardly deed,' and the reader is left to wonder if he knew more than he was saying.

This is a book about boxing, not the underworld; but in writing Ted's story it would be remiss not to include his connection with Britain's most notorious gangsters. So, while his impressive boxing career (he retired unbeaten after 19 pro fights) is the chief subject of the interview, I arrive at Ted's home hoping to also shed light on his life outside the ring.

I am not sure what to expect when I meet a former Kray associate, but I find Ted to be a hospitable, patient and friendly man. He is also a natural conversationalist and his reminiscences make enthralling listening. I can easily picture him regaling customers at the Old Horns, a Bethnal Green pub he ran for many years, with stories of his ring career.

In his boxing days Ted boasted a thick thatch of dark wavy hair, and today, though his hair is greyer and slightly thinner, he bears a resemblance to his younger self and looks more youthful than his 84 years. Though mobility is an issue for him these days and he spends much of his time indoors, there is a youthful vibrancy to Ted's speech and mannerisms, and his long wiry arms, which move rapidly as he talks, still carry a look of latent power, as if ready to spring into action should the need arise.

Though his time in the fight game was all too brief, Ted's recollections provide a fascinating insight into the mindset of a hungry 1940s fighter. Here was a boxer from an underprivileged background who took up fighting both out of family tradition and to attain a better life. His was a raw, budding talent cut frustratingly short – a great promise unfulfilled.

Made in Bethnal Green

'I'm a self-made person. No one taught me nothing, no one give me nothing – I've never been dishonest, that's for sure. But I'm a known person in Bethnal Green, and I'm respected,' says Ted Berry, looking back on his remarkable life. 'You have to fight for respect, but… you get it.'

He says, 'I was born Edward Henry Berry – Edward after my grandfather and Henry after my dad. My mum's history goes back, many years ago, to Italian Sicily – her mother was half Sicilian – but my father was of Irish descent. I was born in the City of London Maternity Hospital, 1 September 1928, and I moved from there, when I come out of hospital, to Satchwell Street in Bethnal Green. We lived there till '41, when we got bombed out by the Nazis, and then we moved here.'

'Here' is Canrobert Street where Ted and his wife Joyce live in a house just a few doors from Ted's old family home, where incidentally Ted's sister now lives. 'My other sister lives round the corner,' he tells me, 'my daughter lives round the corner from there, my son lives in Bow and my brother lives in Covent Garden, so we all live in close proximity to each other.'

This is the traditional East End way. In days gone by, after leaving home, sons and daughters moved into houses near to their parents and other family members, which created a close-knit community.

'The East End was a wonderful place,' recalls Ted, casting his mind back to his childhood. 'From the Salmon and Ball to

Cambridge Heath Station, from there to Shoreditch Church, and from there to the top of Bishopsgate and back down to the Salmon and Ball, was like a village – everyone knew each other. My aunty lived four streets away and an uncle of mine lived a couple of streets away.

'Everyone got married but they all stayed in the same area, until the war started. The war cleaned everything up. A lot of people were evacuated and stayed there. A lot of our local boys got killed in the war and a lot of our places got bombed and the people had to move out the district, and from there it fell away.'

As a boy Ted attended Daniel Street Infants' School and then as he matured, Columbia Road School, before switching to St Matthias School – all of which were in Bethnal Green. 'My education's come from what I've learnt myself, not from school,' he declares. 'I learnt to read and write at school but I never learnt anything else.'

Ted tells me that Bethnal Green was a tough place to grow up and he remembers gang wars between Bethnal Green youngsters and kids from Hoxton. I ask if he was involved in these skirmishes and he replies, 'Well, when you're a kid you get caught up in anything exciting – you just follow the crowd. I never got injured, thank God.' I suspect there hang some interesting tales, but Ted will say no more on the subject. However, as I discover, there are other fascinating aspects of his life that he *will* discuss – in detail.

Wartime

'The war came along when I was 11, and all the schools closed and I never went back to school,' remembers Ted. 'My dad had got discharged out the army for medical reasons and we needed the cash, so I went to work. I see this wanted notice in the window in Ingram's in Bethnal Green Road, a radio shop. I went in and I told them I was 14 and they asked for the cards. I said, "Well, the war's on, you can't get no cards." So they stood for me, kind of thing, and I worked there till I was 14.'

Ted's job was to charge radio accumulators, which he tells me were 'glass things filled with acid. You had batteries as well but these were accumulators. People used to come in with their old accumulator to be charged and we used to rent them one while it was being charged. Sometimes I'd have 20 or 30 accumulators all lined up ready to charge for the next day.'

I recall Sid Nathan's unpleasant experiences of wartime London and wonder, knowing that Bethnal Green was among the most heavily bombed districts of the city, whether Ted suffered similar trauma. For him, however, the freedom afforded by the sudden termination of school, and the excitement of being plunged into a unique and unpredictable world event, came as a boon.

'I can say truthfully – I know it's sad – but the war was the best time of my life,' reveals Ted. 'I was only 11 and I was a free soul; I was working and I was getting wages. And I could go to the pictures; I could go and do whatever I liked. I had tailor-made clothes when I was 12 – I had suits made.

'During the war there was a fellowship,' he adds. 'If there was an air raid, which my mum used to get nervous about, she'd run to the woman next door and she'd let us sit in her passage. Half the street'd be sitting in her passage having tea! We were no more safe there than in our own places, but we'd all be sitting keeping each other company.'

At 14 Ted left the radio shop and worked for a time at a wholesale warehouse, before settling in to the Berry family trade.

Family Traditions

The Berry family had two traditions – and both were passed on to Ted. The first was the now defunct trade of hawking or wardrobe dealing, as it was also known. Bethnal Green was renowned for its hawkers, and entire families took part in the trade. The Smiths, Krays, Kellys, Harpers, and of course the Berrys, were the East End's best-known hawking families. Unlike the pedlar, who sells items from door to door, the hawker bought unwanted items from the householder and resold them, usually from a market stall.

'My dad was a hawker, bought second-hand clothes, sold second-hand clothes. It's been the family profession since my great-grandparents' time – they'd always had stalls in Brick Lane,

FIGHTING MEN OF LONDON

selling clothes and items,' says Ted. 'We used to go out when I was a kid: my father and my uncle, almost all my family, and we'd call it "on the knocker". We used to drop leaflets, then go back and pick the leaflets up and buy old clothes, jewellery, antiques and such at the door.

'When the demob was on after the war we was going out buying all the demob suits. But the clothes had to be proper second-hand clothes – we didn't buy rag and bone – and we had a stall in the market where we used to sell them, at Brick Lane. There was a market on Cutlers Street where all the dealers buying clothes used to go, and we used to take our clothes there and sell them to the dealers. I did it from a kid. It's part of the family tradition. But then all these villains and thieves got around and it finished the trade – people wouldn't open their doors. That's the way of the world today.'

The second Berry family tradition that Ted was destined to follow was prize fighting. His grandfather had been a bare-knuckle fighter of Irish gypsy stock, and his father, Harry Kid Berry, was a top-line feather and lightweight of the 1920s and 30s under the management of Jack Burns.

'Everyone knew Harry Kid Berry,' Ted says proudly. 'He was a top fighter my dad, in his time.' As an amateur Ted's father won the London Federation of Boys' Clubs championships, capturing the junior and senior titles in the same year. 'The juniors was a couple of days, or a month, before his birthday,' remembers Ted, 'and when the seniors came along, he was old enough to be a senior and he entered that.' As a pro Harry Kid Berry took on such pre-war stars as Al Foreman and Nipper Pat Daly, and scored wins over top men such as Kid Socks and Lew Pinkus.

I'm curious to know what type of fighter Harry Kid Berry was and whether he and Ted had similar styles. 'He was a boxer, but I was made different to him,' Ted explains. 'He couldn't punch, the old man, you know, *I could punch*. He had a slippery style – ducking and diving, you've gotta find him to catch him – there he goes, where is he now? One of them type of fighters. He had speed; but I never had speed – I weren't a speedy fighter.'

The Webbe and the Repton

'In our situation, in the East End – I'm going back to the old East End – you had to either be a fighter, a footballer or a cricketer; anything else, you got beaten up,' chuckles Ted. 'And so I followed in my father's footsteps and became a fighter.'

Like so many other East End lads, Ted's introduction to boxing arrived through a local boys' club, the Webbe, for which his father had boxed a decade before him. Founded in memory of the cricketer and philanthropist Herbert Webbe in 1888, the Webbe Institute (to give it its full name) was run by the Oxford House Club, a religious institution set up to promote recreation and education among underprivileged men and boys.

When Ted joined, aged eight, the Webbe was on the corner of Cheshire Street and Hereford Street, but when the war arrived its premises moved to Oxford House. 'As a kid you had nowhere to go,' he tells me. 'There was no entertainment and so you joined your local club. With the Webbe was a boxing club so automatically, whether you wanted to be a fighter or not, you joined the club. They had a canteen where you could have a cup of tea or a sandwich or cake and you'd have a spar in the ring. It was very popular. The Webbe was the Repton of its day.

'When the Webbe moved into Oxford House it had a hall downstairs and they had a portable ring. They'd have inter-club boxing, like the Hoxton club would fight Bethnal Green club, Stepney club would fight them, you know. We used to have our own shows. You joined a club and if you were in the boxing team and they had a show going, you were automatically put down on the show. You was told you was boxing so and so somewhere and that was it.'

At the Webbe at the same time as Ted was a tall, slightly older lad with a fine physique and a special talent for boxing. Ted and the other boys sat and watched in awe whenever Jimmy Davis took to the ring. 'He was poetry to watch, and as an ex-fighter I can say that,' says Ted with affection. 'He had the greatest left-hand you've ever fucking seen. There was a guy at the club who used to call him pop-pop Jimmy. So when he was fighting he says, "Pop-pop, Jim, pop-pop", meaning jab-jab-jab-jab. He was out of this world.

'We grew up together as kids. Jimmy was a pigeon fancier, and pigeons was his life. When we was kids, there was the old Truman Brewery in Brick Lane and Jimmy used to go round there catching pigeons. He was so cute with it, you know. He'd put a little bit of seed down and he had this coat with a hole in the pocket. And he'd start going "Coo-coo, coo-coo", doing a pigeon noise, then boomp, he snatched it. And he used to sell them to the Asians down Cable Street, 'cause they used to love pigeon pie.

'We belonged to Father Jones's church down the bottom of Old Bethnal Green Road, and every year all the church kids, church goers, used to get two weeks down at Chelmsford. You'd get your name picked out of the hat and have two weeks' holiday. We'd never go to church until the holidays come up and all of a sudden we'd start going to church, to get picked out. Jimmy Davis, me and a load of the East End kids used to go down there for a fortnight's holiday.'

Jimmy Davis, an uncle of the well-known trainer Tony Sims, reached the ABA welterweight final in 1944 but lost on a casting vote to future British welterweight champion Henry Hall of Sheffield (whom Davis, incidentally, later beat as a pro). Jimmy turned pro in September 1945 and was soon juggling his day job in Spitalfields Market, where he would work for 40 years, with a busy prize-fighting career.

'How he never won a title I will never know. That man was a genius – he had everything,' reflects Ted. 'He could *move*, he was *clever* and he could read a fight. He wasn't cagey or nothing like that; he didn't have a knockout punch, but he had a damaging punch. He ended up as a middleweight, fought loads of big names. He was one of my idols actually. Great guy.'

Ted had a number of amateur fights before and during the Second World War, but then he gave up the game for a while. By the time he returned to boxing he was dating Joyce, his wife-to-be, and had joined the Repton boxing club (the Webbe by then had closed) purely to keep busy on the days he didn't see Joyce.

He was to meet a man, however, who helped him see boxing as a more serious endeavour.

'My father was an ex-professional fighter but he wasn't much interested in me boxing – he didn't want me to be a boxer,' says Ted. 'The chap who used to take me to boxing and started teaching me and working with me was a man called Ginger Owen – Ginger Charlie Owen, who lived across the road here in Canrobert Street. He was a well-known man in the fight trade; he was a steward at all the shows.

'It started off, the first fights I had before I come back as an amateur, were at an open lightweight contest at the York Hall, and I were on my own. So I gets up in the ring on my own. There were three fights and I won the three fights. Anyway, I had the first fight and who happened to be sitting in the audience but Charlie. I was down in the dressing room waiting to get ready for the next one and he come down. We had a chat and he said "Who's looking after you?" I said, "No one – I'm on me own." So he says, "Mind if I come up in the corner?" I said, "It'd be my pleasure." And Charlie looked after me. I won the contests, got the cup and for all my fights from then Charlie was with me.

'He took me down all the gyms and I sparred with all the professionals. We used to go down to Klein's gym and there was another one, the Torbay, over the water in Rotherhythe. And he spent a lot of time with me, took me to all these gyms and I sparred with *everyone* – I've gotta attribute the beginning of my career to him.

'But my father, like anything else, you have a few fights, you win 'em – now they wanna take over. And that's what happened: he wanted to take over and I didn't want him to, but blood's thicker than water. I had to tell Ginger, "I'm going with the old man now" and it hurt him. He used to go everywhere with me. He used to go to Ilford or wherever I was boxing. It was one of the saddest things in my career when I had to give Charlie up. I can't live with it now even. Sad thing.'

Ted's second amateur club, the Repton, is today among the most famous amateur boxing clubs in the world. With funding from Repton public school, Oxford House had established the Repton in 1895 to cater for 'a lower class of boys than the Webbe Institute'. At the Repton at the same time as Ted were several other future pros including Joe Lucy, Dennis Booty, Duggie Dugard and Ted's cousin Pat Berry.

'I was never much good as an amateur,' Ted says modestly. 'I can't explain it to you but it wasn't my style. There was too many rules and regulations and I could never settle down as an amateur. When you got in the ring and you got busy and all of a sudden the referee calls "hold it – you're doing this or you're doing that", and you ain't doing nothing intentional, it's just how boxing goes on. And it would take your concentration away.

'But I tried amateur, I went through to the ABAs [reaching the North-East London Divisional Championships at Bethnal Green, 8 April 1948]. Me and Joe Lucy got to the finals and he beat me on a casting vote. He was southpaw and I could never manage a southpaw. They make me not even wanna watch them: they seem so awkward and yet I'm left-handed myself.

'He beat me on points but then Joe was an exceptional boy. He *was fast*, and you spent half your time running after him, and when you're amateur you've only got three rounds to do it in. Of course Joe turned pro, he won the lightweight championship and he won a belt outright. So I wasn't beat by nothing.'

Turning Professional

After the Joe Lucy defeat Ted weighed up his future in the unpaid ranks and decided it was time to turn professional. He asked Charlie Owen to find him a manager and Owen introduced him to Jack Jordan, an experienced man based at Wembley who had managed Bethnal Green's famous British champion brothers, Dick and Harry Corbett. Ted's father, meanwhile, would act as his trainer.

Were his parents concerned about him boxing professionally? 'Mum – she'd been used to the old man, hadn't she, so she took it in her stride. The old man, I think he was glad he had something to go and blab with his friends about – that I was a professional fighter.'

Ted's pro debut took place on 16 September 1948, against Tommy Wallace (Camberwell), at a venue that was effectively his home turf. 'It was Mile End Arena, which is local, and I was an ex-member of the Repton, so all the Repton boys was over there to cheer me on,' Ted recalls. 'And all the local people who went to Mile End Arena knew me, so it was quite a nice experience. I knew the difference between amateur and professional boxing that day. I felt more natural, I felt more free and easy, that I could let it flow. And I did let it flow and I knocked the guy out in three rounds. And that's how it went on – fight after fight I was turning them over.'

Ted squeezed eight fights into the last three months of 1948 – all of them wins – appearing at the Mile End Arena, Rochester Casino, Poplar's East India Hall, Manor Place Baths, Caledonian Road Baths and Bermondsey Baths. But as an undercard fighter his bouts received little press attention, and the first time *Boxing News* reported more than just the result was in his fifth contest, against Billy Lee. 'Berry gave Lee a boxing lesson that he will not forget for a long time,' observed the trade paper, 'and demonstrated the correct way to use a straight left.'

Of these initial contests the only one that stands out for Ted is his fourth fight, but for all the wrong reasons. 'It was against Johnny O'Neill. He was a hang-on kind of fighter. You'd catch him, then he'd clinch. And as it went on I got tireder and tireder, and after the fifth round I went back to my corner and I was knackered. Not hurt, but knackered. Tired. But I went out and I pulled meself together in the sixth round and I won on points. It ain't the hardest fight, but it's one of the most horrible fights I've had.'

As the weeks passed, Ted settled into a structured routine of work and boxing training. 'At six o'clock in the morning I did me road work round Victoria Park with my Alsatian, Prince. Then I'd come home, put my dressing gown on, lay in bed and sweat out for an hour. Then I'd get up, have a wash all over – we never had showers in our houses in them days – and go out on the knocker with me dad. We used to finish lunchtime – one o'clock or two o'clock – then we'd come home, I'd pick me bag up and we'd go to the gym, Klein's, and start our training session.'

Professor Bill Klein's

Klein's Olympic Gymnasium was halfway along Fitzroy Street, in a cellar tucked beneath 18 steep stone steps. Ted visited every London gym of note during his career but Klein's was easily his favourite.

'We got off the Tube at Great Portland Street, walked round the back, where they had the car sales market, and you went down the cellar into the gym. Many's the time I've got me bag and I'm on the Tube and I've thought, I don't fancy it today. But as you walked in Klein's the atmosphere hit you and it was like putting a needle in your arm. Woah, you was there mate – and that's how *I* felt; I don't know how anyone else felt. It had a lovely atmosphere about it. I trained at Solomons's gym and so many gyms, but no, Klein's had a sweaty attitude. With fighters, you get the smell of oils and the smell of sweat – you get that smell – and the old urge comes up,' explains Ted, moving his fists expressively.

The gym was run by self-styled 'Professor' Bill Klein, an octogenarian with a bushy, white nicotine-stained moustache and a suitably quirky life story. He was born William Hugo Klein into a circus family in Bochum, Germany, on 26 October 1866, and as a child took to the air as a trapeze artist. On one occasion he narrowly escaped death when he fell 30 feet on to safety nets, landing on his left side. The doctor who examined him said that if Bill had his heart on his left side he would have died. 'I'm one of those unusual people with their insides reversed,' he told *Boxing News* decades later when relating the incident. 'Your heart's on the left – mine's on the right.'

Klein was taught to box when he was 20 by the English lightweight champion Bat Mullins, but made his name as a wrestler and weightlifter, billed as William Atories as part of the Roman Gladiators or Fin de Siecle Athletes troupe. He settled in London around the turn of the century, married, was twice widowed, and fathered 22 children. In 1912 he took the British wrestling team to the Olympic Games in Stockholm.

Klein ran gyms in various parts of London and had famous names such as Georges Carpentier, Joe Jeanette, Bombardier Billy

Wells, Gunner Moir, Primo Carnera, Joe Louis, Billy Conn and Freddie Mills through his doors. He opened his last gym, where Ted trained, in the basement of 46 Fitzroy Street in 1930 and kept it running until his death, at age 90, in 1957.

'I think Bill Klein had rheumatics or something 'cause he could hardly walk. His favourite saying was, "You haven't paid!"' chuckles Ted, adopting a stern, gravelly voice. 'It used to be half a crown a day gym money and you'd go in there and you'd peel off, do your work, have your cup of tea and he'd come round and he'd go, "You haven't paid!" and I'd say, "Oh, sorry Bill", and give him his half a crown. Wonderful old man he was.

'How he managed that place I don't know. His gym wasn't modernised in any way. But I don't s'pose it would have been successful if it was prettied up. And it *was* successful – many a fighter used to train there. Al Phillips used to train there. You had a three-sided ring – one side was mirrors and against the wall. It was a bit congregated – if you had four fighters working out in there it would have been enough. But I was lucky – I used to go in the afternoons when it was quieter.

'Me dad was a trainer in the old-fashioned way,' Ted tells me when I ask about their training sessions. 'He trained me as he'd been trained. A lot of what he taught me were old-fashioned things that people today don't even remember. 'Cause the old-fashioned trainers were the greatest you could wish to meet: they worked on you and they'd watch every movement. The old man was a good trainer.'

Sparring Reminiscences

Visiting Klein's during the quieter afternoon period, Ted was often obliged to spar with heavier men, including middleweights and light-heavyweights such as Harry Davis, Ben Valentine and Joe Quigley, all veterans at the time. Davis was the man Sid Nathan had watched lose gallantly to Kid Berg a decade before, while Valentine was a Fijian who beat many of Britain's best middle and light-heavyweights. Naturally all three were happy to share their experience with an up-and-coming fighter like Ted, who learnt much from sparring with them.

Nearer to Ted's own weight was his Jack Jordan stablemate Eddie Cardew (Holloway), a hard-hitting welterweight and one of a trio of brothers who boxed professionally. 'Eddie was a KO guy and exciting to watch. I think on every card I was on with him, he won,' remembers Ted. 'Jordan found Eddie at the Caledonian Road Baths. Jordan had a couple of fighters there and Eddie was about 16, and he was hanging about there, they got chatting and he says he wants a fight. And Jordan took him over, like, and managed him.

'I sparred with Eddie a *few* times. I was faster than him so I could move about and jab him. But he could hit and he caught me a few times – *bang* on the fucking chin. The story is – I don't know if this is true, this is hearsay – that he got with a girl and they split up, and he's s'posed to have committed suicide.'

Although Ted could not always find sparring partners of his own weight at Klein's, there was the alternative option of finding work as a sparring partner for a champion or top-liner, which involved travelling to their home gym. 'You'd get so much a round, and you earned your money. I think you used to get 30 bob, two quid, something like that, 'cause you was training with champions. When you spar with anyone else it's nothing, but when you're training with champions the expense is paid by the manager. As you've done three rounds, the manager will come up and give you the three rounds' money,' says Ted, switching from past to present tense as the memory becomes vivid.

Just a few fights into his career Ted had the opportunity to spar with the reigning British and European lightweight champion, Billy Thompson. This stocky, curly-haired Yorkshireman had a glittering amateur career, beating most of Britain's leading lights before carrying off the 1944 ABA lightweight title. He turned pro in 1945 to support his family, after his father, a coal miner, was pensioned off from the pits after developing silicosis. Thompson rapidly rose up the ranks, won the British and European lightweight titles in just over two years, and was the first post-war champion to win a Lonsdale belt outright. Eventually, after much sweating and saving, he was able to buy his family a farm with his ring earnings.

Ted knew that sparring with Thompson could be an invaluable learning experience, but equally there was a danger he was taking on too big a job too soon. Thompson, after all, was a powerful and ferocious fighter who never held back in fights or sparring. 'Ooh he was a rough man,' recalls Ted. 'I was offered a sparring job with him but the old man said, "No, you don't wanna know." I'd only had about eight or nine fights, but I wanted to fight with everyone, and being headstrong I went ahead with it. I sparred with him at Solomons's in Great Windmill Street 'cause that was his gym.

'Jesus Christ, did he give me a seeing to. I had rope burns across my back like I'd been lashed – that's from moving to get away from him. He was a body puncher and he kept on top of you all the time: every time you moved he was on top of you. He took no prisoners!

'That was on a Saturday and on the Monday I went back for more punishment,' laughs Ted. 'But Jack Burns, his manager, said, "No, Ted, leave it out" kinda thing. And we had a talk, me and Billy. "I'm sorry I went rough with you," he said. "I just can't help it." And I understood.

'Then, after I'd had another six or seven fights, I felt I had improved a hundred per cent; and I longed for the day I could spar with him again. But it never ever happened. He lost his title, then he went up north – where he lived – become a welterweight, had a few more fights and skipped out.'

Although Ted never got the chance to spar with Thompson again, he did spar with a man who took away Thompson's British title with a first-round knockout in 1951. That man was Tommy McGovern.

Bermondsey-born McGovern learnt to box at the Fitzroy Lodge amateur club and in 1942, at White Hart Lane, won the London ABA lightweight title. Thereafter he joined the RAF and after a year's training found himself stationed in the Algerian city of Oran, where he came to the notice of the world heavyweight champion, Joe Louis, who had arrived with a team of boxers to give a show for the Allied forces. McGovern was picked to box a three-round exhibition with Californian Jackie Wilson, and performed so well that Louis gave a keen speech praising the Britisher, whom he said was the best lightweight prospect he had seen for a long time.

In 1945 McGovern won the Allied welterweight championship and returned to Britain with big things expected of him, not least due to Joe Louis's pronouncement. Managers were queuing up to sign the Bermondsey lad as a professional, but for some reason the BBB of C turned down his licence application – a decision that made headlines – and so, in April 1947 he sailed to America instead. Training at the famous Stillman's gym, Tommy turned pro in the States and won 11 of 15 fights before returning to Britain.

Finally granted a BBB of C licence, he had his first pro contest on British soil on 25 March 1948, but afterwards suffered a few defeats, causing some critics to doubt his championship potential. At the time Ted sparred with McGovern, the jury were still out on whether the Bermondsey boxer could reach the top. At that stage McGovern had the Southern Area title – rather than the British title – in his sights.

'I remember he was a hell of a nice fella and we become pals,' says Ted. 'We used to spar at a gym in Covent Garden – O'Doherty's – which was in a little cellar.' Billy O'Doherty founded the gym in the closing years of the Second World War as a welcome-home present to his son Terry, who was taken prisoner of war at Anzio. Sited on Neal Street in a basement beneath the family's barrow-making shop, father and son ran the gym until 1959, when a boom in trade forced them to use the basement for storage.

'They had a small ring and we used to go hell for leather, me and Tommy. He was the same type of fighter as what I was, but he was more experienced than I was,' Ted explains. 'Dave Crowley was his manager and we were going at it one day, McGovern was training for a title eliminator fight, and Crowley come in and he done his nut. He shouted, "Stop! Stop!" and he give him such a bollocking.

'He says "*What* you trynna do? You're sparring with someone. You're trying to hurt him but you're not gonna fucking hurt him. What are you doing? You're gonna get yourself hurt and you're training for a title eliminator." He laid the law down to him. No disrespect to Tommy, but I was holding *more* than me own.'

In July 1949 McGovern beat the veteran George Daly to win the South-Eastern Area lightweight title, and challenged Billy Thompson unsuccessfully a year later for the British championship. His one-round defeat of Thompson (inside 45 seconds) in a return title fight in August 1951 caused a sensation, but weight trouble undoubtedly played a part in the outcome. 'Thompson couldn't make the weight,' recalls Ted. 'They carried him into the ring; so McGovern had nothing to beat really. Even when I sparred with Thompson he was over ten stone, and he was gonna defend his title but found it hard to make nine-nine.'

McGovern lost the British lightweight title in his first defence, to Manchester's Frank Johnson, and retired from boxing 14 months later. Had he still been fighting in the early 1950s, one wonders if it might have been Ted – who was four or five years younger – in McGovern's place.

Rules of the Game

Training every day and fighting often helped Ted refine his ring skills. 'I learnt a hell of a lot,' he tells me. 'I can honestly say, I learnt with every fight. Everyone that I sparred with and everything I did in boxing was a lesson, and it all went into my head. I used to work like from a book. The book was my head. What do I do here? What do I do now? And there were rules that I fought by that I learnt from my father. You come out the first round, you get loosened up and you watch what your opponent's doing – watch this and watch that. The second round, you go out and try them out, see what they can do. Third round, anything goes.

'But my number one rule, before you come out, hands up so you see the thumb of each hand,' says Ted, raising his hands in a boxing attitude. 'Whatever you do – if you go on the floor, the referee pulls you back, stops the fight for a moment, talks to you – the first thing you do is bring your hands up: it's automatic. And that's gotta be ingrained in your head, 'cause while your hands are there you're not gonna get injured, you can only get bashed in the belly.'

As more fights were made, the wins quickly stacked up. Sticking to his usual fight plan, Ted started 1949 with three consecutive third-round KO wins – Dennis Ford, Johnny Sage and Eddie Oliver his victims. 'Picking his punches well, Berry had his man down for counts of seven and eight, before applying the closure with a perfectly delivered solar plexus punch,' fight scribe Leslie Bell wrote of the Ford bout.

These Ted followed with a third-round stoppage of the game Harry Ruff, who was down three times and then rescued by the referee. Somehow, in Ted's fifth fight that year, Arthur Wright managed to stay the six-round distance. 'In what was probably his stiffest fight so far, Ted fully justified the confidence of his connections. We are looking forward to a quick jump into the front line of this Bethnal Green boy, and he appears to be capable of storing the knowledge gained in each fight,' wrote the *Weekly Sporting Review*.

I ask Ted if he ever felt nervous before a fight and his answer surprises me. 'Always,' he tells me. 'You show me a fighter who's never gone in a ring nervous and he must be a drug addict or something. You always wanna pee when you're gloved up – you have 64 pees before you get there. Many a manager or trainer, as a fighter's been gloved up and wanted a pee, has got his piddly out and done it in a bottle for him!'

While some boxers may underperform when struck by nervous tension directly before a fight, Ted seemed to thrive on it and turned it to his advantage. 'A quarter of an hour before a fight I used to shut me door – I didn't want no one in there. Then I used to buzz myself up, buzz me mind up. I used to take it as an affront. "*You* fighting me; *you* took a match against me; you think you can knock me out!" And I made a war out of it. So then when I went into the ring there was a war. Shake hands, yes; but it was a war. Every fight I had was a war, and the ones I beat on points, I don't know how they got away with it!'

After knocking out Benny Richards in two rounds, Ted stopped Pat Crawford in four and Freddie Evans in six. Then came a needle fight; a match with a strong significance in Bethnal Green.

'My old man's drinking place used to be over the Broadway, London Fields way, and they had a kid come out the Broadway called Joe Rock,' recalls Ted. 'He was a local fighter and I was a local fighter so it become a local derby. Me dad used to booze over that way and they're all sportsmen kind of thing, so they started having bets over who's gonna win, and I think the old man was getting a bit nervous. But we went there and I stopped him in four rounds.

'The first time my old man ever showed me any approbation was when I beat Joe Rock. After the fight he got hold of me, grabbed me tight and said, "My Teddy!" It was the first time I'd ever heard him say anything of the kind. The first time he'd ever been pleased.'

Ted does not recall the detail of many of his fights, as the outcome (an early finish) was usually the same. To him they were essentially a prelude to the more important matches that seemed destined to come. 'There's only one other that I remember,' he informs me. 'I can't think of his bloody name, but it's the only time I'd really been hurt, and when I say hurt I mean when you don't know where you are. That's hurt.

'As I told you, I used to feel them out, then in the second round test out what they can do, and I see what he can do, and did he do it! Jesus Christ. I walked into my own trap. Just before the end of the round he caught me with a right hand and I can honestly say I did not know where I was. I never went on the floor but I was walking about unconscious, I don't know what happened, can't say, but thank God the bell went. It was only instinct that guided me to my corner.

'And I got to the corner – it's only a minute, you know – I sat down, they was dousing me with cold water, and all of a sudden me brain come back. And as it come back I looked across and I see him sitting there and a hatred come out of me and I thought, "*You bastard* – I'm gonna kill you for this." I went out the next round and destroyed him. And I mean destroyed him. That's the first time I'd ever felt rage in a fight. Three rounds I won it in. Stopped him in that round.'

Although Ted, by his own testimony, treated every fight as a 'war', the submission to such unbridled rage was not his usual style. His was a more methodical approach, as he explains:

> I was an orthodox fighter – I'd come out behind a straight left. My habit was to follow and back him up all the time. Jab, go forward, jab, go forward, jab, and I'd try to corner him. If I didn't, I'd do a sidestep. You figure out in your brain what the guy's gonna do. You've gotta think about what he's gonna do before he does it. Once I'd got that confident buzz in my head – this is it, I know what to do, then it was all systems go.
>
> I was a fury fighter. We're there to bash each other – if I don't bash you, you're gonna bash me, and we're getting paid to do it. Amateurs it's all pat on the head and good boy, you know, here's a little medal for you. My intention – and I know it's not sportsmanlike, but if you're a professional you're not a sportsman, you do it for money – was to do the job properly. Don't take liberties or foul, but do the job to the rules, and win.
>
> And I was a hard puncher. I didn't realise how much I could punch. I remember Mickey Duff – we was kids together, we boxed each other at the People's Palace – and later, when I was fighting, he come down to Klein's and asked to spar with me. I sparred with him and when we was finished he went, 'Cor Ted, you can punch!' And I thought, coming from him, I must be able to punch.[2]

I ask Ted if there were any pet punches in his repertoire and he says very quickly, 'Left hook. I was born with a natural left hook, and I could hook off a straight left. Straight left, come back and hook off it, in the same motion. And in one motion I could hook under the belly and come over on top,' he says demonstrating with

---

his left arm a hook to the body seamlessly followed by a hook to the head. 'I was gifted with it; it wasn't taught, it just happened.'

After the Joe Rock win, there are just two more fights on Ted's distinguished record: a fourth-round stoppage of Tommy Swannell at Watford Town Hall and a fourth-round stoppage of Billy Caldicott at Dartford Football Ground.

After his last fight (not knowing then that it was his last), *Boxing News* published an article by R. Gee assessing Ted's prospects:

> At this stage of his career Berry can only be classed as an honest-to-goodness eight-rounder, but in my opinion he is one of our brightest prospects and should reach championship class within the next 12 months…
>
> One of the tallest lightweights around – he stands 5ft 10in – Ted is not built on compact lines like most fighters, but has long arms and lanky legs, and is rawboned. ('I love a rawboned fighter,' says manager Jack Jordan.) He boxes in the orthodox style, and I have seen him KO opponents with copybook punches – especially with his short left-hook to the solar plexus…
>
> He has one of the biggest followings of any preliminary fighter in town because he is jovial, unspoiled and tremendously popular with the local inhabitants. He wants nothing more out of boxing than to be able to buy a home for his family, but it will have to be in dear old Bethnal Green! He is a non-smoker, teetotaller, and makes no secret about the fact that he is obsessed with the sport.

With his long unbeaten pro record, his tireless work ethic and a growing army of fans attesting to his box office appeal, a step into British boxing's top echelon seemed just around the corner for Ted. But it wasn't to be.

'I had a shadow in my eye,' explains Ted with palpable sadness. 'I went to the local doctor and they said there was a cold in my eye or something. But Joycie's mum said I should go to Moorfields, so Joycie took me there. I went to Moorfields, sat down, spoke to the surgeon and he said, "You've got a detachment." I didn't even know what a detachment was so I said, "What is it?" He said, "Well, something's come unhooked in your eye." He said, "What is your profession?" I said, "I'm a professional fighter." "Oh," he said, "you won't fight no more." Well, I tell you, you could have took my legs away from me. I could have collapsed. Oh I was *ill* – physically and mentally ill.

'So I had a detached retina, and I went into the hospital to have it done, and there are people now who have the operation that can still fight. Some of them can. But they said I would never fight again. Anyway, the operation was terrible. They cover your eyes up and you can't see nothing for six weeks. You're covered up for four weeks and you can't see nothing, and after four weeks they come round every so often and take the bandages off and let you have a look round, then they put them back on. It was horrible. Even now I drive past Moorfields Hospital and I feel sick. Honestly, I look and I feel sick.

'It's a wonderful hospital but they never saved me eye. They saved it at the time and everything was all right, I didn't fight no more, obviously, but a couple of months later it happened again. I went back and they said the detachment had come back, and I lost me sight in the eye.'

Having spoken to Ted for well over an hour, it is only at this point that I become aware he is blind in his right eye, and has been since 1949.

Ted was then a 21-year-old in the prime of fitness and strength, and having just faced the devastating news that his boxing career was over, he now had to come to terms with the fact that half his vision was gone too. It is difficult to imagine how hard this must have been.

Career Reflections

'To me it was a wonderful life being a fighter – I loved it – but it was too short a career for me and I've mourned it ever since,' says Ted. One of the most intriguing aspects of Ted's career is its sudden termination while he was still an unbeaten prospect. Gifted competitors from any sport who finish before their time leave behind them a trail of unanswered questions. And though Ted was never famous outside of small-hall London fight shows, his talent and record suggest he was bound for bigger things.

Octogenarian Nobby Clarke (ring name Harold Clarke), who himself fought in the 1940s and 50s and watched Ted box numerous times, told me that Ted would have probably been British champion.

I put this to Ted and he quickly replies, 'Without a doubt. With all modesty I say without a doubt. I had 19 fights and I won them all. Unfortunately a blow caught me a certain way and I got a detached retina. I was broken-hearted. With another two fights I'd have been in the area championship class, you know, lightweight. And that's a step from the top. 'Cause I'd sparred with all the top fighters. I sparred with Billy Thompson when he was lightweight champion, I sparred with Tommy McGovern, and I reckon, with all respect to Tommy, I could have took him any time.'

As we discuss the venues where Ted fought I ask first about a place that was probably London's most unusual boxing arena of the post-war era, the Mile End Arena. 'It was a dump,' he says. 'In the summer they had open air boxing there, and in the winter they had a fairground going on there. If you wanted to see fights you could climb over the side – people'd just climb over. It was like a great big car site, if you can imagine, made into an arena for boxing. They had a ring and chairs, a shed was your dressing room. It was a put-up kind of place. They used to run it on a shoestring. But there was always a good crowd at Mile End Arena. They was enthusiasts, you know.

'Bermondsey Baths had a good crowd, West Ham Baths had a good crowd; Leyton Baths didn't always have a good crowd, it all depends, it was a bigger place. The promoters all cried, "We lost our money, we lost our money," but they all came back with another show the next week,' Ted chuckles.

'The purse at these places was a fixed rate: four-rounders got fivers, six-rounders got 12 and a half quid, eight-rounders got

£30 upwards, all depends who they were, and top of the bill got a top of the bill purse. And you used to have to sell tickets. I was a big ticket-seller. I had a load of friends who used to get all me tickets. I used to sell £150, £200 worth of tickets for every fight I had. They was all ten bob a ticket or five shilling ones circles, and I used to sell 'em all.'

By the time he retired a lack of good purse money was becoming an issue for Ted, and while he was fond of his manager, Jack Jordan, frustration was setting in. 'Jack was a nice man, a quiet man – gentleman Jack – but I didn't see me going anywhere. After you've had, say, eight or nine fights and you've won them all, you expect a bit more cash. I mean I was selling tickets wherever I was, so I thought he should have been a bit more forceful and got me more money. But he never got it.

'When I had to finish, that was the end of our association. He never phoned to see if I was all right. And I was disappointed; I thought he'd do more for me, 'cause I used to like him, he was like my father, you know. He did try and get me a couple of jobs but they fell through.

'I was in trouble then,' continues Ted. 'I'd finished fighting, I was married to Joyce, she was expecting Rocky, our son, and we had nothing.[3*] We didn't have a penny between us. We lived in one room in an aunt of mine's house for a while and Joyce worked almost up till she had the baby. She used to be an upholstery machinist. Brilliant girl. But I wasn't allowed to work. I wasn't allowed to do any manual labour – that's from the hospital. So how am I gonna live? There was no social security them days.

'If you couldn't live, you went to what they called the bun house – the local National Assistance Board. I remember I went up there once and the bloke came up to test us for our finances. And Joycie had a little pedal machine, which she used to do a bit of work on, repair jobs, only to make a penny, you know. I said,

---

3   Ted had married Joyce in late 1949 and their first son, Edward (affectionately known as Rocky), was born the following year. Another son, Daniel, followed in 1952 and a daughter, Sharon, in 1955.

"Well, we've got nothing." "That machine," he said. "Sell that." That's the treatment you got then.'

Coaching

For a long time Ted was a broken man. When his own future in the sport was cruelly snatched away from him, his interest in boxing waned for a while. But before long the boxing bug returned. 'I loved the game,' Ted enthuses, 'so I took out a trainer and second's licence, and I used to help the old man out in the ring sometimes, just for the sake of being there. And I tried to get fighters, but to me it was a closed shop. Trainers was a closed shop. They didn't want any kids, any new ones – I was only a kid. What do they want kids for? "We've gotta get our living, *they* can get a job".

'But you tell me what trainer, anyway, is worth his salt,' Ted adds, turning his attention to trainers who lack proper boxing credentials. 'If you've never been in the ring, how could you understand the experience of getting hit on the chin? I don't mean no disrespect to anybody. But it's like, if you've never driven, how can you get in my car and tell me how to drive? But if you've been through the game, you can tell people and educate them.

'You see the trainers today, and you'd see the trainers in the 40s and 50s even, and all they'd do is hold the towel. Someone's got a cut eye, they don't know what to bloody do. In my time, there was a guy, a well-known trainer, looking after an up-and-coming fighter down Klein's. He was standing, holding a towel and the kid was doing his workout and he never took a bit of notice of him; he was talking to us; talking to me and me dad about this and that. 'Cause an automatic bell used to ring at the end of time, so he didn't even look to see what the kid was doing. It's all money.

'Patience, observing and getting to know the person' are all key facets of a trainer's job according to Ted. 'You have to talk and get to know what he's thinking about. You've got to understand the person. You know what move he's gonna do next. You've got to know what they're capable of before they get in the ring. It's no good sitting in the corner going, "Hold your hands up. Jab-jab-jab-jab."'

Although Ted's career as a trainer never took off, he did coach one pro fighter, bantamweight Harry Alley, who was managed by Morrie Fletcher. 'Young Harry was from Paddington – he was a lovely kid. I had him for about four or five fights. But I think he was spoilt from the start. He was a very aggressive fighter, a non-stop fighter, but with the aggressiveness he never had no defence. And I tried to make a bit of defence with him but unfortunately I got the sack,' Ted laughs. 'If he'd had defence, he could have gone somewhere.'

In addition, Ted's younger brother, Checker (real name Henry) Berry, boxed twice as a professional in 1952. 'I started training me brother but he really didn't wanna know about the game – it was too hard for him,' chuckles Ted. Later Ted trained his cousin Pat Berry, who Ted says was a good amateur who turned pro too late and consequently did not progress far.

The Krays

With his boxing career over, Ted carried on hawking with his father, and as already mentioned, in his spare time helped him to train and second fighters. Under Ted's father's care at that time were a pair of twin brothers from Bethnal Green who in a few years would be household names. They were of course the infamous Krays, Reggie and Ronnie.

The Berry family's connection with the Kray family goes back several generations. The Kray family, like the Berrys, were well-known hawkers, and in their younger days, like Ted, Reggie and Ronnie went out with their father and uncles 'on the knocker', buying clothes, jewellery and other items from householders. Their paternal grandfather, Jim Kray, was known to Ted and his brother as 'Uncle Jim', so familiar were the two families.

The twins' elder brother Charlie Kray (also coached by Harry Kid Berry) had done well as an amateur and won numerous trophies, which took pride of place on the mantelpiece at the family's 178 Vallance Road home. As a pro – fighting between 1948 and 1951 – he won 11, drew one and lost six of 18 bouts. Naturally the twins wanted to emulate their elder brother, and had their first boxing lessons at the Robert Browning Youth Club in Camberwell, south London, before moving to the Webbe club, the Oxford House and eventually the Repton.

In a bid to learn from the pros, Ronnie and Reggie visited gyms such as Bill Klein's and Jack Solomons's where they sparred with the likes of British champion Dickie O'Sullivan, world flyweight champion Terry Allen and Ben Valentine, who were all happy to box a few rounds with these eager young amateurs. In his autobiography, Reggie recalls Harry Kid Berry (who was by then training the Krays) having to pull his volatile brother Ron and Trinidadian featherweight Rolly Blyce apart when a sparring session at Klein's turned explosive.

As amateur schoolboys the twins won various titles, with Reggie the more successful, then at 17 both turned professional under Ted's old manager, Jack Jordan. They made their debuts on the same bill at the Mile End Arena on 31 July 1951, Ronnie stopping his opponent in two rounds and Reggie boxing his way to a points win over six. The twins, still in their boxing gear, were photographed with Ted and their brother Charlie straight after the fight. In the photo, Ted (dressed in a dark suit) rests one hand in a fatherly fashion on a boyish-looking Reggie's shoulder, while Charlie stands next to brother Ronnie.

Between July and December 1951 Ronnie had six pro fights, winning four and losing two, while Reggie won all seven of his. On 11 December 1951 the twins and their brother Charlie appeared on the same bill at the Royal Albert Hall. Charlie, who had been out of the ring for nearly two years, was not in the best of shape and took the fight against Harry Kid Berry's advice. Unsurprisingly he was knocked out in three rounds by Lew Lazar, a younger brother of Sid Nathan's brilliant stablemate Harry Lazar. Ronnie, meanwhile, was well out-pointed by Bill Sliney (who brother Reggie had twice out-pointed, which indicates Reggie's superior boxing ability), while Reggie beat his opponent, Bobby Manito, on points.

By the time they started boxing the Kray twins were well known around the East End, where they and their teenage gang wreaked havoc, carrying choppers, swords and knives and battling with other gangs. As a result, the twins had been barred from most of the area's dance halls and cinemas and had narrowly escaped prison sentences several times.

Boxing seemed to be the only activity that might have steered the twins away from a life of crime and notoriety, in theory at least. With hindsight, however, it seems likely Ronnie's psychopathic tendencies would have always carried him and his inseparable twin down a felonious path, regardless of how their ring careers panned out. In any case, their boxing days were about to be cut short; and that night at the Albert Hall was the last time any of the three Kray brothers appeared in a pro ring.

In 1952 the twins were called into the army for national service. They went on the run, were recaptured several times, and assaulted a police officer who tried to arrest them for desertion. After a term in both the Tower of London and a military prison they were given dishonourable discharges.

Over the next few years the twins built their criminal empire. Starting with the ownership of a Bethnal Green snooker hall and local protection rackets, by the late 1950s they owned numerous clubs and properties and were involved via their gang, 'the firm', in various criminal activities. Eventually, as is well documented, both twins graduated to murder.

Ted does not wish to go into detail about his connection with the Krays, but it seems he worked for them both as a driver and club doorman and also ran a Kray-owned spieler (or gambling club). Ted was five years older than the twins but his brother, Checker, was just a year older and had been pals with them from boyhood.

With the benefit of hindsight it's clear that the Krays' empire was toxic, but in the 1950s the full extent of their activity had yet to be realised, and it's easy to see how a life working for these outwardly glamorous figures, who hobnobbed with stars of sport and entertainment, may have appealed to Ted in his poverty-stricken state. Once aboard this lethal rollercoaster, it would be hard to jump off.

The Shooting

On the evening of Friday 10 January 1964 Ted was in a pub about 200 yards from his home at the Hadrian Estate, Hackney Road, Bethnal Green, drinking with his brother. At about 9pm he left the pub and went home to fetch his tobacco tin. As he left his house to return to the pub a car containing two men – a white driver and a black passenger – pulled up alongside him.

As the window was wound down, the passenger aimed a 12-bore shotgun at Ted's legs and opened fire. Ted fell to the ground in agony and his assailant leaped from the car, stood over him, and fired another shot just inches from Ted's right knee. The man then jumped back in the car and it sped away.

Ted was rushed to hospital, where the damage to his right leg was deemed so severe that it had to be amputated. His left leg was also injured and still bears the scars.

As word spread, the shooting made headlines in the following Monday's national papers, and the *Daily Mirror* and *Daily Express* ran sensationalist stories stating that Scotland Yard was bracing itself for revenge attacks and an outbreak of gang warfare.

The papers suggested that the shooting of Ted, whom the *Daily Express* called a 'friend of the underworld "controllers" in the East End of London', was the work of a gang that could not frighten him into paying them protection money. The *Daily Mirror* noted that Ted worked at a betting shop in Green Dragon Yard, off Commercial Road, and linked the shooting to a series of petrol bomb attacks on East End betting shops.

But it seems the papers got no further with their speculation, the promised gang war never materialised, and the police investigations into the incident reached a dead end. In Kray-related books of recent years it has been claimed that Ronnie Kray was the gunman who shot Ted, though Ted insists this is 'cobblers'. 'I was hit,' he explains, 'and that's all I can tell you. It was a paid-for hit.'

My interviews for this book were recorded with a camcorder, and at this point in our discussion Ted informs me he's willing to tell me more about the incident but doesn't wish to do so on camera. Accordingly, I switch off the camera and Ted gives his version of events.

He tells me that the shooting stemmed from an incident that happened a few weeks earlier in a club he and his brother were paid to protect. Most of the club's patrons knew who Ted and Checker were and usually their presence alone, or at most a quiet word from them, was enough to deter troublemakers. On this particular night, a pair of men were causing trouble and took no notice when Ted and Checker warned them about their behaviour. Outside the club a huge fight ensued and the Berry brothers gave the men a severe beating. Unfortunately the men were close associates of the Krays.

Sensing trouble, Ted visited Reggie and Ronnie Kray and explained that the fracas was not intended as an insult to them. Reggie seemed to accept this, but days later Ted heard through the grapevine that Ronnie viewed the incident as an affront and planned to take revenge.

Ted purchased a gun, which he carried with him constantly and fully intended to use if the need to defend himself arose. As fate would have it, on the night he was shot he had relaxed a little and for the first time decided to leave the gun indoors instead of carrying it to the pub.

Afterwards Ted discovered the shooting was a professional hit, bankrolled by Ronnie Kray. Ted says the hitmen were not locals and he suspects they may have been hired from overseas. The thought of revenge on Ronnie entered Ted's mind immediately, but when he weighed this up against a probable long prison sentence and the danger this would mean for Joyce and their three children, he decided to take no action.

Needless to say, the permanent injury Ted had suffered left him feeling very depressed, but that summer his mood brightened a little when he took a holiday with friends to Italy, France and Switzerland.

The Old Horns

After hearing about his plight, the people of Bethnal Green rallied around Ted. 'They had collections all round Bethnal Green,' he tells me. 'There were boxing shows and one thing and another, and they got me a nice few quid and I bought a pub.'

In 1966 Ted went into the licensed trade with a pub called the Bridge House in Bow, but within two years he moved to the Old Horns on Warner Place in Bethnal Green. It has been written that the Kray twins helped raise some of the money for the purchase of Ted's pub as a gesture of atonement.

And it seems the Krays and the Berrys eventually reached a reconciliation of sorts, as the Old Horns became the Kray firm's HQ.

'While I was there, there was ten murderers that used the pub,' Ted informs me. 'The Krays and all the villains. And there was two people before I took it, just at the beginning of the war I think, two of the pub's customers got done for murder. One got hung and the other one turned King's evidence.'

A photo taken at the pub while the twins were at large shows Ted and Checker sitting with the Krays' biographer, John Pearson, and the famous photographer David Bailey. And a trawl through several Kray books suggests the pub was also the site of several attacks by Reggie and Ronnie on other villains.

In May 1968, the Krays and numerous other members of their firm were arrested and given famously long prison sentences. Ted, meanwhile, remained the landlord of the Old Horns until 1979. 'I retired when I was 50. It was a good life while it lasted,' he says, 'but I'd been long enough in it and I got fed up with it, so I just got out the business. It was too tiring, seven days a week.'

Boxing Today

Today, Ted remains a follower of the sport that was always his first love, and he still has strong feelings about it.

When I ask Ted how the fight game today compares with his own day, he tells me, 'It doesn't. Today I couldn't tell you who was the champion of what, because there's so many divisions and so many titles – it ain't like years ago. You've got four different title-holders at every weight and they're all champions of the world.

Where's the Joe Louises? That's why a lot of older people don't really bother, 'cause it's foreign to them, which is sad because boxing's a part of our past – boxing started in England.

'In our day everyone knew who the champions were – they were household names. A British champion stood out. Everyone knew them. But they don't stand out no more. People don't know them.'

'There's not enough fights going today,' he adds. 'In my day there was fights every week. You had Leyton Baths, you had Manor Place Baths, Plumstead Baths, you had so many venues. I boxed 19 fights in ten months. That's a fight a fortnight.'

I ask Ted if he felt fighting this often placed an undue strain on his body and he answers rationally, 'No, not really. If I didn't feel I'd recovered I wouldn't take the fight. And if I've stopped somebody in three rounds it can't be a hard fight, can it? So you can book me up next week, can't you? If I've gone to points with someone I should have knocked out, and it's been a bit of a strenuous fight, then my manager could say, "Leave him out this week." You go by the way the fighter acts.'

However, Ted acknowledges that in the hands of unscrupulous managers this kind of fight schedule would lead to exploitation and could prove hazardous to a fighter's health. 'You'd look round and you'd see the old-time fighters, all got cauliflower ear-holes and slurred speech, and they couldn't get a penny off no one,' he says, referring to some of the boxers from the pre-war era, who were appallingly overworked.

But the ingredients for success in boxing are the same in any era, and Ted readily proffers these words of advice that boxers at any level would do well to heed:

> You never know enough. A wise fighter would say that every fight he takes is a teaching. The fight game's the hardest game in the world, and no matter how great you are, every day's a lesson. There's always some Joe Bloggings out there who's gonna come up and hit you on the chin and over you're gonna go, which has happened so many times.

So every fight is a lesson, every part of training is a lesson. It's like life. Every day you learn something, and if you're wise enough or clever enough you keep it in your head.

%% %% %%

My interview with Ted took place on 20 May 2012. Later that year he was taken into hospital, where he remained for several months, returning home briefly before being taken ill again. After a long fight to regain his health, sadly Ted (known as Teddy to his close friends and family) passed away on 11 May 2013. By this point I had already finished a first draft of his story, and I have therefore left it just as I had written it: in the present tense.

Ted wanted his story to be told and contacted me for that purpose after hearing about my planned book. I hope he would have been pleased with the result.

JOCK TAYLOR (SIDCUP) 1943–51

IT is 1 March 1948 and we are at the Plumstead Baths on Plumstead High Street for a sell-out Monday night boxing show.

Jack Streek, a promising 15-year-old amateur boxer, watches tentatively from the crowd as his hometown hero, Jock Taylor of Sidcup, enters the ring for the fight of his life. Secretly young Streek wishes it was him in the ring and dreams that in a few years he will be in Jock's place, boxing before an admiring crowd for titles, money and glory. But right now all his hopes are with Jock, whom he greatly admires and knows has the strength and tenacity to win.

Jock, meanwhile, is raring to be let loose by the bell. He has drawn with the man before him in a previous encounter and knows that an extra effort this time will see him go home victorious, with an area title to his name and possibly a shot at Freddie Mills's British light-heavyweight crown in the offing.

His opponent is Al Marson of Canning Town, a clever, rangy man who is taller than Jock and a better boxer. But Jock possesses that equaliser that can wipe out any number of boxing points instantaneously – an innate knockout punch. This is a classic boxer–fighter confrontation.

The bell clangs for the start of round one and the fight is on. From his seat in the crowd Streek grits his teeth and casts his full attention to his friend in the ring, willing him on to victory.

Two rounds pass and the fight is open and closely contested. Marson has held Jock off with his fine left lead, but Jock's aggressive assault is relentless and his opponent has to fight at full pace to keep him at bay. Already Marson has been rocked several times and blood streams from a cut on his right eye.

Midway through the fourth Jock crowds his opponent into a corner and fires a vicious right into the pit of his stomach. Streek screams encouragement from his seat in the crowd and Marson crumples to the canvas in agony. Shakily he makes it to his feet at the count of eight, but Jock is poised to put him down again.

Then, inexplicably, the referee turns to Jock and whispers something into his ear. The expression on the Sidcup man's face alters from one of focus to one of anxiety, and at once the pattern of the fight (and possibly its outcome) is changed.

Five years of dedication have led the Sidcup fighter to this make or break fight, and afterwards he will not be quite the same.

%. %. %.

Sixty-five years have passed but Jock still remembers that night with some emotion. It was, after all, the pinnacle of his ring career, a unique period of his life that he looks back on with a mixture of pride, sentiment and regret. Today, in his late 80s, he leads a calm existence and lives in a small, quiet town on the Sussex coast.

I visit the former light-heavyweight contender at his home on several occasions and he eagerly talks me through his boxing life. Due to his age Jock's memory of recent events sometimes wavers, but his recall of his time at the top of the hardest of sports is excellent.

When one first meets Jock it is hard to mistake him for anything but a former professional fighter. At 5ft 10in he is not a giant in stature, but his wide shoulders, large workmanlike hands and broad, flattened nose combined with a self-possessed demeanour give him a powerful presence. When he speaks this is accentuated by the deep nasal tone of his voice.

He is, however, friendly and good-natured and although his unsteady legs mean he can't get out as often as he used to, he remains in good spirits with his deadpan sense of humour intact. I get the impression when talking to him that he is an inherently moral man.

There is no pretence about him and what he tells me I invariably feel is sincere. If he cannot remember a particular event or detail, he will not fictionalise. 'I just don't remember,' he answers to several questions. 'There's no point pretending I do.' Jock is a realist who does not romanticise his ring days, but he also exhibits an endearing innocence.

Sidcup is not renowned for its boxing talent, but for a few years in the late 1940s Jock gave the area a fighter to be proud of and really cheer about. After I had interviewed Jock, his younger stablemate Jack Streek kindly spoke to me at length and gave me a broader insight into both their careers, while Jock's daughter June gave me more information about his life after boxing.

In the late 1940s Britain possessed a pack of extremely good middleweights and light-heavyweights, whom, had they boxed separately during a less competitive period, could have all been British champions. These men included Ginger Sadd, Al Marson, Reg Spring, Don Cockell, Albert Finch, Mark Hart, Ernie Woodman, Pat Stribling and – by no means least – Jock Taylor.

Jock fought each of the others in that exciting group but sadly he is now its sole surviving member. His recollections resurrect an exciting period in British ring history that is not well documented and has almost faded from living memory.

Early Life

> He was a terrific bloke. Great fighter. Never frightened of anybody – he used to give 'em all he could. And he was a fine-built bloke. Beautiful body he had on him – bronzed he was.

He was quite the business actually... he was a fitness fanatic,
you know.

These are the words of Jack Streek, spoken as he describes Jock
Taylor, a boyhood hero who became his friend and stablemate
when Streek boxed professionally in the early 1950s. To many
who remember them, those days seem like a lifetime ago, but to
Streek and Taylor they remain vividly clear.

※ ※ ※

'I was born at 38 Clarence Crescent, Sidcup – a home birth – on
2 August 1925,' Jock informs me as our interview begins. 'I lived
there with my mum and dad and my brother Derrick, who was four
years older than me. Frederick Ernest was my name but when I was
a baby my brother couldn't pronounce it and he used to call me
this name that sounded like Jock. I don't think my mother liked
my name, Frederick, very much, so Jock I became and it's stuck
with me all my life. A Scots bloke once asked me, "So what part
of Scotland are you from, Jock?" I said ... "Sidcup".'

It is open to debate whether Sidcup truly belongs to Kent or
London: today it's officially part of Greater London, but it used to
be known as the gateway to Kent. In the 18th and 19th centuries
the area had been popular with the landed gentry, and several
substantial houses with large estates sprung up there.

It remained a predominantly rural place until the late 1920s
and early 30s when developers bought up large portions of its land.
The fields that had once belonged to Sidcup's great estates were
then replaced with road upon road of new homes, built to cater
for middle-class commuters in search of pleasant surroundings
close to the City.

It was therefore not an area apt to produce professional
boxers. There is no known history of boxing – either amateur or
professional – in Jock's family, and being born into a financially
secure household, it hardly seemed likely he would grow up to be
a professional fighter. 'My mother was born in Malta,' he recalls.

'Her dad, who'd been an army major, was well-off and mum had been well-educated. Her sister was a teacher and her brother was a top civil servant. My father, who was from Tunbridge Wells, was a clerical officer in the civil service, so he was reasonably well off.'

Despite his relatively comfortable beginnings, Jock's was not an entirely happy childhood. 'My dad wouldn't accept me for years because of my looks,' he states, 'because I wasn't a pretty boy. My brother had got a lovely bright complexion, curly hair and then there was me. In fact, he even went as far as to say that mum'd had a love affair with somebody else. But I think that helps you fight – it makes you antagonistic.

'My brother and me always fought. He was older than me and used to take advantage quite a lot, and when I got to school I was still fighting. I was automatically the best fighter in junior school and when I got to senior school I was the best fighter there.'

Jock's junior school was just 100 yards from his Clarence Crescent home, and his senior school – the newly built Sidcup Central Boys' School – was on Alma Road, around 300 yards from his home. By the time he reached senior school, however, Jock's fighting had become controlled and he was rarely called on to prove his capability. 'I was accepted as being the best boy in the school and that was that, you know what kids are like – nobody really challenged me.'

He had developed this self-control from the age of eight, after joining the local boxing club, as he recalls, 'Me dad belonged to a working men's club on the Main Road, which had boxing shows about once a month. He saw these boys boxing and knew I was always fighting me brother – the good-looking elder brother – so he got me going up there to learn to box. I started boxing at these shows, mostly against the local boys, and I had eight fights there and won six of them. The trainer was an old army man called Alf Pearcy.'

After these initial schoolboy bouts, Jock took a break from boxing for a few years. The outbreak of war in 1939 coincided with his leaving school at the statutory age of 14 and he found a job, a short bike ride away, at a garage in New Eltham. 'They were doing war work, and I was being trained as a steel turner supposedly – I used to make valves for anti-tank guns, any job that needed to be turned on a lathe – but I was doing any odd job and I was more a cleaner really.'

While we are on the subject, I ask Jock what he remembers of the effect of the war locally and he recalls sitting in Danson Park in nearby Welling with his future wife, Barbara, and watching 'dog fights' light up the sky. 'Sidcup got quite a lot of bombing,' he says. 'At night you'd hear the bombs coming down and the planes flying over. If a bomb went off you accepted it, you lived with it and put up with it. What else could you do?'

To keep active in his spare time, Jock resumed boxing when he was aged 15 or 16. He started to train at a local gym run by a man named Dod Rickner. 'I used to go down this gym and practise and practise,' Jock recalls, 'and I was a sparring partner to this very strong featherweight called Tich Parsons. He was a bundle of muscles and he was very good – *and he could punch*. He was a top-line amateur and he could box rings round me at the time, and I was used more or less as a punch bag. It didn't do me any harm though and I learnt a bit from him.'

At the time, regular amateur shows were being staged in and around Sidcup under the banner of Sidcup's Home Guard Battalion. With his boxing interest reignited, Jock began to box on these bills and soon became acquainted with the matchmaker, Rex J. Manning, a Home Guard Lieutenant who was also a senior figure in the London Transport Passenger Board.

'He hadn't got any children and he more or less adopted me,' Jock says, 'and he got me fights all over the place. Because Rex Manning was a Home Guard officer, he was allowed to use the Drill Hall in Halfway Street for the boys to train in. I used to train there and that was a short bike ride for me, near Sidcup station.'

Jock boxed regularly on shows at venues such as Croydon Civic Hall, Ladywell Baths, Sidcup Football Club, St John's Hall in Sidcup and Southend Hall in Eltham. Sometimes styled as 'the Home Guard Champion' and at other times billed as representing Sidcup and District Boxing Club, Magenta Boxing

Club or Croydon ABC, in reality Jock did not belong to an amateur club. 'Sidcup hadn't got an amateur boxing club, not as such,' he explains, 'and Croydon, I wasn't anything to do with Croydon. But you had to have a club, so Rex Manning used to put these club names in to get me fights.'

Although Jock was only in his mid teens, he already had a powerful physique and was soon being matched with full-grown men. Grenadier Guards, police constables, firemen and military physical training instructors all wilted under the whirlwind attacks of this extremely strong and aggressive youth, and many were knocked out or saved by the referee.

But on 24 August 1942 Jock met an opponent who proved to him that brute force alone was not always enough in the ring. Harry Watson, a black man who lived in nearby Welling, showed Jock that skill and experience could overcome raw power and youth.

'He was about 50 I s'pose but hard as nails and fit as a fiddle. He beat me, at that time, with one simple move,' remembers Jock. 'He put his left arm across my left to knock my wrist down and expose my chin, then clonked me with his right. A few blows like that was enough to disorientate me and he beat me on points.'

Photos in Jock's collection of him and Harry Watson together show that Watson was in remarkable shape for a man of 50 (if indeed he was that old). After the fight he and Jock trained regularly together, before Rex Manning astutely suggested Watson become Jock's regular coach.

'I used to spar with him every night,' says Jock, 'and I picked up lots of little tips. Then gradually I got accustomed to his style and I could manage him quite easily in the end. But through boxing so much with him I was able to manage people that I probably never would have been able to manage, 'cause Harry was so experienced. He was a very nice man but it was hard for him, being coloured in those days.'

Notwithstanding the Watson defeat Jock went from success to success in the amateur ranks. In June 1943 the London *Evening News* called him 'one of the hardest hitters among present London amateur middleweights', noting that he 'has knocked out most of the men he has so far met'.

By now Rex Manning was keenly telling all and sundry that he had unearthed a potential future British champion. To an area like Sidcup, with a less than lustrous fistic past, this was exciting news indeed.

By his own estimation Jock had around 40 unpaid bouts then, just as he was starting to get recognition in the amateur world, Manning advised him that the time was right to turn professional. A contract was promptly signed and, with Manning as his manager and Harry Watson as his trainer, Jock had his first paid fight on 29 June 1943, at age 17.

Pro Debut

Jock made his pro debut at Watford Town Hall where for the princely sum of £2 he stopped George Hatton (Watford) inside a round. Did he find moving from the amateurs to the pros difficult? 'No, it didn't worry me at all. In the early days it wasn't much different from the amateurs, apart from the fact you didn't wear a vest.'

Having made short work of his first professional opponent, Manning entered Jock into a fight the following day. He was to meet Canada's Harry Bartin at the Queensberry All Services Club, a venue which for a newcomer to pro boxing it was a privilege to box at.

The Queensberry Club on Old Compton Street had been founded the previous year (1942) by the 11th Marquess of Queensberry (whose grandfather had fashioned the rules of modern boxing) and lasted until the end of the war. It was a members-only club ostensibly for servicemen, although membership was open to civilians too. Housed in what was formerly the Prince Edward Theatre (where in the 1930s stars such as Josephine Baker had once performed), the club was a grandiose setting for professional boxing.

During its short reign the Queensberry Club staged performances by the likes of Bing Crosby, the Glenn Miller Dance Band, Flannagan & Allen, Ann Shelton, Arthur Askey and Mark Hambourg. On boxing nights some of the country's leading fighters – many of them serving in the forces – performed there when granted leave.[4*]

On the bill with Jock that evening were former British welterweight champion Jake Kilrain, Arthur Danahar (whom Jock rates as the best boxer he ever watched live), future British featherweight champion Al Phillips and the talented Harry Lazar. It was a swift step up in class from the local halls Jock was used to. Disappointingly, however, he lost his four three-minute rounds bout on points, but received the improved purse of £5.

His performance, though, must have pleased the services crowd as he was invited back to the Queensberry Club three months later. This time he comfortably out-pointed his opponent (who was billed as the Polish amateur champion), but when he returned home he got a surprise when his mother handed him an envelope.

'These are your call-up papers,' she said. 'I didn't want to tell you before, in case it upset you for the fight.' He had been called into the Royal Navy's Fleet Air Arm, in which he would serve for three years as an armourer.

Military Exploits

Although being called into the forces was a setback to his fighting ambitions, Jock was relieved to discover that, despite turning pro, he was sufficiently unknown to be able to box as a member of the services.

'I was 18 when my call-up papers came and away I went,' he recalls. 'Within a few weeks we were all sorted out, and when we first got together as a mob the warrant officer asked if anybody could run, dance or sing, et cetera. Then he said, "Can anybody box?" I said, "Yes, I can," and I showed him the programme from my last fight before I got called up, fighting the Polish champion at the Queensberry Club. It was only a four three-minute round curtain-raiser, but people like Arthur Danahar and Peter Kane, the world flyweight champion, were on the bill.

4 After the war the building again became a theatre and survives today under its original name, the Prince Edward.

'"Oh," he said, "how d'you get on?" I said, "I beat him." He said, "You're fighting tonight. Not a word to anybody – you'll be our little secret!" Then the fella who was due to fight, they threw him out and put me in.

'I disposed of my opponent quickly, in the first round, so the warrant officer was quite happy about that. I was immediately made "boxing captain", whatever that meant, and I carried on boxing right through my time in the forces. They were only too pleased to have me fighting for them, but I was already a pro of course, so I had to be very careful.'

As an armourer Jock learned the intricacies of various weapons and how to service them. He was eventually posted up north, where he became friendly with future British, Commonwealth and European featherweight champion Ronnie Clayton, who was also serving in the Fleet Air Arm. Also while in the north Jock met a man who would tempt him back into the professional ring. He would, however, fall foul of a reckless type of matchmaking that was not uncommon in British boxing at that time.

'When I got up near Blackpool I met a man called Tom Hurst, who was Bruce Woodcock's manager,' Jock recalls. 'Now Bruce Woodcock was the heavyweight champion of Great Britain, so of course I thought I'm in good company here, and Tom Hurst fixed me up with a fight at Liverpool Stadium.

'I didn't know anything about the fight until I got to the stadium; I thought it'd be another little four-rounder, you know. But when I get there, it's the chief supporting bout – eight three-minute rounds – against the Irish middleweight champion, Bert Hyland! I nearly fell through the floor, 'cause I'd only had a couple of four-round bouts and eight threes compared with four threes was a different class altogether.

'Anyway, I went all the way with him and lost on points. I got 15 quid, which was a fortune to me 'cause I was only on about three quid a week in the mob. So I sent mum home a tenner and told her to put it into the bank for me.

'I made quite an impression at the stadium so they fixed me up with another fight there. When I got there this time I was fighting a heavyweight – he was 14st 10lb and I was only a middleweight. They said, "Well, we'll say he's 13st 10lb", and that's what they announced him as. But anyway he flattened me – he beat me in about three rounds. Bloke called Butler: he was a huge man. I should have never gone in with him – it was all wrong – but I'm stupid like that. I'd fought big men before and beaten them, but I didn't beat this bloke: blimey, he *clonked me*.'

Luckily word of Jock's pro excursions did not reach his Fleet Air Arm superiors and he was able to carry on his services boxing. At Kirkham he took on the 1944 ABA heavyweight champion Mark Hart. 'He was in the RAF,' Jock recalls, 'which we were attached to being the Fleet Air Arm. I remember seeing him fight beforehand. He wasn't all that big but he'd got this terrific left hook and he knocked everybody out with it. He'd won the ABA heavyweight title with three one-round knockouts if I remember rightly. He put me down with his left hook but I got up and carried on and he beat me on points. I gave him a stone and a half in weight.'[5]

Notwithstanding defeats to heavyweights, when Jock fought men of his own weight he was usually the winner. The highlight of his services boxing career was when he competed in the middleweight finals of the Fleet Air Arm championships, which were held on the evening of 14 November 1945 at the Royal Naval barracks at Lee-on-Solent.

Fighting in his usual ferocious style, Jock reached the final, but his previous battles that evening had taken their toll. 'I'd got a shut black eye 'cause I'd been headed in the eye in the semi-final. And the fella I was fighting in the final turned to me laughing and said, "It's a pity about your eye, it would have been a good fight." Anyway, we shook hands then – bang – I threw a left hook and knocked him out. So it *was* a good fight!' Jock chuckles. The recipient of Jock's left hook, Petty Officer Lowndes, no doubt rued his rash remark.

---

5 Although a heavyweight as an amateur, when he left the RAF Mark Hart (Croydon) surprised the boxing world by slimming down to 11st 6lb and turning professional as a middleweight. He won area titles at middle and light-heavyweight, but a British title eluded him.

Back in Sidcup news of Jock's service championship win soon reached Rex Manning, who was quick to alert the local press. In a newspaper report headlined 'Jock Taylor's First Championship', Manning described Jock as 'a clean-living and intelligent young man' and made it clear that this title was merely a first step 'towards far greater achievements'.

Duels with Don Cockell

By the time of his next recorded fight in August 1946, Jock had left the forces and had just turned 21. His military training had kept him in good shape, and his numerous services fights had given him invaluable experience. With Manning still his manager and Harry Watson his trainer it was time to launch a serious campaign as a professional fighter.

He decided, however, to abandon the middleweight division. 'I was a big middle and to save boiling down to middleweight I decided to fight at light-heavy and give the weight away,' Jock explains. His natural fighting weight was around 11st 12lb, which would make him a comfortable super-middleweight if he were boxing today. But with only eight weight classes to choose from in the 1940s, he was obliged to take on fully fledged light-heavies – often men who were half a stone or more heavier than him.

On 17 August Jock stopped the 1943 ABA middleweight champion George Page (who later trained the famous Henry Cooper and his twin brother George) in two rounds at Orpington. Then on 20 September he demolished Barnsley's Bob McArdle inside three at Watford Town Hall while conceding 11lb to the Yorkshireman.

At the same hall, 20 days later, Jock was pitted against a rising young star in future world heavyweight title challenger Don Cockell, who at the time was a light-heavyweight. 'It was 1946 and Cockell was coming up. He was unbeaten and I was supposed to be just another victim for him – or so they thought,' grins Jock.

Jock stepped out that evening to a chorus of boos before a decidedly pro-Cockell crowd who heartily cheered his unbeaten

18-year-old opponent. But unlike other fledgling fighters, Jock was unfazed by icy receptions. 'Once you're in that ring you're on your own; it don't matter about anything else,' he says as we discuss the topic of crowd interference. 'They cheer or they boo but it doesn't make any difference, not to me anyway.' At this fight, at any rate, the crowd were in for a surprise.

'Cockell started as if he was out for a KO, but found Taylor ready to join in,' wrote *Boxing News*. 'Gradually Taylor got on top and, connecting with well-placed body blows, had Cockell taking counts in the fifth, sixth and seventh rounds.'

'I don't know why but he was made for me,' Jock reveals. 'For all his cleverness I could beat him to the punch, and that's everything in the game. I could slip his left hand over my shoulder and hit him in the body every time. His style suited me and I won on points; I thought I beat him quite easily, but he of course wanted a return.'

The return match was set to be staged at High Wycombe Town Hall three months later, but in the interim both men squeezed in several fights.

Rex Manning entered Jock into an open light-heavyweight competition at Luton, spread over two dates, which comprised a series of four-round eliminating bouts with three wins needed to reach the final. Jock fought his way to the final where he faced a wily veteran called Jack Beech of Bletchley. 'I bounced out and walloped him one and put him down,' Jock recalls, 'and then he started boxing clever. I went right-hand crazy and of course he was picking me off with his left hand, and he beat me on points, much to my manager's annoyance. I got 20 quid for it.'

Three days after the competition, Jock was matched at Watford Town Hall against a hard-hitting opponent in Jimmy Carroll (Stockport). The Sidcup fighter started well and did most of the forcing, but in the third he walked onto a crisp right-hand counter and was knocked to the canvas. Bravely Jock rose at nine but was knocked down three more times before the referee stopped the fight.

This stoppage loss was a bad result psychologically, especially directly before Jock's rematch with Don Cockell. Since their first fight Cockell had notched up six more wins, including a victory over Jock's recent conqueror, Jimmy Carroll. Both Cockell and his supporters were now supremely confident he would turn the tables on Jock, and the crowd once more were on the Battersea boxer's side.

Having found success in their first fight with counters to the body, Jock knew this was his key to victory. 'Again I found that I could slip his left hand and clonk him in his body with my right,' he tells me. 'I did that in the first round and put him straight on the floor, and then at the end of the fourth I knocked him down again, and in the fifth I knocked him out.' It was a rewarding win in both reputation and financial terms. 'We had a £25 side-stake on it and 25 quid was a month's pay then,' Jock reveals.

As the history books show, Cockell was not deterred by his two defeats to Jock. Rarely losing thereafter, the Battersea man blazed his way through Britain's best light-heavyweights, won the British title in 1950, then moved up to heavyweight in 1952, when a glandular disorder caused him to put on a great deal of surplus weight. He then won the British heavyweight title and, after defeating top Americans Roland LaStarza and Harry Kid Matthews, took the legendary Rocky Marciano nine rounds in a challenge for boxing's greatest prize, the heavyweight championship of the world.

After his second win over Cockell, Jock was matched in concurrent fights with some of the best light-heavyweights in the country, yet he remained unbeaten against them. He avenged his loss to Jimmy Carroll with a second-round knockout of Carroll, and beat other leading men such as Reg Spring (Southall), Dave Goodwin (Shirebrook) and Len Fowler (Barnet). With this success came formal recognition: by August 1947 Jock was ranked sixth among Britain's light-heavyweights in the *Boxing News* ratings and had become a serious aspirant to the British title, which was held by the famous Freddie Mills.

By now Jock had settled into a comfortable training routine, basing himself at Sidcup's Halfway Street Drill Hall. For his roadwork he ran to Chislehurst or to his trainer Harry Watson's home at 36 The Green in Welling, whereupon Watson would give him a massage and drive him home.

'I never had any trainers apart from Harry at the beginning,' Jock recalls. He'd got a car and he could take me all over the place. He used to take me to this club at Brixton where I'd spar with various people. But I used to train meself more or less – punch the bag, skipping, sparring – though mainly you learn fighting by fighting of course.'

Jack Streek's reminiscences, which appear later in this book, attest to Jock's dedication to training and the first-class condition he got into for every fight. In this aspect of boxing there were few who could match him.

Among Jock's sparring partners was Harry Watson's son – also called Harry Watson – a talented professional middleweight under the management of Jack Burns. Jock remembers Watson Jnr fondly.

'He was an exceedingly good boy, young Harry. He was army professional champion and he was the first boy to beat [future British champion] Albert Finch. He could box rings round me,' Jock admits modestly. 'It was unfortunate he got in with a girl – he married her it's true – but I think that finished him. He started losing fights and then Alby Hollister knocked him out and that more or less put a stop to his career.'

Controversies

In late 1947 Jock started boxing at Plumstead Baths, a popular local venue where he proved an instant crowd favourite. Earning £50 a fight, he was a top-of-the-bill attraction. 'I s'pose they liked me 'cause I had this punch,' he says when I ask him about his popularity at Plumstead. 'If there's a puncher going people love to see him in action.'

By virtue of his win at the Baths over Dave Goodwin (Shirebrook) he was matched there with Battersea's Ernie Woodman in a final eliminator for the South-Eastern Area (the equivalent of today's Southern Area) light-heavyweight title, in January 1948. In customary fashion Jock (weighing 11st 9lb) conceded eight pounds to Woodman, who twice floored him during the fight. But Jock fought back bravely and secured the verdict after ten tough three-minute rounds, and with it the right to meet Sid Nathan's old stablemate Al Marson for the area title two months later.

In the interim Jock had a warm-up fight at Plumstead Baths against the wily Norwich veteran Ginger Sadd, who as a welter and middleweight had beaten such notables as Freddie Mills, Dave McCleave, Dick Turpin, Harry Mason and Jack Hyams, and was now going strong at light-heavyweight. 'He was clever, crafty and very experienced. He was the most experienced boxer in the country I would say – but when I was on song I could beat him,' Jock opines.

Covering the contest, the London *Evening Standard* observed, 'Sadd, who received a damaged eye in the first round, had boxed well, but could not keep his younger and stronger opponent at distance.'

Going into the fourth round the paper had Jock 'well in front', but then something surprising happened, as Jock explains with palpable exasperation:

> I knocked him down with a body blow – hit him fair and square – then the referee came over and disqualified me for an alleged low blow. I'm certain it was a fiddle. I was on top in the fight, I hadn't been beaten for ages and I was rated number two to Mills. I think somebody must have made a lot of money on it.

Whether unseen forces were at work that evening is now impossible to know; but the press at least doubted the legitimacy of the disqualification and referred to the offending punch as 'an alleged low blow'. It was a frustrating end to a fight Jock seemed on the verge of winning, but luckily it did not affect his right to fight Al Marson for the area title in his next contest. The Sadd disqualification, however, would come back to haunt him.

Demand for tickets to see the Taylor–Marson area title clash was unprecedented for Plumstead Baths, and to the disappointment of many fans the show was sold out days in advance.

Going into the fight Jock had every reason to think he would win. At 22 and having trained tirelessly, he was in the pink of physical condition; while Marson, at 34, was old in boxing terms. The pair had fought at Croydon six months earlier and on that occasion Jock's strategy of non-stop attack had seemingly won him the fight. But the referee had called it a draw and was booed vociferously by the large crowd.

This time far more was at stake. The winner would not only win an area title (a notable achievement then), but would qualify as the official challenger to Freddie Mills's British title.

As described in the opening of this part of the book, in the return match Jock took the fight to Marson and seemed on the way to victory until a bizarre incident in the fourth round. This, Jock is convinced, was an underhanded attempt to influence the outcome of the fight.

'My idea was to slip his blows and counter to the body,' he says. 'I was doing that all the time and I was beating Marson, until I put him down in the fourth round with a body blow. The referee came over and said, "I'll have to disqualify you," and as soon as he said it that finished me. I just left him alone after that. It frightened me to death, the thought of being disqualified for something that wasn't even low and in a title fight.

'See I'd been disqualified for an alleged low blow against Sadd, and that was I s'pose to put the wind up me when I fought Marson for the title, which it did. They know what they're doing these people.

'Consequently I reverted to boxing, against a bigger man with a longer reach. I mean, I'm not a boxer, I'm a puncher; I just stayed on the end of Marson's left hand for the other eight rounds – it was a 12-rounder – and I ended up with a shut eye, black and blue. I lost on points, and I lost my confidence with it.'

Boxing News supported Jock's opinion that he was greatly troubling Marson in the early rounds and the body blow that floored the older man in the fourth, the paper said, had Marson 'in agony'. But it proved a turning point. Regardless of whether the referee had actually been 'leaned on' to influence the fight, it seems his words to Jock at that crucial moment changed the Sidcup man's fight plan and perhaps the outcome of the fight too. Later he would revisit that fourth-round incident repeatedly in a recurrent dream, which shows how much this title-fight defeat – and the apparent injustice of it – affected him.

To this day Jock is convinced foul play was at work both in his disqualification loss to Sadd and the area title defeat to Marson.

A Challenge to Albert Finch

Despite Rex Manning's inexperience and apparent shortcomings as a manager (which are discussed more later), he was at least an able publicist and well aware of the importance of press coverage in raising a fighter's profile.

In March 1947, for example, he had gained valuable column inches by concocting a quirky story to explain the source of Jock's punching power. The story made the national papers, Frank Butler writing in his *Daily Express* column, 'Up-and-coming cruiserweight Jock Taylor (Sidcup) attributes his physical fitness and powerful punching to horse meat.[6] For all his recent KO victories he has been on a horse-meat diet. In fact, there is a kick in every Taylor punch.'

Jock tells me that Manning secured this particular piece of publicity through a freemasonry connection with Butler's father, another well-known boxing writer called James Butler, who at the time lived near Sidcup, in New Eltham.

I ask Jock whether there was any truth in the claims. 'I did eat horse, yeah. That's how Rex Manning got the idea. Some people ate it 'cause we were terribly rationed and meat was in such short supply, and after all what's the difference, really, truly?'

But was it the source of his powerful punch or fitness? 'No,' he laughs, 'that was a gimmick.'

---

6 In the first half of the 20th century, the 12st 7lb division was known as cruiserweight in Britain and light-heavyweight in America. Eventually the British Boxing Board of Control changed the division's title to light-heavyweight to bring it in line with the USA. Britain's original 12st 7lb cruiserweight class should not be confused with the modern cruiserweight division, which sits between heavyweight and light-heavyweight, and was introduced by the WBC in 1979.

Having previously used the press to good advantage, Manning again employed his skill as a publicist for Jock, this time to drum up interest in a fight he felt would be a sure way to get his fighter recognition. Although Jock had lost in his area title bid, thanks to Manning's persistence he already had another big fight in the offing.

For some time Manning had wanted to match Jock in a catchweights contest with rising middleweight star Albert Finch (Croydon) and various challenges had been issued. A letter printed in the *Weekly Sporting Review*, purporting to be from Jock, had offered 'Albert Finch an opportunity to rehabilitate himself in the eyes of the British sporting public after his pathetic exhibition at Olympia recently' by agreeing to fight Jock.

A response via the same paper from Finch's manager, Jack Burns, had affirmed that 'no promoter would want to use the Taylor–Finch fight as a top-liner, so it is a waste of good time to consider it'. But an even more abrasive follow-up letter, again purportedly penned by Jock, seemingly had the desired effect, as finally the match was made.

'It was my manager's bright idea to *challenge* Finch,' remembers Jock. 'I wasn't interested at all – he was a middleweight and I was a cruiserweight. But the manager kept on nagging and nagging with his perpetual letters and in the end he got it; but it was nothing to do with me. I didn't challenge Finch, *he* challenged Finch. But I had to beat Ginger Sadd to fight Finch.'

The 'qualifying' contest Jock refers to was a return fight with Sadd at Croydon a month after the area title fight with Marson. Their meeting once more pitted an exceptionally clever veteran against an exceedingly fit, strong and aggressive youth.

Jock set a fast pace and forced the fight throughout, finishing the eight rounds a narrow but worthy winner. 'I thought, I've gotta beat him to get the Finch fight, and I pressed him hard and beat him. But again, that was a wanted fight. *They* wanted me to fight Finch,' Jock says with emphasis on the word 'they'. 'I was wanted to win because the fight with Finch was a good thing, a must come and see.'

'They' in this instance presumably means the promotional duo of Bill Goodwin and Alf Hart (Goodwin–Hart Promotions), who staged Jock's Croydon contest with Sadd as well as his fight with Finch.

The Taylor–Finch contest was joint-top of the bill along with a match between Mark Hart (promoter Alf's brother) and Emile de Greef of Belgium. The promoters had recently agreed terms with Crystal Palace Football Club to stage regular summer shows at the club's home ground, Selhurst Park. The future use of the stadium depended on the success of this, their first show staged there, so there was added pressure to pull in the crowds.

Finch, a clever boxer and future British middleweight champion, was in scorching-hot form and must have entered the fight brimming with confidence. In his last bout, six weeks before facing Jock, he had become the first man to beat the gifted future world middleweight champion Randy Turpin (who would defeat the legendary Sugar Ray Robinson for the title). Then three fights prior to that Finch had out-pointed Jock's bogeyman Al Marson, despite conceding 13lb. Clearly, tackling light-heavyweights was no problem for Finch.

On 8 June 1948 a large and expectant crowd filed in to Selhurst Park to watch this intriguing open-air south London derby, which pitched a marauding all-action puncher – Jock – against a fast, orthodox but safety-first boxer in Finch.

Jock is characteristically honest as he turns his mind back to that summer evening of over 65 years ago. 'Finch out-boxed me,' he sighs. 'He was too fast for me. He caught me on the whiskers, around about the seventh round, and put me down and that was that. Finch wasn't a puncher but you've only gotta get somebody in the right place at the right time and they're gone. You've got your weight coming forward, an experienced punch coming in; they land together and down you go.'

'This was one of Finch's best displays,' wrote *Boxing News*. 'He had Taylor puzzled by a fast-moving left for which the Sidcup boxer had but a poor defence. These lefts were solid punches which had the desired effect of weakening his opponent and though Taylor made valiant efforts with strong attacks to the body he found Finch in devastating form.'

'Taylor's main asset against Finch was a fighting heart and a tremendous load of pluck,' noted another paper. 'The Sidcup fighter never ceased trying and a gamer lad I have yet to see… In the seventh round Finch unleashed a battery of right crosses to the jaw and Taylor went down for counts of "7", "7", "8", "3" and "8" – and just when the gallant fighter from Sidcup was shaping up again to continue, referee Mickey Fox quite rightly intervened.'

'I should never have fought him,' Jock declares dolefully, 'it was only my manager's idea: 'cause Harry Watson, my trainer's son, had beaten Finch, he thought I was gonna beat Finch. But Harry's boy was so good. When I sparred with Finch later he told me Harry's son had been too good for him. But Finch was too good for me, especially at that time – I'd lost my confidence as I say, and losing to Finch was part of my undoing.'

At this point, I ask Jock how important confidence is to a fighter and his answer is revealing. 'You get confidence by winning fights, it snowballs and it always makes that slight bit of difference between winning and losing. It gets you there instead of there,' he says, indicating two differing lengths. 'But if you lose fights, you lose confidence, especially when you lose like that [meaning his one-sided loss to Finch]. You're so keyed up to win fights, your whole being is winning: you're trained mentally and physically *to win*, and if you don't win it all explodes.'

Turning to the financial implications of the defeat, Jock reveals, 'It was a side-stake match – £50 of mine and £10 of my manager's – and £60 was a lot of money at the time, but the purse was £100 so that covered it. He wasn't in my weight class – he was a middleweight and I was a cruiserweight – so it didn't affect the ratings at all.'

The *Boxing News* ratings published a month after the Finch defeat still placed Jock as the number two light-heavyweight contender (just behind Al Marson) to champion Freddie Mills. In theory Jock was still in a credible position to challenge Mills for the British title, and at 22 he was certainly young enough to revive his career. But in reality the psychological damage of the

Sadd, Marson and Finch defeats would have a lasting detrimental effect on him.

Jock's next three fights – against Ginger Sadd, Johnny Williams (a future British heavyweight champion) and Reg Spring (whom he had previously beaten) – were all points defeats. He carried on boxing for another three years with mixed success, but never again found the form that had taken him close to the top of the light-heavyweight ratings, and tantalisingly near to a potentially career-changing – and life-changing – fight with Freddie Mills.

But Jock kept on fighting because, aside from the hope he might turn his career around, above all – having recently married his childhood sweetheart, Barbara – he was fastidiously saving to buy his own home.

Though by comparison with many boxers of those days, Jock came from a comfortable background, his father gave him no help financially and he had to scrimp and save as much as the next pro fighter. Accordingly his fistic raison d'etre was principally financial. 'I was only in it to win money,' he says candidly, 'that was why I fought. That's why you turn professional.'

However, he does acknowledge there is a special thrill attached to being a successful pro fighter. 'If you're beating people, especially if you beat them easily or knock them out, and it was *somebody*, then you're on a cloud,' he smiles. 'A lot of people don't realise you're a boxer, but as far as you're concerned you're a king, you know.'

Although Jock's best fighting days were now behind him, he still had one more outstanding performance ahead of him: a fight that he regards as his finest.

Fighting Finale

In November 1950 Jock was hired as a late substitute to box on a show at Empress Hall. His opponent was an up-and-coming light-heavyweight prospect called Alf Hines, who hailed from West Ham but belonged to manager Teddy Lewis's Dagenham stable. 'He'd never been beaten,' Jock recalls, 'I think he'd had 24 fights and 24 wins, and I was 4 to 1 against winning, which are terrific odds in boxing. So you can imagine the state I was in, knowing how good he was and that I was four to one against.'

'This was a hard, gruelling fight,' observed one reporter. 'Hines had the skill and the punching power, but Taylor, who has amazed me before by his capacity to take punishment, just would not give in and proceeded to paint Hines's face a bloody mess from the second on… Hines's best punch was a right uppercut to the chin as Taylor led with his left. Against many opponents this punch would have spelt finish, but as I have said before, and it's worth repeating, Taylor is an extremely tough customer.'

Taking up the story, Jock reveals how he got on top in the fight. 'Alfie Hines had a good left hand but when I got in there with him I noticed after he flicked his left out, he dropped it. So I waited for his left hand to go down, then crossed him with my right. I caught him every time with it and I shut both his eyes up.'

At the end of the seventh round, with two badly damaged eyes impeding his vision, Hines was forced to retire from the fight. 'It was a great fight and a wonderful win,' Jock says proudly. 'They stopped it 'cause he was bleeding from the eye so much, but I was winning all right.'

Jock's stablemate, Jack Streek, also remembers the occasion. 'I watched a lot of Jock's fights and that was the best I'd seen him,' he says enthusiastically. 'It was a great fight and I think Jock was more surprised than anyone with the result. He was a right underdog in that particular fight, but he was star of the show that night. He was so calm and collected and he did everything right. And cor, when he won it he brought the house down 'cause it was the first time this Hines had been beaten.'

Jock believes this defeat caused Hines to suffer the same psychological damage that had hampered his own career. 'That fight finished Hines,' he says. 'It was a terrific fight and he took a bashing, but he was never the same after that. Later he went and worked on the films. He was in *The Square Ring* [Ealing Studios, 1953] with Robert Beatty – he's the one who fought Beatty in the film.' Jock then admits that he also took a good deal of punishment in the fight, which he feels may have shortened his career.

Despite the morale boost of the Hines win, Jock lost his next four fights and then called time on his career. His last bout took place in the open air on a Freddie Mills promotion at Bristol City FC's ground on 28 May 1951. His opponent was a hitherto unheralded fighter called Vic Phayer (Woolwich), who by coincidence was a stablemate of Alf Hines's.

'I was confident and quite sure that I was gonna win that fight,' remembers Jock. 'He'd been beaten by other people who I'd beaten and I thought, well, it'll be a bit of cake really – I wonder what round I'll knock him out in. But I don't even remember coming out for the first round. Next minute I'm back in the dressing room, and he got the *Boxing News* Certificate of Merit for the best performance in the world of boxing.' For the first time in his career Jock had been knocked out inside a round.

Had he underestimated his opponent? 'Absolutely. You get complacent sometimes. You're both in there to win and if you get in the way of one, you'll go out like anybody else – you're flesh and blood. I mean, I've been laughed at and scoffed at and beat blokes who thought they were gonna kill me. Then I've had the same thing done to me. The last bloke that done it to me was Jimmy Carroll, and I fought a return with him and knocked him clean out. But this time I thought, well, I'm getting old and I think I better stop, so I did. I was 26 years old.'

One pressure that Jock acknowledges played a part in his decision to quit boxing and had made his ring career a good deal harder, was holding down a full-time job while training and fighting. Each day he travelled into London – often hitchhiking to save money – where he worked as a maintenance fitter at a stationery office in Old Street.

'It was one long slog,' he recalls with a weary smile. 'I was up at seven, a bit of breakfast and away I'd go to work and I didn't get home till seven or eight at night. I had to work quite a lot of overtime to get the money to live on, and it was always all day Saturdays – *and* we were rationed in those days.

'I used to train in the evenings, do roadwork at the weekend: on Sundays get up early and run. It was too much to have to do all that, so it was a bit of a relief to be able to give it up. You can't really do a job and fight like that. I mean, I was fighting top-liners. When I think back to the amount of training I put in, I earned *every penny* of that boxing money.'

But Jock's hard training at one point brought him close to a shot at big money and big-time boxing. As he leafs through his career scrapbook he stops at a page and points to his name at number two in the *Boxing News* ratings, directly beneath Al Marson and champion Freddie Mills. 'So near and yet so far,' he sighs. 'I was building up to a fight with Mills and Mills came down to watch one of my fights – 'cause I was getting so near to him, he wanted to see me fight.'

At the time Jock is referring to there was criticism in the press over Mills's failure to defend his British light-heavyweight title since winning it from Len Harvey in 1942. 'In fairness to the other light-heavyweights in the country,' wrote one journalist, 'Mills should be ordered to put his championship on the line. It is obviously disheartening to cruisers like Jock Taylor, Ernie Woodman and a few more to be able to get no higher up the fistic ladder than the stage where they keep throwing out challenges to Mills which are always ignored.'

As it turned out nobody got a shot at the British light-heavyweight crown while Mills was champion. Although Mills had won other championships – including world honours – his failure to defend his British title created a frustrating eight-year hiatus for fans and would-be challengers alike. The next British light-heavyweight title fight was staged in October 1950, when Don Cockell fought Mark Hart for Mills's vacated crown, with Cockell the winner.

Life After Boxing

'Your wages were £7 a week then,' says Jock in reference to the late 1940s and early 50s. 'A good, top man could get £7 a week, but I could get £50 a fight for boxing, so it was quite a good bonus. I never earned a lot of money. The most I ever got was £100 for a fight – that was for the Southern Area championship and the Finch fight – but I hung on to my money as much as I could and I ended up with about £1,200.

'Two thousand pounds bought you a house and you had to put down a quarter of that to be able to borrow the rest of the money. I put down £550 on the house, then of course you've got your expenses to pay, and then your furniture, and I ended up with about 20 quid in the bank,' he laughs.

'But I was in… I was in a house: three bedrooms, bathroom, garden, and I laid concrete down, had a nice driveway, put the garage up, and I sold it for £159,000. I thought about all the training and fighting I did just for a few quid, and you can make all that money just from the sale of a house. It does bring it home to you.'

The house Jock bought with his ring earnings was at 16 Fleet Avenue in Dartford, and he, Barbara and their three daughters lived there for many years. Again thanks to Jock's ring earnings, they were the first family on the street to own a television, and they and their neighbours crowded round the TV set to watch the Queen's coronation in 1953.

After boxing, Jock continued to work in the City for several years before finding a local position as a baker's roundsman. But Jock's kind nature put him at odds with the firm's proprietors, as he would drive round after his shift giving away surplus stock, which would otherwise have been thrown away, to poorer customers.

While in the job, he also took the time to befriend a deaf-dumb couple, learning to communicate with them through sign. The final straw came when Jock dented the roof of his delivery van on a low-ceilinged structure in the firm's yard. On seeing the state of the van, his boss sacked him on the spot.

But as one door shut another opened and Jock found a steady job as a fitter at the Amalgamated Oxides company in Dartford, where he worked for many years with a 4pm finish and decent pay.

To earn extra cash, in the 1960s Jock took on two bouncing jobs, also in Dartford. His evening began as a doorman at the Scala Ballroom (today the Air & Breathe nightclub), before he moved on to work at the late-night Sun Do Chinese restaurant, where his presence served as a deterrent to troublesome drunks.

A host of trendy 60s singers and bands performed at the Scala, but to Jock their names were unfamiliar, which led to some comedic situations such as when Jock challenged well-known singer Georgie Fame to produce his ticket. When Georgie told Jock, 'I'm the star of the show!', the Sidcup man replied nonchalantly, 'I don't care who you are. You're not coming in without a ticket.'

On another occasion the four-piece Merseybeat band the Swinging Blue Jeans were refused entry by Jock – aptly enough – for wearing jeans. Yet Jock turned a blind eye to patrons who regularly snuck in to the ballroom partway through the evening via a lavatory window.

The Sun Do restaurant job was, on the whole, an easy proposition, but there was at least one occasion when Jock's fighting prowess was needed: when an irate man entered the restaurant brandishing a knife.

The owner – a small Chinese man – looked on in astonishment as Jock calmly approached the yob and said, 'Don't be silly, mate – put that away.' When the thug ignored Jock's appeal, the Sidcup fighter slung a swift blow at his unguarded chin and he fell to the ground unconscious. The stunned restaurateur was reverential in his praise for Jock, and treated the Taylor family like royalty whenever they visited his restaurant.

Always a grafter, Jock worked on until he was 74 and three or four years after that moved from Dartford to East Sussex.

Away from boxing, Jock has always enjoyed the gentler game of chess and for a while had a keen interest in motorbikes, owning a string of them. He was obliged to curtail his motorcycling activities, however, after several accidents in the late 1950s, one of which left him in hospital for three months. Afterwards he bought a car and, as his daughter June tells me, would kindly offer people lifts when he saw them waiting for buses.

When I ask Jock if he stayed involved with boxing, he explains that for a time he trained fighters at his old base, the Sidcup Drill Hall, but this was not a success. 'We were there for anybody who wanted to come,' he says, 'but very few did come. There was no great interest.'

Regrets

Jock readily admits that he has regrets about his boxing career, but he does not make excuses lightly. When I point out that regularly giving away half a stone in weight to opponents put him at a disadvantage, he shrugs off the suggestion and says, 'That's something you just accept. It might even have given me a bit of speed on them.'

But there are some carefully considered regrets. 'I'm only sorry television wasn't around so much,' he tells me. 'Some of my fights would have made me a bomb; and getting televised makes such a difference. Billy Walker got £3,000 [as a signing-on fee] – that's twice as much money as I got in all the fights I had. He got that just for turning pro, 'cause they televised him knocking that big Yank out.'[7*]

Jock's only other evident regret is an obvious one. 'My manager had never managed anyone in his life until I came along,' he says. 'He was a beginner like me, and I think that, personally looking back, I missed out quite a lot.

'Rex Manning was a freemason but he was outside the boxing sphere – all the managers and promoters who knew each other and scratched each other's backs. With anything to do with money there's fiddles, whether it's bankers, businesses or boxing. They'd pull strings and you'd find that they'd get decisions that you should have got, and things happened that I couldn't do anything about. I could have got on far better if I'd had a known manager, one that could put you in the right place at the right time.'

At the same time, however, Jock retains a genuine fondness for Manning and describes him as 'a gentleman'. He acknowledges that in Manning he at least had a conscientious

---

7 Billy Walker's televised knockout of the giant American Cornelius Perry in 1961 indeed put him on the boxing map, and left the leading managers queuing up to sign him as a pro. However, the fee Harry Levene paid Walker to sign as a pro was in fact a staggering £9,000.

manager who, unlike some of his contemporaries, tried to do right by his fighter.

'He was well educated, well spoken, well dressed, had an executive job in the London Transport and owned his own house in Sidcup,' Jock reveals. 'He'd got a great interest in boxing and I was like a son to him – everybody thought he was me dad actually.

'Legally 25 per cent of a boxer's purse went to his manager, but Rex Manning never used to take it. He took *some* but he was generous. All he was interested in was getting somewhere in the boxing world. He wasn't interested in making money; he was quite rich already. He just wanted to be my manager and for me to win the championship.

'He did the same thing with Jack Streek when I packed up. Streek got on quite well, didn't get quite as far as I got, but he had a string of victories. Then he started to lose fights, stopped boxing, and the manager just packed up. He never managed anyone else.'

A Question of Style

'He was so strong, he was like a bull,' says Jack Streek when I ask him about Jock. 'But he was a bit too strong and fit for his own good really. He boxed a lot of good boys and with him being so fit and strong, he'd hold his own with most; and if he got the better of a bloke he'd probably stop him, 'cause he certainly had a punch on him. But he had some terrific, hard fights and he took a few good hidings, like off of Albert Finch, for instance, who out-boxed him completely.

'He fought for the area title, which was quite a big thing to have in those days. Now you get these second-bout boys fighting for an area title, but in those days you had to be one of the top boys to get an area title, and there were so many good boys. If only Jock had been a bit more scientific, he would have really gone places.'

Jock's lack of boxing finesse was a criticism sometimes levelled against him (although no one ever questioned his heart, fitness, punch-power or strength). Jock admits he was 'not good as a boxer', but disagrees with the idea that he could have altered his style to be more scientific.

'Every boxer's got his style,' he tells me, 'but you can't really alter that style because it's not that man any more. My style didn't please some people, but you are what you are and I was a fighter, not a boxer. I could knock a man out with a left hand, and I'd got a terrific right hand and I could knock them out with that with one blow. My main idea was: one hit and I've won the fight.'

If strength, courage and tenacity are qualities that you admire then it is hard not to be impressed by Jock Taylor. With his dark, wavy hair, bronzed skin, never-say-die spirit and ferocious fighting style, he was a fighter reminiscent of the great Jack Dempsey. BBC sports commentator W. Barrington Dalby called one of Jock's fights with Reg Spring 'one of the greatest cruiserweight scraps I've ever seen', and by studying newspaper reports of Jock's various contests it's easy to see he was rarely – if ever – involved in a dull fight.

The following 1940s newspaper extract, which I found proudly pasted in Jock's career scrapbook, explains exactly why boxing needs men like Jock Taylor:

> Present-day fighters like Freddie Mills, Jock Taylor, Eric Boon and Claude Dennington will always draw the great crowds, despite their possible limitations as purely scientific boxers. For these fighters are the unpredictables of the ring: it is their kind who almost always provide the unexpected and nearly all the thrills.
>
> In the very sweat and passion of their struggle to master the orthodox by the unorthodox, they create a colourful sense of drama which at once communicates itself to the far reaches of the arena, to stir, in turn, primeval instincts buried deep within the breast of every man... without the Mills, Taylors, Boons and Denningtons of this or any age, man-fighting would not be the fascinating sport and entertainment it has been, and still is to the paying public.

JACK STREEK (SIDCUP) 1950–53

A FTER my interview with Jock Taylor, boxing historian and writer Derek O'Dell kindly put me in contact with Jock's former stablemate Jack Streek. Taylor and Streek had lost touch back in the 1950s after they both moved away from Sidcup. In recent years Streek had tried to track down his old pal via the ex-boxers' associations, but his search had been to no avail. It was therefore a pleasure to be able to reunite them.

When I interviewed Jack Streek about his memories of Jock Taylor, I quickly realised that he too had an interesting story to tell. I asked if he would share his own fighting reminiscences with me and he readily agreed. After speaking with him at length on the phone, I visited him at his home on the outskirts of Bournemouth to conduct a fuller interview and meet him in person.

※ ※ ※

Jack lives with his second wife, Sylvia, in a retirement park where every resident is over 55. When I arrive, after a long drive along the coast, I am struck at once by its tranquil and friendly atmosphere.

It is a bright spring day and I observe several residents cheerfully going about their business before an affable elderly man directs me to a parking space. I then stroll a short distance down a one-way track to reach Jack's home.

When he opens his door I am met (for the only time during the course of these interviews) by a man of about my height, and of a considerably bigger build. Now tipping the scales at 16st, it has been some years since Jack made the middleweight limit. He carries the weight well, though, across thick, powerful shoulders and arms. There is a solid look about him – not a flabby one – and he moves nimbly for his age and size. The thick, dark, wavy hair of his fighting days remains thick and wavy but is now strikingly white and sited above a bushy white moustache.

Although he has lived in Dorset since the 1980s Jack retains that south London accent that is native to Sidcup. He is a cheerful, good-natured man with a positive outlook on life and a fine sense of humour. He speaks with a thoughtful, laid-back cadence.

Eltham, Sidcup and Leysdown

Jack was born in Eltham, south London, on 19 December 1932, and lived the first five years of his life in a house two doors down from a childhood home of the legendary entertainer Bob Hope, who incidentally did some boxing himself before he became famous. The Streek family briefly lived at another Eltham address and then moved to 103 Days Lane in nearby Sidcup, when Jack was six.

Like Jock Taylor, Jack did not box under his birth name. 'Edward Victor Streek is my real name,' he explains. '"Jack" was my manager's idea. He said, "I think J is lucky in boxing, so if you don't mind and if your parents don't mind, we'll put you down as Jack." But eventually even me dad called me Jack. Nowadays me wife calls me Ted but all me neighbours, they all know me as Jack.'

Unlike Jock Taylor, there was some boxing history in Jack's family: his father, uncles and grandfather had all boxed as amateurs or in the services. Yet his only sibling – his elder brother, Roy – did not pursue a ring career despite some natural talent. 'Roy was a good boxer, same as me: tall, with a good left hand,' Jack recalls, 'but he never took it up seriously. Me granddad did a lot of boxing in the forces and he was supposed to be pretty good.'

Although Jack says his father – a coal merchant – was never 'well off', it seems the family were at least comfortable financially. 'Me dad always had a car,' he says, 'and back then *nobody* had a car. We never wanted for anything: he looked after us well.'

The Streek family's arrival in Sidcup was around the time of the outbreak of the Second World War, an event of which, despite his young age at the time, Jack retains strong memories.

'It was very exciting,' he tells me. 'Especially when you'd see a big plane going over, very low, with a big German swastika on it. Some of them used to drop their bombs over Sidcup, turn round and go back home. We had doodlebugs flying over: I remember one nearly landed on top of us. With the doodlebugs there was like a big halo at the back and that's where their jet propulsion came from. They used to make a terrible noise and then it stopped; and that was it. They used to just drop down. Some of them used to glide a bit, but most of them, soon as that engine stopped, down they came.

'We had a doodlebug land about 200 yards from our house; we had a rocket, massive great thing, and there was no end of incendiary bombs. We had another 2,000lb bomb at the top of the road, and we never even got a cracked window. We were lucky.'

But Jack is quick to point out that not everyone was so lucky. 'A lot of me mates were killed. Two of me best mates lived about 200 yards from us and they saw a flash, which was a rocket landing down the road in Days Lane, where I lived. They run in their garden, under this big apple tree, and a big steel girder came flying through the air and killed them both, landed right on top of them. Terrible that was. If it'd dropped down on the path, outside, they'd have been all right.

'We had a chance of being evacuated but me mum wouldn't let us go. She was one of the old school I s'pose saying that if we're gonna get killed, we'll be killed together sort of thing. She didn't want us to leave; she wanted us to stay together as a family.

'Most weekends we used to go down to Leysdown on the Isle of Sheppey 'cause me dad had a smallholding down there with a little bungalow and me uncle had this little farm down there as well. We went there to get out the way of the bombing, but we used to see more there than we did up in Sidcup. There's a big airfield in Leysdown, which was a target for the German bombers.

'We used to see dog fights with spitfires. I saw a spitfire coming down and saw the pilot standing on the wing, hanging on to the cockpit, ready to jump off. And when the spitfire crashed we went over and had a look at it, got bits of the plane off and brought them home as souvenirs. As kids we thought it was wonderful.'

Amateur Days

As the war was coming to a close Jack was taking his first steps as an amateur boxer. When his father insisted that he and his brother join a club of some sort, Jack made his way to a boxing gym he had heard about on the outskirts of Sidcup. 'A little old boy called Dod Rickner used to run it,' he recalls. 'He was quite well known in the amateur game in those days. He was a potman at one of the pubs in Eltham High Street. He had this little old barn, you used to walk in and it stunk of white oils – it was right atmospheric. I loved it; I couldn't wait for Tuesdays and Fridays, which were the training nights.

'At that time Sidcup had their own club, there was Eltham club, Mottingham club and old Dod had opened this little barn place, completely away from everybody. So we was surrounded by clubs and that's how we used to get fights. Although we was boxing with Dod Rickner in his little barn, we was still under Sidcup club. Dod was a bit of a fly-by-night: he used to look after us but he'd get us as many fights as he could. If Mottingham, Eltham or Downham club was holding a competition then we was billed as belonging to them. We was always on call – we had no end of fights.

'We had all these clubs so some nights, instead of training at our little barn, we'd go to Sidcup to get sparring with different boys or to the Drill Hall on Halfway Street, which is where I first saw Jock Taylor. Jock had his own gym there and we used to go in there a lot to watch him train, when I was 12, 13 and 14 I s'pose. He was a bit of a hero to us 'cause being professional was beyond our wildest dreams.

'We'd look on in amazement when he trained, 'cause watching Jock train, Christ, you'd never seen anything like it. He was a fanatic and his fitness was wonderful. I can see him now skipping and you couldn't get anywhere near the rope 'cause you'd get blown away! I thought, perhaps one day I could be like that. We used to train there as well, of course, out the way of Jock, and it's also where the Sidcup club held their shows.'

When Dod Rickner closed his gym, Jack moved to the Sidcup club whose training base – at the Sidcup Working Men's Club – was run by Alf Pearcy. With Pearcy's blessing Rickner continued to train Jack and a couple of other boxers there.

'I had me first fight when I was 12 or 13,' Jack recalls. 'I had 100-odd amateur fights and I can't remember them all; but I can remember the ones where I got beaten and I can only remember losing six. Once I had nine fights in a week. Unheard of nowadays, but in those days they didn't worry about how many fights you had.' Jack explains that to accumulate the nine fights he had entered three competitions that week – and won them all.

'Every week I was in the paper 'cause hardly a week went by without me going somewhere and boxing. I was mad on it, you know, you couldn't keep me away from the gym, and me dad encouraged me every bit of the way. He used to buy all me gear: he'd buy me the gloves and the boots, 'cause kids then used to box more or less in plimsolls, but he bought me the old Yankee-style boxing boots. He put up a boxing ring in our garden and all me mates used to come round and have a spar. The house used to be an orchard, so we had big apple trees and pear trees in the garden and they was handy for hanging the punch bags up.'

The pinnacle of Jack's boyhood boxing career arrived a month after his 15th birthday: on 30 January 1948 he won the Class A South-East London Divisional Youth Championships, in the 9st division, at Woolwich's Royal Ordnance Factory. But he then lost in the all-London championships, held a couple of weeks later at Marylebone's Seymour Hall. 'I lost on points to a boy called Charlie Page,' he recalls. 'I thought I'd won but he got the decision, and he went on to Wembley and won the title – won the overall ABA juniors at nine stone. He turned pro later and did quite well.'

It was the first and only time Jack entered the junior ABA championships, and as it turned out he would not get the chance to enter the senior equivalent. He had been unlucky to lose to Page, but nonetheless his capture of the South-East London Divisional title gave him valuable exposure and brought him to the notice of Jock Taylor's manager, Rex Manning.

Earmarked for Success

'Rex Manning was our amateur matchmaker,' says Jack, 'so he had his eye open for any decent lads that come along, which fortunately or unfortunately turned out to be me. As I said, we used to train at this drill hall where Jock trained. One night me dad got chatting to Manning, and he gave Manning a lift to his house on the way home to our place.

'When we got home indoors I said, "What were you talking about then dad?" He said, "He wants to know if you'd turn pro when you get a bit older." I said, "Cor, what d'you tell him dad?" He said, "I told him it was entirely up to you; I'm not gonna sway you either way." I was about 15 at the time.'

From that point it was taken for granted that Jack would turn professional and Rex Manning would be his manager. And Manning, it transpired, was keen to get the arrangement underway.

'I really started training as a pro when I was 16 and a half, although I was still an amateur,' Jack reveals. 'Manning used to take me up to London, he used to pay all me train fares, and he took me down all the pro gyms to get me used to a different class of training.

'The very first pro gym my manager took me to was a place in Brixton called Dale Martin's. It was a wrestling gym off Brixton High Street. The wrestlers used to use it during the day and the boxers took it over at night. I was working mainly up in London, so I used to always take me bag with me, with all me gear, and go straight to Dale Martin's on a 133 bus, which stopped right outside the gym.'

Other gyms Jack trained at included The Torbay in Rotherhithe, Bill Klein's in Fitzroy Street and Jack Solomons's in Great Windmill Street. After this initial indoctrination period ('His idea was to blood me in to the professional sport,' Jack recalls), under Manning's direction Jack turned pro at 17 – coincidentally the same age that Jock had seven years before him.

When Jack had his first paid fight in 1950 Jock's career had hit a downward spiral and it seems Manning saw Jack as Jock's successor; someone good enough to take the mantle from him and perhaps even win Sidcup a British title.

Aside from sharing their manager and home district, however, the two were very different – physically and stylistically. While Jock relied on his strength, fitness and two-fisted punch-power to win fights, Jack was conversely referred to by *Boxing News* as 'a copybook exponent of the straight left'. At 6ft 2in and with correspondingly long arms, he out-reached most opponents and made the left lead his weapon of choice.

'I was a pure boxer,' he tells me. 'I had a terrific left hand and I was very fast. I hardly ever used me right hand: because I was winning fights so well with me left, I thought, well, why bother? It was only towards the end that I started to use me right hand more and became more of an all-rounder.'

Naturally, as the only two members of Manning's stable, the pair started to train and spar together, and the experience proved eye-opening for Jack. 'We both lived in Sidcup about ten minutes' walk away from each other and we used to do a lot of training together. He was much too strong for me at the beginning, but towards the end I could handle him more – me being a better boxer than he was. But he was so bloody strong and he could n'alf punch – if he caught ya, you knew all about it!

'He could n'alf run too, I tell you that. When we first went on runs together, I said, "Christ, how far you going, Jock?" He said, "Oh, this is only halfway through yet. You'll get used to it." He taught me a lot in roadwork and training. He was a right fitness fanatic. I never saw him drink, I've never known him to go to a disco – or dances was what they were called then… didn't have discos.

'Jock used to come round my house on a Sunday and we'd go out for a run. When we got back we had a wash down and then an almighty breakfast. The only thing was, my mum used to do these breakfasts with everything that's not good for you: two eggs, bacon and sausages, fried tomatoes and chips – she thought she was doing us proud,' Jack laughs. 'But we used to fight all right on it anyway.

'We used to sit around the rest of the day, playing records and talking about fights and different things. Then obviously we'd see each other during the week, do a bit of sparring together and train… great bloke.'

Into a Man's World

'My dad was a bit dubious when I turned pro so early,' Jack reveals. 'I remember him saying to Manning, "Look, I don't want none of this over-matching. He's only a boy and he's going into a man's world, so you look after him!" Me dad was a bit protective of me I think. He'd heard so much about boxers getting over-matched.'

Was Jack himself nervous about entering the professional ring? 'No, I wasn't actually. I don't think I ever was nervous really, though I s'pose I had a few butterflies, otherwise I wouldn't be normal, would I? I looked on it as a learning opportunity. I never worried about losing; it was all to do with learning. After 100-odd amateur contests you wouldn't have thought I'd have much to learn, but it's a different sport altogether really, professional boxing.'

Jack made his pro debut at Watford Town Hall on 15 May 1950 and was paid £5 in purse money. 'My opponent was a bloke called Bob Dover from Canning Town,' he recalls. 'I knocked him out in the first round, two minutes 50 seconds I think it was, put him down three times. He was made for me really; I don't know what his record was or how many fights he'd had, but I shouldn't think he'd had many.'

Jack weighed just 10st 7lb (dead on the welterweight limit) for that fight, so it is curious to find he quickly moved up to middleweight, and then to light-heavyweight. 'When I turned pro, at just over 17, I was a welterweight,' Jack confirms. 'But Rex Manning had *something* about light-heavyweights, and after about two fights as a welterweight he said, "Oh, you're a middleweight now." Then a few more fights as a middleweight and I was bloody boxing light-heavyweights!'

Fighting at Watford, Luton and the Mile End Arena, Jack had mixed success in his first seven bouts, but at least one of the four losses he suffered was entirely unwarranted: that is, his reverse to Johnny Godfrey (Walworth), as Jack explains. 'He was my sparring partner; although Manning didn't manage him he was more or less looking after him. He was a tough fighter but I was quite a good boxer, so I just played with him when we sparred.

'One night at Mile End Arena my opponent or his opponent didn't turn up, and I think one of us was there but not down to box, so they said to my manager, "Do you mind if these two lads box each other? We're a bit short of bouts." So the manager agreed. He said to me, "Take it easy on him" – which I did – and I won it hands down.

'Then a week later we were back at Mile End Arena and the same thing happened: my opponent or Godfrey's opponent never turned up. We boxed again and I thought I'd beaten him easier than when we'd first met, but they gave him the decision. Then the referee come over to us in the dressing room afterwards. "I've got something to say," he says. "I've never done it before and I shouldn't tell you this but I made a mistake. I meant to raise *your* hand. I raised the wrong hand and I couldn't do anything about it!" I said, "That's all right, mate. Don't worry about it." I got a good write-up in the paper at least, saying I should have won it, easy. That was quite comical.'

By this time Manning had found Jack a coach called Harry 'Gus' Harris, who accompanied him to various gyms to supervise his training. 'If he was telling you anything he'd use an f-word every other word,' Jack chuckles, 'but it didn't matter to me. A right Cockney he was. He'd been around a lot and was quite a good trainer; he lived up in London somewhere. My manager used to look after him as well as a little bit I gave him out of my earnings.'

Jack's nearest gym was Manning's Halfway Street base, 'an ex-army billet place', as he recalls. 'It was a great big building with a lovely big hall. But mainly I used to go up London to train, 'cause that was where you'd get all the sparring. It was no good staying in Sidcup just sparring with the amateur club boys; you had to take it easy on them. So I used to travel up to London – it was only 20 minutes on the train from Sidcup – do me training, get home about nine o'clock at night, go to bed. Wonderful life!'

At Jack Solomons's Great Windmill Street gym Jack sparred with visiting world-class heavyweights such as Nino Valdes and Lee Savold. 'All you could do with them was just dance around and keep out the way,' Jack tells me. 'Some of them threw a couple of bombs but I managed to keep away. I was a bit too quick for 'em. They were big lads – bloody great arms – and it was like boxing a windmill.

'When I sparred with Nino Valdes my manager said, "Look, he's only a young lad, so I don't want him put through the mill." But I don't think Valdes could speak English, so he had to speak to him through an interpreter. He didn't take liberties anyway; he never hit me properly, but his little taps were hard enough.

'I was in Solomons's one day when this bloke came in, he had all the gear on and he looked the part, and I thought, "I bet he's American." But then I found out who he was: George Walker, Billy's brother. I sparred with him and I thought, he's not so good as I thought he was. I managed him quite well. I think he was number one or number two in the ratings and everybody wanted to know who I was. I was the talk of the gym at the time. I was quite surprised.'

None of the aforementioned sparring partners particularly impressed Jack, but a man of his own weight whom he first met at Dale Martin's gym in Brixton certainly did. The most gifted of four fighting brothers, Alex Buxton of Watford (whose mother was English and father Antiguan), was British light-heavyweight champion and one of the stars of 40s and 50s British rings.

'I first started sparring with Alex Buxton when I was 16 and a half,' Jack tells me. 'What a great fighter he was! If I'm asked who was the best boxer you've ever seen or known, Alex Buxton comes to mind. He was tremendous, and what he taught me was nobody's business. I used to spar five or six rounds most nights with him in the course of the week and I had ten rounds with him one night. He was me main sparring partner.

'Whenever he had a big fight on he used to have a training camp, one of them was in Surrey in the open air. He had a big barn place he used to spar in if the weather was bad, but mainly he used to spar in this open-air ring 'cause it was summertime. I used to go down there every day and have three or four rounds with him. And I reckon in all I must have had a couple of thousand rounds with Alex.

'He won the British title, had some bloody hard fights and fought some terrific boys. I more-or-less grew up with Alex. He was such a great bloke and I was really sad when he died.'

Jack's recollections of Buxton tell of the close bonds and friendships that are often formed between sparring partners who spend hours together spilling blood and sweat in that lonely roped-off space.

Following Jack's first seven fights, from November 1950 he began an impressive unbeaten run and squeezed 16 fights into his first year as a pro. Like most up-and-coming boxers of his era, he needed a full-time job to augment his ring earnings; but in this regard he was luckier than most.

'I was a plumber with the London Transport when I was boxing,' Jack says. 'Funnily enough, my manager was a chief executive to the London Transport and if I wanted any time off, I just had to mention Rex Manning and they'd say, "Well, yes, yes, you can have it off. Is that all you want?" He was quite feared; he was one of the top-notchers in the London Transport at the time.'

Unfortunately, just as Jack's ring career was gathering momentum (he was unbeaten in 12 fights) he was called upon to complete his national service in the RAF. 'I had a couple of fights on when I got me call-up papers,' he recalls, 'and my manager wrote to them and said, "He can't go in yet, he's got a couple of fights." So they gave me a deferment and I went in at 18 and a half instead of 18.'

National Service

'I was looking forward to going in actually,' Jack says of his military call-up. 'My brother went in before me – he was nearly two years older than me – and he seemed to like it all right.

'We went to Padgate in Lancashire and did our six weeks' square bashing – training and marching up and down – and then they asked us what part of the RAF we hoped to join. Me and a lot of me mates put in for the RAF Regiment [the ground fighting force of the RAF], which was like the army really. We thought if we put our names down for that, we'd all stay together 'cause nobody wants to join the RAF Regiment 'cause it's all drills and marches – and nobody likes that. And that's what happened. About six of us joined the RAF Regiment and we went through our two-year stint together. It was quite good having your mates together.

'The first camp we went to was RAF Wunstorf, about three miles outside Hannover in Germany, and I thought, I wonder if they've got a gym at this camp. Lo and behold, just round the corner from the camp was this beautiful gym, which had a boxing ring as well, and I started training the first day I got to the camp.

'There was a PTI there. He said, "Christ, you look a bit handy. I've been at this camp five years now and I've been trying to get a boxing team together, 'cause you get special food, you don't do any sort of work, you just train every day. You can forget your uniform, just get a good tracksuit that'll last you for two years." I said, "Look, before you say any more, I'm a professional. Obviously I'll help you get a team up, spar with them and everything, but I can't fight." He said, "Leave it with me. Have a couple of fights and see what the situation is then." I said, "Well I'm quite well known now in London 'cause I was in the *Boxing News* a lot, but of course I'm not known here."'

After six months stationed in Britain, Jack spent 18 months of his two-year service in Germany and had numerous services fights. 'I got roped in for a very cushy life,' he laughs. 'I had a terrific time – I'd love it again; I was completely left alone and they more-or-less made me their trainer. I was boxing more than I was doing gunnery work. I could just please myself: the PT instructors and that didn't say anything to me.'

But the danger of being exposed as a professional boxer was ever present, as this anecdote shows:

> One time an English team flew over to box us and this trainer bloke was chatting to 'em and they kept looking over to me. He called me over and said, 'Streek, one of our team recognises your name as being professional.' I said, 'Ah God, not again. If I was pro, how could I box here? Me brother's Jack. My name's Ted, or Edward if you like.' That got me out of a lot of trouble, having a different name from the one I boxed under!
>
> But this bloke I was due to box was evidently pretty good, some sort of amateur champion; might even have been an ABA champion, I can't remember. So I decided I was gonna box as though I didn't feel like boxing and they gave him the decision. He was a good boy but I felt I could have beaten him.

Deliberately boxing below his usual standard, Jack lost the fight but saved himself from further awkward questions about his professional status. 'I think I had 18 fights out there; shouldn't have had any really,' he chuckles. 'Luckily I got away with it. Nobody said anything more.'

Although some would say Jack's professional experience gave him an unfair advantage over services opponents, to some degree this was offset by the fact he often fought full-blown heavyweights while no more than a middleweight himself. He won the RAF Second Tactical Air Force Championship at heavyweight, defeating the much larger Service Police Constable Ridgley in the final.

Aside from his defeat to the boxer from the visiting English team, Jack suffered only one other loss while boxing in the mob – to a future top-line pro called Tony Dove.

'He was based in Germany but in a different squadron than me, and we both boxed for the English services team,' remembers Jack. 'We had a terrific scrap and he beat me on points, but I was quite pleased with my performance. I knew him quite well actually

Sid Nathan pictured in 1939 as a 17-year-old professional boxer.

Sid in the twilight years of his refereeing career.

Sid (now in his 90s) proudly displays the lifetime achievement award presented to him by the British Boxing Board of Control in 2011.

Sid referees a Southern Area title clash between welterweights Ricky Porter and Bernie Terrell at Walworth's Manor Place Baths in April 1971.

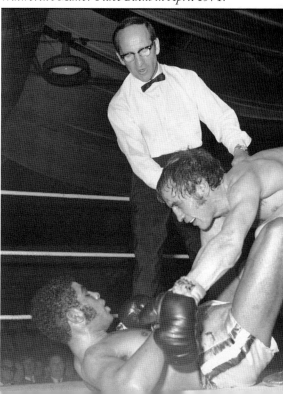

TED BERRY
BETHNAL GREEN

Mgr. Jack Jordan
PHONE: WEM. 1676

The late Teddy Berry as a professional boxer in the late 1940s.

The dilapidated but atmospheric Mile End Arena, a leading London fight venue of the 1940s and early 50s. Six of the fighters in the book boxed there.

Left to right: Charlie Kray, Ronnie Kray, Reggie Kray and Ted Berry, pictured after the Kray twins' professional boxing debut at the Mile End Arena in July 1951.

Left to right: Ted Berry, the writer John Pearson, the famous photographer David Bailey and Checker Berry, pictured at Ted's pub, the Old Horns, in 1968.

Ted pictured in 2012.

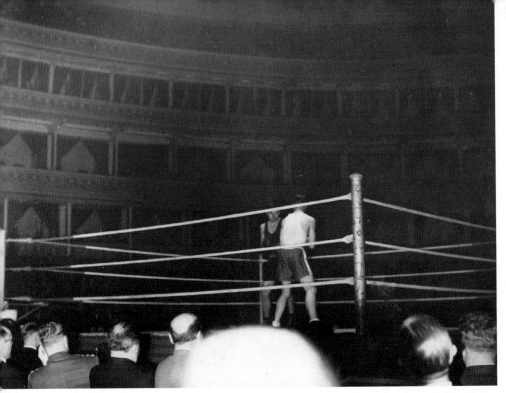

Jock Taylor (facing the camera) outpoints M. C. White (West Hendon BC) in an amateur bout at the Royal Albert Hall in April 1943.

Jock as a 17-year-old professional in 1943, with Rex Manning (manager) and Harry Watson (trainer).

Jock in his fighting prime.

Jock (back row, centre) with the Fleet Air Arm boxing team.

Jock (right) spars with trainer Harry Watson.

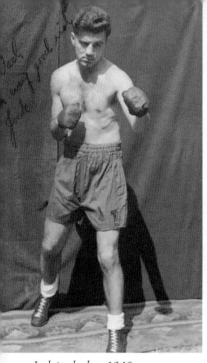

Jock in the late 1940s.

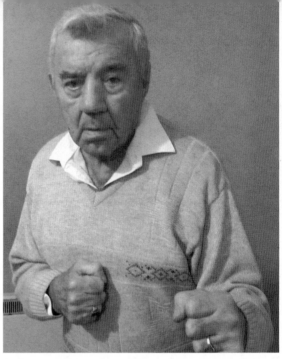

Jock in 2014.

A 14-year-old Jack Streek on his way to a points win at Sidcup's Lamorbey Hall.

Jack (age 15) in his garden at Days Lane, Sidcup, after winning the 1948 SE London Divisional Youth Championships (Class A) at 9st.

Jack at the Torbay pub gym at Rotherhithe in late 1949, just before turning pro.

A promotional postcard showing Jack as a young pro boxer.

Jack in 2014.

Jack (only a middleweight), representing the RAF versus the Army, knocks out the Army's heavyweight representative in the third round, in Germany, 1953.

Jack coaching at Orpington ABC in 1980.

Two Albert Carroll publicity cards.

March 1955: members of the National Association for the Paralysed look on as Albert trains for a charity bout in aid of the association.

September 1959: Albert trains for his British welterweight title fight with Tommy Molloy (Liverpool).

Albert in 2014.

Teddy Lewis as a young pro boxer.

Ted in 2014.

A fighting family: Ted's father (right) with Ted's uncles Bill and George Lewis, pictured during their boxing days.

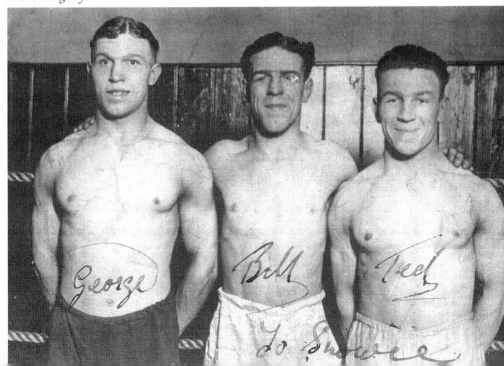

Ted's grandfather Bill Lewis.

Ted with his father (right) and manager George Morris, pictured at Southend in the late 1940s.

Ted's boxing licence.

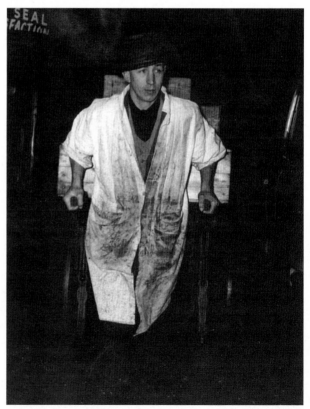

Fighter by night, market porter by day: Ted hard at work at Billingsgate Fish Market.

Sammy McCarthy in his tenth pro fight, about to become the first boxer to stop the teak-tough Guyanese fighter Hugh Mackie (Manor Place Baths, January 1952).

White City Stadium, June 1952: Sammy takes on Jackie Turpin, brother of world middleweight champion Randolph Turpin.

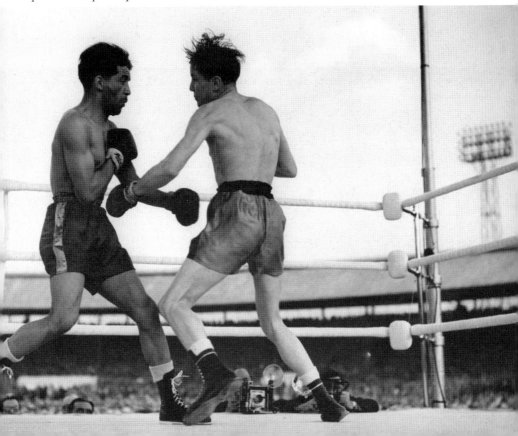

Sammy lands a short left to the face of the reigning British featherweight champion Ronnie Clayton in a non-title affair, December 1952.

Prince Philip, Duke of Edinburgh, congratulates Sammy after watching him fight reigning feathe champion Clayton in December 1952.

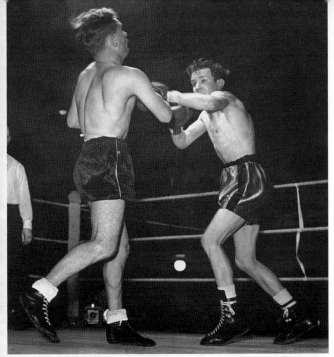

A swift left from Sammy knocks back the head of Eugene Servais (Belgium), Seymour Hall, Marylebone, February 1953.

February 1954: Sammy spars with welterweight Hector Constance as he prepares for a fight with European featherweight champion Jean Sneyers.

Sammy and Jean Sneyers (Belgium) weigh in at Jack Solomons's Windmill Street gym for their European featherweight title clash in February 1954.

White City Stadium, June 1954: Sammy is crowned British featherweight champion, pictured here with his new Lonsdale belt alongside trainer Snowy Buckingham (left) and manager Jack King.

Battered and bruised but still smiling: Sammy enjoys a cup of tea after winning the British featherweight title.

Sammy, fresh from winning his British title, with actor Norman Wisdom at Pinewood Studios, on the set of One Good Turn, released in 1955.

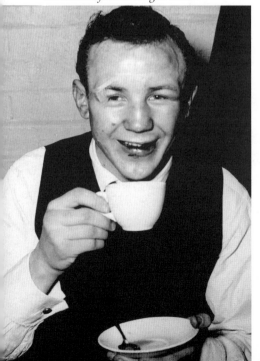

Left to right: Yolande Pompey, Snowy Buckingham, Sammy and Lew Lazar training at Brighton as Sammy prepares for his fight with Roy Ankrah.

December 1954: Sammy and the Gold Coast fighting fury Roy Ankrah weigh in at Jack Solomons's gym ahead of their bout at Harringay Arena.

Sammy trains at the Thomas a' Becket in June 1955 as he prepares for his return fight with Bournemouth's Teddy Peckham.

Royal Albert Hall, October 1956: Sammy lands a left to the body of Johnny Miller (South Shields)

Sammy stops Frenchman Jacques Dumesnil, Streatham Ice Rink, November 1956.

Sammy, as he is today, reading a 1954 issue of The Ring *magazine with a familiar boxer on the cover – himself.*

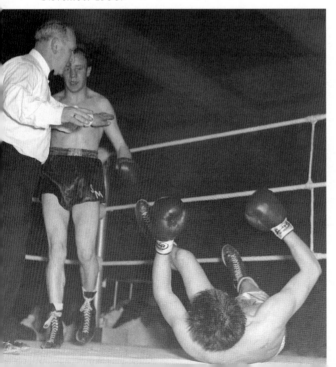

'cause we'd sparred a lot beforehand. We used to show each other moves and it was always close between us.

'The next time I saw him, I turned on the telly one day, after I'd got demobbed, and there was Tony Dove in one corner and Albert Finch in the other, and Albert Finch beat him on points.'

Sparring Partner to Don Cockell

'I was 20 when I got demobbed and when I come out I thought, I'll have a nice rest now before I start training again. I got home on the Saturday then on the Sunday morning I went to see Rex Manning, who lived just round the corner from me, and he said, "I've got a nice little holiday down in Brighton for you. You're gonna be Don Cockell's chief sparring partner!"

'He was gonna box Johnny Williams for the British heavyweight title and his trainer or manager had seen me box at Mile End Arena and thought that I boxed very much like Johnny Williams. He was a tall left-hand boxer, so they thought I'd be good for Cockell to spar with. Rex told me, "We're going down to Brighton. Will your dad take us in the car?" So me, Manning and me dad went down to this hotel in Brighton where Cockell was training.[8*]

'And when we got there, who should open the door to the hotel but Frank Bell – amateur champion, turned pro and did quite well as a professional – he was one of the top boys. He had a big plaster right across his nose. "You've come to spar with Don, have you? The bastard – look what he's done to my nose!" He said, "He's all yours now." And he left, I didn't see him again… it was funny. I had a couple of rounds with Cockell that day, then me dad and Manning drove home and picked me up a week later.

'I already knew Don quite well 'cause he used to come down to Sidcup and spar with Jock after Jock had beaten him twice; Don lived in Battersea at the time, and I hadn't turned pro then. I was about 15 and used to go down there just to watch them train. He sparred with Jock a lot.

---

8   The Crown and Anchor Hotel (and public house), near Preston Park.

'Anyway, we had a great time in Brighton. We went to several places in the evening as guests of honour and got introduced up on the stage. As for the sparring, whether he didn't like tall, upright boxers, I don't know, but I found him very easy to hit. I don't wanna sound big-headed but I was quite a good boxer, he was five foot ten or five foot 11 and I was six foot two, and after Buxton and all the other boys I'd sparred with, I found him easy to box.

'It was the only time I got paid to spar: I got three pounds a round. In the week I was down there I had 15 rounds with him, so I got £45 – that was like winning the pools!

'When me dad come and picked us up and I left Don at Brighton, I wished him all the best for his fight with Johnny Williams – "Give him what for" sort of thing – but I was surprised he actually beat Williams, 'cause Williams was a fantastic boxer.'

On 12 May 1953, Cockell out-pointed Williams to capture the British and Commonwealth heavyweight titles. This win was a springboard to a series of world-class heavyweight fights, culminating, as previously mentioned, in a contest with the great Rocky Marciano for the world heavyweight crown. Such a match-up would have seemed improbable when Jack sparred with Cockell two years before that memorable fight.

Back to Boxing

Jack's first fight after leaving the forces was a tough assignment at an open-air show at Epson Town FC's ground. Jack scaled 11st 8lb but his opponent, Les Bristow (Walworth), weighed a whopping 12st 8lb. 'He was really strong,' Jack recalls. 'I was trying to get to him, but I couldn't, you know, he was such a big bastard.' Nonetheless Jack managed to floor his man with a right to the body in the third round before Bristow was disqualified for fouling in the sixth and final round.

Having yet to be convinced that matching Jack against far heavier men was unwise, Manning then entered him in a light-heavyweight competition, just as he had done with Jock Taylor seven years earlier after Jock had left the military. Even the promoter of the two tournaments – Eddie Mallet – was the same.

'That was ridiculous,' remembers Jack, 'bad management that was, putting me in for that. It's a light-heavyweight competition and I was just about a middleweight. But 'cause I was six foot two tall, long reach and that, and my manager had managed Jock Taylor – light-heavyweight – he was trying to work me the same as Jock.'

In November 1946, at a similar stage in his career, Jock had reached the final of a 12st 7lb competition at Luton and received good publicity as a result. But Jock had been heavier than Jack and was a different type of fighter.

The open light-heavyweight competition Jack entered, in September 1953, was at Watford Town Hall and he was over a stone lighter than every other entrant. Jack weighed only 11st 1lb for his opening bout, while his opponent, Tony Monaghan (County Mayo), tipped the scales at 12st 6lb.

'Streek had been highly fancied by locals to win the competition outright,' wrote *Boxing News*, 'but though fast and skilful with both left lead and evasive tactics, the Sidcup man had neither the weight nor punch to offset Monaghan's strong-punching, sustained attack.

'Streek has a nice stance, a pleasing style, and is invariably superbly cool and fit. When last the writer saw him (over a year ago), he sighed "If only that boy could punch!" Today, as then, the kayo punch is lacking. Coupled with his weight disadvantage, this factor kept him from at any time looking a likely winner. Monaghan won on points.'

When criticising Jack's alleged lack of a punch the reporter fails to consider the full enormity of his opponent's weight advantage. 'He was a great big bloke and so strong,' Jack recalls. 'He didn't out-box me but he out-fought me and he got the decision. The promoter gave me a fiver as the best loser.'

The eminent sports writer A. J. Liebling, when writing of weight advantages in his classic boxing tome *The Sweet Science*, reflected, 'If the difference amounts to no more than a couple of pounds, it can be offset by a number of other factors, including luck, but when it goes up to five or six or seven, it takes a lot of beating. The span between the top limit of one weight class and the next represents the margin that history has proved is almost impossible to overcome.'

While describing the obstacle of a full weight class between two well-matched, well-conditioned boxers as 'almost impossible to overcome' may be an exaggeration, Liebling's observation at least sheds perspective on the disadvantage Jack endured when taking on fully-fledged light-heavyweights.

In his next fight, at Empress Hall, Jack was finally matched with a man of his own weight in middleweight Johnny Byrne (Bristol). Their bout was on a prestigious bill, which saw Mile End southpaw Joe Lucy out-point Bermondsey's Tommy McGovern for the vacant British lightweight crown. For Jack it was a step closer to boxing's big time and this was reflected in his purse money – £35, which was a decent sum to a young man earning just £5 or £6 per week. It was to be the biggest purse he ever earned for a fight.

An impressive win on this bill would have provided good exposure for Jack, but his fight was cut frustratingly short. 'Johnny Byrne was quite a high-rated boy,' Jack remembers, 'but he nutted me in the second round and cut all me eye open and I packed it in at the end of the round.'

His next fight, on 30 November 1953, which took place a couple of weeks before his 21st birthday, turned out to be his last. In this he lost on points to Dennis Bebbington (West Ham), who was part of a well-known boxing family. 'I didn't put enough into it and he probably just about earned the decision,' Jack admits. 'That was when I walked out the ring and said to me manager, "Right, that's it. I'm finished." I was right browned off with it all.' Jack's weight for his final encounter was just 11st 1lb, well below even the middleweight limit, while his opponent was 5.5lb heavier.

I ask Jack why he stopped boxing at this point and he says there were a number of factors that influenced his decision.

'When I first started it was like an adventure,' he tells me, 'but like anything else the newness wears off. I didn't wanna let anybody down when I packed up, but I thought, ah, sod it, it's my life – I'm the one who's gotta do all the work. My dad was very upset when I said I was gonna pack up 'cause he was one of my staunch supporters. Me dad and me granddad, they was me ardent supporters. But I started courting and lost a bit of interest – that puts you off of boxing – you've gotta go training every night and you wanna go out with your girlfriend.

'Also, I wasn't happy with me manager, quite honestly. He was the only one we ever knew. "He's a *professional manager*" we'd say when we was young kids, and I sort of grew up with that. Although I met a load of managers and trainers, he was our main man. We didn't even think of going with somebody else.

'I think he could have got me on better. Where I was learning most was in the gym with all these top-line boys. Sparring with blokes like Alex Buxton when I was 16 was great for me, a great learning phase. All these American heavyweights that was coming over – Lee Savold, Nino Valdes – I sparred with them all.

'Some of the boys I was sparring with, they was ten- or 12-round fighters and I handled them easy. I found that with a lot of boys. I thought, Christ, he's in the top ten this kid! I fought a couple of eight-rounders but my manager kept me on six-rounders mainly, which was silly really.

'When I did retire, I told the manager I was packing it in and he didn't like it, but after about six months I started to get the bug again. I was still only 21, so I went and saw Jim Wicks. He lived in the same road as me, Foots Cray Road, but it's a long winding road, about seven or eight mile long. I lived in the Sidcup end and he lived the Eltham end.

'I went to his house and he opened the door to me and said, "Hello Jack, how you going? All right?" And I thought, I'm in here, you know, and I showed him me record. "Oh," he said, "you've boxed a lot of these small halls." I said, "What's wrong with that? Long as they paid well."'

At this point I ask Jack how much of a difference being signed by a manager like Jim Wicks (who handled Henry Cooper and other stars) could make to an up-and-coming boxer, and he explains:

If you went with him, a promoter would ring up and say, 'I want Henry Cooper or Joe Lucy' or whoever he had. But if they wanted them on the bill, they'd have to accommodate some of his other boys as well, the lesser-known boys. So if you wanted to get on, you'd get in with a big manager, 'cause you'd get on all those shows at places like Harringay and Earls Court – the big places. You get a manager like that who's got a few real good boys, British champions and that, and you get on these big shows; and of course, that's where the money is.

So, anyway, he said he'd take me on but he didn't like the way I'd been handled. He said I'd more or less have to start again. I went back to where me dad lived and he said, 'I wouldn't bother, Jack. Pack it in altogether. It's not worth it. You get blokes like that, think they own the place. I wouldn't bother if I was you, Jack.' So I took his advice and that was it.

Jack finished his career with a final tally of 23 professional fights: 14 wins, seven losses and two draws. This raw data, however, does not do him justice. It is not a true reflection of his talent and it does not take account of the sometimes huge weight disadvantages he endured. Nor does it tell of the two-year disruption of military service that broke up his unbeaten run. It is a testament to his defensive skill that (excepting a retirement due to a cut eye) Jack was never knocked out or stopped as either an amateur or pro, and he tells me he was never floored either.

'My record's not brilliant but with the losses I had, I thought I won most of them,' Jack opines, 'but I expect we all think that. The only time I thought I was lucky to get the decision was against Rocco Long. He was a black boy, hard bastard he was. I thought to give him justice it could have at least been a draw or him winning it. But anyway they gave it to me so that was it; I didn't complain. But that was the only lucky win I had.

'I enjoyed me boxing life,' Jack adds. 'Probably the only thing I regretted was turning pro too early. Rex Manning wanted me to turn pro before I was even 17. I'd have liked to have had a lot more amateur fights as a senior, gone into the forces as an amateur and carried on from there when I came out. If I'd turned pro when I was, say, 20 or even older, I'd have been more mature physically and mentally.'

Life After Boxing

'When I was 15 or 16, I was training in the garden and I saw this girl on a swing next door but one – so that was 99 Days Lane – swinging away. I said "Hello" and I got chatting to her, and in the end I married her. But unfortunately we got divorced after 25 or 26 years, and so I married again, and I've been married to Sylvia about 26 or 27 years.'

Jack moved from Sidcup to Sevenoaks in Kent and worked for many years as a foreman for the London Electricity Board at Sydenham. In the late 1980s he moved to Bournemouth. 'When I moved here I tried to carry on from where I'd left off working for the electricity board, but they never had any vacancies so I joined a contracting firm, which was contracted to the electricity board anyway. So it was the same thing but I earned a lot more money. It's a lovely quiet place,' Jack says of his current home, 'and the people are very friendly.'

Although Jack's boxing career ended aged 20, his connection with the sport has lasted a lifetime. 'I felt that I could put something back into the game with what I'd learnt in my amateur and pro careers,' he tells me. 'I felt that I had enough to offer a boy – to put him in the right direction and teach him a lot of the things I learnt.'

In 1972 Jack started coaching at the Crescent (Eltham) ABC and then from 1975 until 1985 held the same position at Orpington ABC. While at the Orpington club he formalised his credentials by qualifying as an ABA coach under the guidance of national team coach Kevin Hickey. He finished his coaching career as a trainer to Bournemouth ABC and while at the club qualified as a senior ABA coach (under another national team coach, Ian Irwin).

While Jack has now officially retired from coaching, he is still involved with Bournemouth ABC and has warm memories of the club. 'We'd got this old barn place and we did it all up, made it beautiful,' he tells me, 'then some bastard set fire to it and gutted it completely. All the gloves, all the equipment, the ring and everything was all burnt. But you could say it did us a bit of good, 'cause with the insurance pay-out we got it all re-done and the place was rebuilt virtually: all new equipment, new ring and now it's a gym that any boxer would be proud to go into.

'Actually, I still go down the gym now and again, and David Haye came down our gym one evening. We met him, as him and his trainer were gonna live down here for a while 'cause he wanted to train at the seaside: nice air, running on the beach and all that caper. He came down with his entourage and trainer to inspect the gym, but unfortunately for us the ring wasn't quite big enough. He said, "It's a beautiful gym you've got" – 'cause it was all new and repainted – but the ring was 12 or 13 foot square and he wanted a 17- or 18-foot square one.'

'I took him in the ring,' Jack chuckles. 'I showed him a couple of moves that I thought were good, and I think his manager was having a bit of a laugh, but *he* seemed interested, as actually it was a couple of good moves. I've seen him box a couple of times but I haven't seen him use the moves.

'Boxing took up most of me time when I was coaching,' Jack says, 'but I've got a lot of fond memories of all the boys – and I trained some good boys.'

Away from work and boxing coaching Jack had little time for hobbies, although he did have one other keen interest. 'I used to love fishing – still got all me rods and that, but I haven't been for ages. I used to go a lot down Salcombe in Devon – beautiful place – and I did a lot of shark fishing there. You go out about 12 or 15 miles on a boat for sharking. I caught an 80-pounder – blue shark – once and that was quite an experience. It was the only one caught that week.'

Having been directly involved and interested in boxing from the 1940s and 50s through to the 21st century, I ask Jack how boxing now compares with boxing then. 'I think there were a lot better boys about then – in my day – than there are today,' he says summarily, before adding cheerily, 'I look at the 50s as though it was 20 years ago; I feel as though I'm 40 or 50 meself. Luckily I'm in good health.'

ALBERT CARROLL (BETHNAL GREEN) 1952–62

I WAS a professional boxer from 1952 to 1962 and I won the Southern Area title and fought for the British championship. I fought most of the top-liners of my day, notably Wally Swift, Brian Curvis, Tommy Molloy, Tony Mancini, Tony Smith and Sandy Manuel. But I want to tell you about my first professional fight, at the National Sporting Club.

I turned pro at 17 and my manager, Mr Curly Carr, had the devil of a job to get my mother, who suffered with her heart, to sign the papers. She relented at last, so there I was, a pro boxer at 17, boxing at the famous National Sporting Club: six two-minute rounds against a guy called Ken Scammell for £5 – a week's wages at work!

I won the fight on points after my manager introduced me to that great, great ex-world welterweight champion Ted Kid Lewis, who gave me a few tips. Mr Carr gave me a white £5 note, saying he wouldn't take any commission until I was earning £15 or more. So I got the white £5 note and I said to Ted Kid Lewis, 'Will you sign that, Mr Lewis?' He said, 'Course I will, boy' and signed it. I couldn't wait to get home to show my mum.

I was so excited, I forgot about my black eye: I just couldn't stop talking about the fight and the people I'd met. Mum tried to calm me down, saying, 'Go to bed – you've got work tomorrow. While you're at work I'll go down the market and find a frame for your £5 note.' I went to bed but I had a hell of a job getting to sleep.

Next day I got up and went to work as an apprentice asphalter. I couldn't wait to get home to see my £5 note on the mantelpiece, in its new frame. When I did get home I couldn't stop looking at it. I loved my mum more than anything else in the world that day.

The next day I went to work as usual, as happy as Larry. When I got home the first thing I did was look at the mantelpiece, and there it was – an empty frame.

I screamed, 'Where's my £5 note? Mother, what have you done?'

'Oh, don't start,' she said. 'I only borrowed it. I'll put it back on Friday when I get my pension.'

'Your pension!' I screamed. 'That £5 was signed by the great Ted Kid Lewis.'

'Who's he?' she cried.

I told her he was the greatest world champion Britain has ever produced.

'Don't worry,' she said, 'you're bound to bump into him again. Perhaps he'll sign another one.'

It didn't enter her head that it was the first money I'd earned through boxing: the most precious £5 I'd ever earn. That frame stayed empty until the day she died.

※ ※ ※

This eloquently penned account is from a letter Albert Carroll sent me in response to an appeal I made through the London Ex-Boxers Association's (LEBA) newsletter for former professional fighters with stories to tell to get in touch. After I had read it, I immediately phoned Albert and asked if I could feature him in this book. To my delight, he agreed. I met him in person at a LEBA meeting the following weekend, and a week later drove to his home for an in-depth interview.

It has been some years since Albert lived in east London but he retains the accent and mannerisms of the place. Today he lives in the leafier borough of Bromley in Greater London, in a pristinely tidy flat he shares with his partner Joan, whom he met in the late 1990s after the death of his wife.

I find Albert an extremely frank man who is willing to speak about every aspect of his life. He talks openly about his mistakes, some of which led to prison time, because, as he puts it, 'it might help someone else in *their* life'.

Today Albert weighs several stone above his old fighting weight. His once-hallmark blonde hair is grey and there are few physical signs of his former trade. As an evasive boxer, he managed to keep his nose in its original shape and avoided cauliflower ears. But his deep, gravelly voice certainly befits someone who earned a living through fighting. He is a man who tells – and appreciates – a good joke, and his reminiscences are peppered with a deadpan Cockney humour that got him through some very tough times.

As I go to leave Albert's flat after the interview, he stops me and unexpectedly hands me a notebook full of his writing. 'Use whatever you want from that,' he says casually before I head to my car. When I arrive home I find it is a detailed account of his life and ring career, written in the same riveting style as his letter. Accordingly, this story features extracts from these memoirs as well as the interview Albert gave.

Beginnings

Albert George Carroll was born on 9 June 1935, at Bancroft Road Hospital in Mile End, within earshot of the crowd's roar at the Mile End Arena, where he would later box. 'My father had left my mother for another women and she had to bring up me and my older sister Doris single-handed,' reveals Albert. 'I can't remember when my mum and dad split up because I was too young, so I had no memories of him, although I did know him later. My mother was lovely, about five feet tall and very poor, but she always managed to put a dinner on the table.'

Shortly after the outbreak of the Second World War, Albert and his sister were evacuated to Wales for their safety, while their mother remained in London. Along with crowds of other kids – with labels on their lapels and gas masks slung over their shoulders – they were herded on to a train at Paddington Station.

Who they would live with when they reached Wales was left entirely to chance, as Albert recalls:

> I remember standing in a school playground holding my sister's hand while all these men and women picked out other kids – my sister and I were the last to be picked out. We were chosen by a Mrs King, who lived in Derrick Street in Tylorstown.[9]* I was never happy there and I remember I was always crying and wetting the bed, for which I was often beaten.
>
> One morning I woke up and sure enough I'd wet my bed again. Mrs King, after giving me a wallop, pinned a note on my back saying, 'I WET THE BED', then sent me to school. All the other kids going to school were laughing at me as I tried to scrape the note off by rubbing my back against the wall. I was crying with shame and confusion when all of a sudden a bloke pulled me away from the wall, ripped the note off my back and went to see Mrs King.
>
> I could hear the row going on from the street outside. It turned out that this man, Mr Billy Fry, was Mrs King's brother and he was taking me to live with him from now on. It was the happiest day of my young life, and to this day I have never wet the bed again. I loved living with Mr and Mrs Fry – Uncle Bill and Auntie Ivy as we called them. They had two children about my age (young Billy and Valerie), we had great fun and I was sorry when my mum came down one day and took us home.

---

9 Interestingly, Tylorstown was once home to the legendary world flyweight champion Jimmy Wilde, who was nicknamed the 'Tylorstown Terror'.

Albert was nine when his mother brought him back to London in 1944, and having lived in Tylorstown for around four years, the East End felt strange and unfamiliar to him. 'I'd never heard of the Tube,' he recalls, 'and I wondered why people were sleeping down there. When we got home to Stepney I couldn't believe the size of the roads.

'I well remember the first Christmas after I came home. For the last three years I'd had a Christmas present from Uncle Bill and Aunt Ivy, so I hung up my stocking as usual. When I woke up I had the biggest disappointment of my life: I found my stocking filled with the biggest potato I'd ever seen. My mum, bless her, didn't have any money, and thinking we would understand she'd put potatoes in our stockings to make us laugh. Instead of that we cried our eyes out.'

The family were bombed out of their Stepney home just after Christmas 1944, and from there moved to Tagg Street in Bethnal Green, where they shared a house with a family named Wheeler. 'The house was the pits,' Albert recalls, 'and water ran down the walls. It was so bad that I ended up with rheumatic fever and had to go into hospital for about eight months.'

When he was finally well enough to leave hospital, Albert joined Bonner Street Primary School before moving on to Cephas Street Secondary School, and the family moved to Whiston Road, Bethnal Green. One of his class-mates was a boy named George Happe (pronounced happy), who became a lifelong friend. 'I grew up with him really. I spent more time round his house than I did me own,' says Albert.

It was through his friendship with George that Albert, quite by chance, discovered he had a gift for boxing:

> We used to go to an evening institute in Morpeth Street where George lived. There was metalwork, woodwork, cooking for girls, football and boxing. They were two-hour classes from seven till nine, then from nine till ten there were records to dance to in the school hall. And that's the reason me and George used to go over there: to go and dance and try to pull

a bird. But the man who ran the institute said, 'You can't just come here and go in there and dance; you've gotta join one of the classes.' So we decided we'd join the boxing class 'cause it was the only thing we knew.

The main reason the boys chose boxing was George's uncle – also called George Happe – a promising amateur and future professional who was four years older than the lads and trained regularly at the evening institute gym.

'We went along and I took to it right away,' says Albert. 'Punching the bag, skipping rope and running round the streets in my boxing shorts, I felt like a world champion, that is until I sparred with Uncle George. He took liberties with me, and I had a few good hidings from him. But I'm glad I did because it toughened me up and he taught me a lot.'

Albert pauses and then laughs, 'He taught me how to fall! Cor he could hit. He had a punch like the kick of a mule. I persevered though and gradually got better and better.

'The institute wasn't affiliated to the ABA so we only had contests with similar institutions, and consequently the prizes weren't much cop. Three two-minute rounds and I got a pair of braces. Another time I got a biscuit barrel. But the best of all was a 2/6 book on how to box. We all had a laugh over that one!

'I boxed for my school and lost in the final of the East London Schoolboy Championships in 1950. Then in 1951 they put me in for the youth championships. I wondered what the youth championships were; I'd never heard of them before but they told me it's a form of ABA championships, but for youths under a certain age.

'I got to the final of the North-East London Divisionals, where I come up against Ronnie Redrup at West Ham Baths, and he was a West Ham boxer. I won the fight – don't worry about that – but I didn't get the decision. It happens a lot. Ron Redrup went on to win the Great Britain Youth title and he finished up fighting for the British light-heavyweight championship when he turned professional.'

In 1950 Albert left school at the then-statutory age of 15 and got a job as a van boy for the City of London Bottling Co, based in Broadway Market, near London Fields. 'I was earning £3 per week old money,' he recalls. 'I liked it because we drove all over London and got home about 5pm. I used to give my mum £2 and 5 shillings and keep 15 shillings myself. Then something went wrong with the driver and I got the push. But young George Happe came to my rescue.

'George, his brothers, his dad and all his uncles – including Uncle George the boxer – were asphalters by trade and young George was an apprentice. George asked his father, whose name was Con, to ask his governor if he would take me on as an apprentice with a starting wage of 9d an hour.

'I loved it from the moment I started: it was hard, heavy work but it kept me fit as a fiddle. We worked really hard for four or five hours then we were on our way home. I could then have my bath and a nice cup of tea before going to the club for training. After training I'd meet June in the school hall for dancing and then take her home.'

Albert had met June – his new girlfriend and future wife – at a New Year's Eve party he had attended with George Happe's parents at the end of 1950. During their courtship much of his asphalting wage was spent on taking her to the cinema two or three times a week.

A Surprise Offer

'I was still sparring with Uncle George and I was getting better all the time: I knew this because I wasn't getting hit so much (George had turned pro by now and was doing well as a welterweight). One night while we were sparring, George's manager, Curly Carr, turned up. He asked me my age. "Seventeen," I said. "Weight?" I said, "Ten stone two pounds." Then he asked me if I wanted to turn pro and I thought he was joking; see I'd only had 20 amateur fights, and I'd lost 11, so I didn't know what to say. But with a bit of encouragement from big George I said yes. The next day was a Saturday and Curly Carr came to my house to see my mum to ask her to sign a consent form for me to box pro, 'cause I was under 18. I'll never forget her first words to him. She listened to him telling her how good he thought I could be then said, "Mr Carr, have you got any children?" "Yes," he said, "I've got a boy and a girl." So she said, "What does your boy do?" "He plays the piano," he said. "I'll tell you what," she said, "you teach my boy to play the piano and let your boy box professionally."

'She meant it too. It took over an hour to convince her that nothing bad would happen to me and it finished up with me pleading with her. But eventually she signed this thing and I was then a professional boxer.'

The agreement was signed on 23 June 1952 and Albert's first pro fight was on 27 October that year. In the interim Albert's girlfriend, June, discovered she was pregnant. 'I was 17 years old, just starting out on a new career and this had to happen,' says Albert, remembering his feelings at the time. 'I told my mum and she was heartbroken, as was June's mother. In those days girls didn't have terminations unless it was a backstreet abortion, and she wasn't going to have one of those, so we decided to get married.

'Over the next couple of weeks it was agreed we should marry on 8 November 1952. I wanted young George Happe to be my best man but my mother had her way and my uncle John was best man. That night, at the reception, June had a miscarriage. What a start to married life.'

A New Routine

After marrying, Albert moved in with June at her mother's house in Poplar where they had an upstairs room. 'I used to get up about 6.30am, go to work, come home between 4.30pm and 5.30pm then go to the gym in Rotherhithe in a pub called The Torbay. I'd train for a couple of hours then get home by 9pm or 9.30pm. By then everyone else had eaten so June had to cook me a meal, which I took upstairs and ate on my own before I went to sleep.

'I wasn't very happy and we were always having rows. One day I decided I'd had enough and went back to my mum's. She was overjoyed and gave me my old room back. June didn't get on too well with my mum so she stayed with her own mum, and we saw each other about two or three times a week.

'I was only at The Torbay for about six months. Danny Holland was running the gym in The Torbay – he trained Henry Cooper to three Lonsdale belts – and then they had to shut the pub down, so they moved the gym to the Thomas a' Becket; and the Thomas a' Becket went on for ever.'

As we talk about The Torbay, I ask Albert whether he met any memorable characters there and he recalls meeting the Kray twins. 'They were in the Torbay when I first went up there and I sparred with them a couple of times: one one day, one another day. But they weren't all that. They didn't hurt me at all. They were in the army when they come up there and everyone was running around for them, "D'you want this done? D'you want that done?" and all that. Anyone would think they were world champions. I found them all right actually, but I never had a lot to do with them.'

Professional Career

Albert made his pro debut at the recently-established National Sporting Club (NSC), which took its name from a famous pre-war members-only establishment that had fashioned the rules of modern boxing and created the Lonsdale belt system. The original club, a majestic yet austere institution where spectators sat in complete silence during rounds, had gone into liquidation in the 1930s.

The post-war NSC was styled on its predecessor – with crowds of cigar-smoking gentlemen and long-gowned ladies gathered at ringside amid clouds of blue smoke and an eerie silence observed during rounds. When Albert boxed there, the club's shows were being held at the Empress Club in Mayfair's Berkeley Street, but soon afterwards the NSC found a long-term home at the Café Royal in Regent Street.

As previously mentioned, Albert's first pro fight was a six-rounder against Ken Scammell (Wandsworth) and a legendary boxer was there to support him. 'I'm in the dressing room then all of a sudden my manager walks in and he's got Ted Kid Lewis with him,' says Albert, grinning as he relates the story. 'He's introduced Ted Kid Lewis and I'm overawed, you know, an ex-world champion talking to little old me – and he's giving me tips. He says you do this and you do that; whether I done it or not I don't know, but I won the fight.'

I ask if Albert found adjusting to the pro ring hard and he says, 'I didn't because longer fights suited me. When you're fighting amateur – three rounds – by the time you get warmed up it's over. But six rounds is double so I found it a lot better. That's why I won 11 of my first 13 pro fights, and the other two I thought I should have won easily. In one I had the bloke down twice and got a draw, and in the other I had him down once and still got beat. Both of them were at the Mile End Arena.'

Despite his success, like many pros, Albert was obliged to continue his day job, which proved an undoubted hindrance. 'If I wasn't married I wouldn't have gone to work,' he says. 'I would have just concentrated on boxing and I'd have probably done a lot better. But at the same time, going to work did keep me fit, 'cause it was heavy work. I broke off me apprenticeship in the asphalt trade because I got married and I couldn't live on the money. I started at ninepence an hour, then it went up to a shilling an hour, then one and nine; but I had to break it off and go as a labourer, which was two and three an hour, still in the asphalt trade, to get some money. And then I was boxing as well.

'I was getting five or six quid for a four- or six-round fight, and I had 13 of them on the trot. So I wasn't earning a lot of money. But I thought: the better I get, the more money I'm gonna get.'

Albert's 14th fight signified a step up in class from the small hall shows he had so far boxed on. He had made it on to the bill at the Empress Hall in Earls Court. 'I fought Ronnie Richardson and beat him over six threes,' he recalls. 'I got 22 quid for it, but by now Curly had started taking his whack, which was 25 per cent, and some went to my trainer; so I finished up with £14 and ten shillings. But that was three weeks' wages back then. I thought, lovely, I've *got* a few quid. And now I'm looking for the eight-round class 'cause I done the six threes easy.'

But the contest was memorable to Albert for more than just the purse and venue. 'As I stepped into the ring I happened to look up at the clock and saw it was eight o'clock. The next day my brother-in-law, Alan, came round to my mum's to tell me that June had had our first baby at eight o'clock the previous night... just as I stepped in the ring. We named her Diana.'

The Thomas a' Becket

By now The Torbay pub gymnasium had closed and Albert was training at the newly opened Thomas a' Becket pub gym, where he remained for the rest of his career.

'When we moved from The Torbay to the Becket I had to get two buses,' Albert recalls, 'a number eight bus down to Shoreditch and then the 78 bus over to the Old Kent Road. Later we moved from Ranwell Close to Henley Buildings in Shoreditch, so then I only had to get one bus. There were some great fighters up the Becket. The Hinson brothers used to train there, Dave Charnley trained there. But some of them – like Charnley and Henry Cooper – used to train in the afternoon, whereas we used to go there at night.

'My trainer was Nobby Wallace – a nice man and a good coach. He had a bit of help from another bloke, his assistant Benny Edwards. Nobby used to work as a paint deliverer and sometimes he was late. If he was late, Benny used to take over until he arrived. Benny Edwards was another nice fella. It was Benny Edwards and Danny Holland – the pair of them – who first took over the Becket and some great, great champions trained there. The Thomas a' Becket's still there and the pub's become a restaurant, but there's no gym there now.'

When you ask Albert about the men he sparred with at the Becket he can proudly mention such notables as the top American middleweight Moses Ward and the legendary world welterweight champion Kid Gavilan of Cuba. 'He was one side of the ring and I was the other side of the ring and he'd still hit me,' laughs Albert when I ask about Gavilan. 'He was a bolo puncher. He was extraordinary.

'What happened, Kid Gavilan came over to fight Peter Waterman, so I sparred with Kid Gavilan and Peter Waterman won the decision, which was a dodgy decision. Then when they fought again, I sparred with Waterman and Gavilan beat him. Peter Waterman was a good fighter: I sparred with Peter a lot.

'I remember his brother Dennis, the actor, coming up the Becket one day. He was only a kid and he'd come there from acting school. I was just getting ready to go in and spar with Peter when Dennis said something to me. I can't remember what he said but it got up my nose – "He'll kill you" or something like that. I never met the boy again but I've disliked him ever since!'

Another regular sparring partner was Albert's stablemate George Happe, the uncle of his boyhood friend. 'He was an aggressive fighter and I used to love them 'cause all I had to do was run round the ring. I had a good left hand and he used to walk onto it all day. I used to love fighting them sort of fighters. They lead with their face to get one in; they take two punches to land one. But if he hit ya, you'd know all about it.

'I wasn't a fighter that went forward all the time,' Albert adds. 'I used to go back. I used to love them to come to me and I'd just pick them off willy nilly. But you've got to be exceptionally fit to fight like that and if you ain't fit you don't last very long, and I learnt that towards the end of my career.'

In his 15th pro fight – his first outside London – Albert boxed at the famous Liverpool Stadium in his first eight-rounder. 'I fought a bloke called Ken Regan,' he tells me, 'and he was from Blackpool. He'd just beaten Ken Bebbington in Liverpool and caused a sensation, so they wanted him back and they asked me to go up there. I got £35 purse money and they paid me for two fares, so I thought, ooh – it's going up, it's going up!'

With only 14 pro bouts to his name, Albert was conceding considerable experience to Regan, who'd had 49 paid fights, of which he'd won 38, drawn one and lost ten. But the gulf in experience did not show.

'We have never seen Regan so perplexed and harassed,' wrote *Boxing News*. 'He stepped inside with vicious left hooks to the head, but Carroll was often like a "Jack in the Box" with his sprightly footwork and excellent use of the ropes. When Carroll moved forward he had Regan hesitating and mystified by weaving and bobbing. Before Regan could launch his expected counter-attack the London boy had zipped home lefts and rights to the head… Carroll never wasted a blow, and his timing and delivery were first-class.'

Perhaps the most surprising aspect of Albert's fight with Regan was that he dropped the Blackpool man several times and then brought matters to an early close. 'I stopped him in seven rounds,' Albert recalls excitedly, 'and I thought, "I've found a punch!" 'Cause I used to win my fights on points.' This was in fact Albert's first inside-the-distance win, but further surprises followed when he fought at the Liverpool Stadium twice the very next month.

'Next time I went up there I fought Charlie Currie, a Scotsman, and I stopped him in *three* rounds. I couldn't believe it,' grins Albert. The referee had rescued Currie in the third round after he'd been down twice. 'He was badly shaken by Carroll's crisp and solid punching,' noted *Boxing News*, 'Carroll, who is only 18, hardly ever wastes a punch and shows excellent judgment and timing.'

'Then the next time in Liverpool I fought Billy Wooding, Midlands Area champion. I thought, well, I'm getting into championship class now. *But I broke his jaw…* four rounds… lovely! I thought – this is brilliant,' chuckles Albert.

'I was becoming a bit of a celebrity around the East End by now, what with the local paper showing my picture and writing about my fights. Being only 18 or 19 years old I suppose I let it all go to my head. I started going out pubbing and clubbing it, pulling birds left, right and centre. It's surprising how easy it is to pull birds when you're a bit of a name.

'I stopped working and wouldn't listen to anybody who tried to advise me. I suppose I became a right Johnny know it all. I started to neglect my training because I couldn't be bothered to get two buses to go there and two buses home.'

Nonetheless Albert won his next two fights, out-pointing the game but outclassed Santos Martins (Nigeria), firstly at Leyton

Baths and then again at Leeds Town Hall – both fights being held in November 1954. In January 1955 Albert topped his first bill at the Liverpool Stadium, where the fans had been clamouring to see him back in action.

'I got up there and I'm fighting a geezer called Sandy Manuel,' says Albert, 'and when he turned up for this fight I couldn't believe it. He had like a Tommy Cooper hat on and robes all round him. This was his local paraphernalia. They said, "That's your opponent." I looked at him and I went, "You're joking!" But he was some fighter. He was in between lightweight and welterweight, around 10st 4lb, and *fast*, unbelievably fast.

'I come out me corner and by the time I'd got me hands up he'd hit me on the chin, and I didn't know no more till the sixth round. That's the truth. He hit me so hard that as I went down he was still going forward, and he fell over me prostrate body. But I didn't know this because I was out like a kipper, but I got up. Somehow I managed to get up – instinct they call it. Next thing I know, they're ringing the bell for the sixth round. I said, "What round is it?" So Nobby Wallace, me trainer, says, "Round six. Come on, you've only got three to go." I went, "Six!" I didn't even know about the others. Anyway, I went out and I held me own in the sixth and I won the last two rounds, but it was too late. He'd well won the fight.'

Sandy Manuel (real name Emmanuel Olu Fumilola Babarinsa) took up boxing in his native Lagos, Nigeria at the age of eight, turned pro in 1949 and in 1952 sailed to Liverpool, where he based himself for the rest of his career. A fans' favourite wherever he boxed, Manuel made Liverpool his adopted home and remained there until his death in 2002, aged 68.

'Cor he was good,' says Albert of Manuel, 'and he beat some good fellas, but I don't think he ever got a chance to fight for the Empire title. I fought him four times and it ended up at two wins each. Next time I fought him I beat him at Streatham. Then he beat me at Hanley, up near Stoke-on-Trent, because of a clash of heads which cut me eye. I wasn't worried really, but it was a big cut that bled a lot and the fight was stopped. Then in our last fight

I beat him at the Liverpool Stadium. He turned out a smashing bloke – he was always laughing. He became the secretary of the Merseyside Former Boxers' Association.'

Albert had a further seven fights in 1955 and won them all bar a KO loss to a tough Trinidadian named Boswell St Louis, whom he out-pointed in a return. In June 1956, Albert won a Southern Area welterweight title eliminator fight against former opponent Ron Richardson (Canning Town), but then suffered consecutive stoppage defeats in September and December, to ex-British lightweight champion Frank Johnson (Manchester) and former Scottish welterweight champion Jimmy Croll (Dundee) respectively.

There follows a nine-month gap in Albert's fight record. When I ask him about this absence from the ring he says solemnly, 'Me mum was ill. She had heart trouble and she didn't want me to box anyway. When I was fighting on the telly my sister made sure she didn't watch it. So I said to me mum, "I'll turn it in," and I did, but I still used to go training. She knew that I wanted to box and I used to tell her, "See that bloke there – I beat him and look where he is now," and all that. Eventually she said I could go and do it again, so I made a comeback. But she was ill and she finished up dying very young.'

A break from boxing apparently did Albert good, as he returned to the ring with renewed vigour. Wins over Terry Gill (West Ham), Wally Swift (Nottingham), Tommy Tagoe (Ghana) and Jimmy Croll (Dundee) preceded a Southern Area title fight with Terry Gill in October 1958. But to the chagrin of many spectators, Gill got the decision. 'Two of the veteran ringside supporters – their names household in boxing – scored only two rounds for Gill with three even,' noted a *Boxing News* reporter who was stunned by the decision.

'I fought Terry Gill three times,' Albert tells me, 'and the first fight I thought Terry won. I got the decision but to be honest with you I didn't win that fight; he won it. So it happens both ways. But our second fight was for the Southern Area championship, 12 rounds at Leyton Baths. If I say I won a fight, I won a fight; if

I say I lost it, I lost it. And *I won that fight*, you know, I won ten rounds out of 12.

'Tommy Little was the referee and he give it to Terry Gill, and there was murder. People were throwing chairs in the ring, throwing telephone directories – there were fights everywhere. The upshot was they give me a rematch with Terry Gill, again for the Southern Area title, and also made it a final eliminator for the British championship.'

The rematch with Gill took place on 11 June 1959. 'It was in Terry Gill's backyard, Canning Town,' recalls Albert. 'So I went down there and boxed his head off. He should have won our first fight but I got the decision; I should have won the second fight but he got it; but I well won the third fight. So I'd won the Southern Area title and I'd also won the final eliminator for the British welterweight title. My next fight was for the title, against Tommy Molloy.'

I ask Albert how it felt to win the Southern Area title. 'It felt great,' he says, 'and I thought I was into money. I got £400 for it and I was well pleased, although I didn't finish up with that. I finished up with £225 after expenses, but it was still a lot of money compared to what I'd been getting. So now I'm thinking I'm gonna get some big money, you know, because I'm the number-one contender. I read in the paper that Dave Charnley was getting £10,000 to fight a ten-rounder against a Frenchman no one's ever heard of. He's getting ten grand so I thought, well, I've gotta get a few quid for fighting Tommy Molloy, even if I lose.

'Molloy had just beaten Jimmy Newman, who was a stablemate at a club I used to go to in Wells Street as an amateur. I used to spar with Jimmy Newman a lot. I'd seen Tommy Molloy fight Jimmy Newman and I thought, well, I can beat this Tommy Molloy.

'The fight went to purse offers and went to Liverpool's Johnny Best, who bid £1,100 – 60 per cent to the champion, Molloy, and 40 per cent to the challenger, me. So I was gonna get the same for a 15-round championship contest as I did for a 12-round eliminator!

'By this time I wasn't at work – I was boxing full-time. I used to borrow on the strength of me fights and I'd borrowed a load.

I'm borrowing off this one, that one and that one, and when I get me fight money I pay it all out. But when I heard how little I was getting, it broke my heart and I didn't even bother. I used to do me road work and that was it. I'd go to the gym about three times a week, when it should have been every day. If ever a man cut off his nose to spite his face it was me.

'At night I was up the West End boozing and birding it and during the day I was knocking about with all the thieves from Hoxton, where my father and uncles lived. I was just lazing about feeling sorry for myself, and sometimes I even went out thieving with them. If we had a tickle, we would all go up west and booze the money away with girls we didn't know. Never a thought for those indoors.

'It was four months between the Gill fight and the Molloy fight and the abuse I did to myself was stupid – and it told in the end.'

British Championship Challenge

Tommy Molloy was a younger brother of Jimmy Molloy, a top-notch 1940s welterweight who managed and trained Tommy after hanging up the gloves himself. As an amateur Tommy lost only 11 of 110 bouts, and won the British Army of the Rhine (BAOR), British Army and Imperial Services Boxing Association (ISBA) championships while completing his national service. Foremost among his amateur wins were two victories over the gifted three-time ABA welterweight champion Nicky Gargano.

Molloy, a powerful two-fisted fighter, turned pro in February 1955 and amassed a 30-fight unbeaten run before beating Jimmy Newman for the British welterweight title, which had been vacated by Peter Waterman. In his climb to the top Molloy's form had been spectacular. But since he'd won the title, in July 1958, questions had been raised as to whether he was still the force he had been.

Fifteen months had elapsed between winning the title and defending it against Albert, and in that time Molloy's form had been unconvincing. He had stopped Ron Jackson (due to a cut eye), lost on a disqualification to Johnny Melfah, been beaten on points by Brian Husband and only managed a draw against Paddy

Graham. Illness and the death of one of his brothers in a road accident were said to have taken a great toll on Tommy, and his aura of invincibility as a pro had somewhat diminished.

But Molloy had trained hard for his fight with Albert and had based himself away from home at the Bosco gym in Belfast to ensure he met with no distractions. The outcome of various championship fights held at the Liverpool Stadium over the years had earned the venue the nickname the 'graveyard of champions', but Tommy Molloy had given himself every chance to prove an exception to the rule.

At 24, Albert was a year younger than Molloy, and going into the fight his record showed just eight defeats in 44 pro bouts. Despite boozing and cutting corners in training, Albert made the 10st 7lb championship weight after several sessions in the Turkish baths. The sports writers, who knew nothing of Albert's reckless lifestyle outside of boxing, considered his chances of victory good.

'This is an even-money battle with stamina playing a leading role,' surmised *Boxing News*. 'If Carroll can keep to a fast pace we expect him to take a close points verdict, but Molloy – deadly determined to win – can pull it out the bag if he regains his dazzling form of last year.'

There were no spare seats at the Liverpool Stadium on the evening of Wednesday 14 October 1959, when Molloy and Albert finally met in the ring. Although this was Molloy's home ground, a fair portion of the crowd, if not actually rooting for Albert, were at least sympathetic towards him, since the Londoner's six previous fights in Liverpool had won him many local fans.

'Carroll, faster, smarter and more convincing, was almost coasting to a comfortable points win,' wrote *Boxing News* when assessing the first ten rounds of the fight. 'He was continually beating Molloy to the punch. He was moving inside, scoring all the time with his flashing straight left to the jaw. The champion looked worried and perplexed, with his left eye cut and swelling... Time and again Carroll stopped Molloy in his tracks with that ramrod straight left, and his prospects were rising high, for the champion showed little sparkle or confident aggression in his own work.'

'I started well, winning the first six or seven rounds,' says Albert, 'but Tommy Molloy had always been a slow starter and knew what he was doing. When you box off the back foot, like I did, you use more energy and have to be extremely fit, which of course I wasn't.

'Going into the tenth round the papers said I was well in front, but then me legs just went. Tommy caught me at the end of the tenth with a tremendous right hand, which shut my left eye completely. I slipped to the canvas then the bell went and saved me... for another one,' he laughs. 'They more or less dragged me back to my corner and I went out for the 11th and managed to stay out of trouble. But in the 12th he caught up with me again.

'He got me on the ropes and he pummelled me, give me a good hiding. I covered up and I thought I'd let him punch himself out on my gloves while I'm ducking and diving. I waited and his punches got lighter and lighter because he was sending so many in. He slackened off a bit, stood back and as he stood back I hit him flush on the jaw. He staggered back and I thought, "I've got him!"

'I went to go forwards but my legs were like lead, I couldn't move. Then Tommy came forward, caught me with another right and I dropped like a stone. The referee stopped it there and then because he saw that it was already over. And he was entitled to stop it because Tommy had done the business.'

But not everyone in the stadium was satisfied with the referee's intervention, and some were under the misapprehension that Albert hadn't been stopped but prematurely counted out. Some spectators seated near ringside thought that the referee, Billy Jones, who was in charge of his first championship fight, had mistaken the timekeeper's shout of 'eight' for 'out'.

'Carroll's supporters, led by his muscular uncle Bobby Carroll, stormed into the ring,' wrote a bemused Desmond Hackett of the *Daily Express*. 'Passionately angry Uncle Bobby looked as though he was going to painfully impress referee Jones that young Albert had been robbed. But relief for the referee came from hefty Merseysiders who tore over the ropes from Molloy's corner. After three minutes of threat and counter-threat, with never a blow struck, the ring was cleared.'

It was then announced to the audience that the referee had stopped the fight, deeming Albert to be unable to defend himself, and had not, as many had thought, counted Albert out. 'Diehard fans are used to breathless thrills and drama at this renowned "graveyard of champions",' wrote *Boxing News*, 'but it is pretty safe to say that they have never known such a fantastic finale as this.'

'Lots of people were pouring into the ring 'cause they thought, because of that last right-hander I threw, that it shouldn't have been stopped – I s'pose they thought I could do it again. But I didn't have the strength to stand up, don't worry about anything else,' admits Albert. 'And it was my own fault: if I'd trained properly I would have won that fight.

'I've seen Tommy since and we had a drink together in Liverpool when I went up to the Merseyside Former Boxers' Association. He had a stick, you know – he was ill – but he came down with his daughter and his grandson just to see me, and I thought it was very nice of him.'

Sadly, Tommy Molloy passed away in April 2013, some months after my interview with Albert.

Final Fights

Four months after the Molloy defeat, Albert lost on points to future British champion and world title challenger Brian Curvis (Cardiff), whom he rates as the best man he faced. Despite losing in his British title challenge, Albert was still the Southern Area welterweight champion. In July 1960 he successfully defended his title at Wembley's Empire Pool against Tony Mancini, son of the famous 1920s welterweight Alf Mancini. But a return Southern Area title fight with Mancini, held at the same venue in March 1961, saw Albert lose the championship and revealed a weakness he had tried to conceal throughout his career.

'There was a clash of heads and he's got a cut eye and I've got a cut eye, but mine was more serious because I couldn't see. Me right eye's cut and I'm fucking gone – I'm blind – and he was hitting me with everything,' Albert recalls.

What Albert had hidden from the boxing world was the fact that his left-eye vision was extremely poor, so poor that he had failed an army medical because of it when called up for national service. With his right-eye vision severely impaired his left was virtually useless in the fight with Mancini. 'I went back to the corner and I said, "I can't see!" They tried to fix it up and I went out again, but I had to retire from the fight. Then it came out about me eye and everyone I fought after that kept throwing right-handers, 'cause I couldn't see them coming!'

Regardless of the defect in Albert's left eye being common knowledge, without the motivation and desire to fight his way back to the top, his career was coming to a close anyway. 'After the Molloy fight I wasn't the same fighter,' he says. 'I had 11 fights after Molloy and I was getting pittances. But it was me own fault 'cause I wasn't training.'

In one of these fights, held in December 1960, Albert had a memorable encounter with the famous referee Harry Gibbs, who was then relatively unknown as a third man.

'There were two jockeys who were brothers,' Albert recalls, 'Manny Mercer and Joe Mercer. Manny Mercer got killed during a race, so they had a benefit boxing show for Joe down at the Corn Exchange in Cambridge. They asked me to box a fella named Johnny Melfah (Ghana), eight rounds we was gonna do, and who was the referee but Harry Gibbs; although I didn't know who Harry Gibbs was at the time.

'Anyway, we get in the ring, I wasn't fit as usual, and this Johnny Melfah had massive long arms and he never stopped throwing punches. I just couldn't get out the way of him. He's hitting me with everything but the kitchen sink for about four rounds. I thought to meself, I'm not having this, so I went down on the floor.

'Gibbs come over and said, "Get up, you're in front!" And I thought, well, perhaps he don't like blacks – he can't do – 'cause the geezer was all over me. So I got up, I went the eight rounds and Gibbs give it to him!

'I come out the ring and Harry followed me, so I turned round and said, "You got me a good hiding there, Harry, didn't ya? I was gonna turn it in in the fourth." He went, "Yeah, I know. That's refereeing!'" laughs Albert. 'I tell people that story and they don't believe it.'

Intrigued by Albert's story, I consult a copy of the late Harry Gibbs's autobiography, *Box On*, to see whether he mentions the incident. Sure enough, on page 76, Gibbs wrote as follows:

> One of my early trips out of town was to the Corn Exchange in Cambridge to referee a bloke from Bethnal Green who was fighting a black kid. The Cockney boy was definitely not in the pink of condition and after five or six rounds he began to run out of gas. Finally he went down claiming a low blow and as I was counting I whispered to him, 'You're in front son, get up.' Up he climbed and when I gave the verdict to the other fellow at the end he called me a choice name... you have to kid fighters and you have to know them, to realise when they are conning you...

Albert lost five of his last six fights, the other a disqualification win over Nottingham's Wally Swift. His final appearance in a professional ring was on 17 January 1962 when he took on Johnny Kramer (West Ham) at West Ham Baths.

'I finished up getting beaten by Johnny Kramer,' says Albert, 'and I'm certain I'd have beaten him if I was fit and well; but he knocked me out in two rounds. Between you and me, I didn't get up because I didn't wanna get up. I threw the fight really. I'd already decided I was gonna retire from boxing, and I saw no point in carrying on. I knew I was gonna finish, so that was it – and I did finish.'

Life After Boxing (mainly taken from Albert's memoirs)
Long Arm of the Law

By the time of Albert's final fight, in addition to his first-born, Diana, he had four other children to support – Tony, Kimberley, Steven and Eddie – so it was the wrong time financially to retire from boxing.

'There I was: 26 years old, married with five children, no job and no prospects,' recalls Albert. 'When I was boxing and I wanted money all I had to do was borrow off my manager till my next fight; or sell some tickets and pay him out of my next purse. Now I had nothing, and it got to the stage where June had to pawn the bed sheets to feed the kids.

'I had started thieving in earnest, so she didn't know from one day to the next if I was coming home. When I had a tickle we lived it up a bit but that wasn't very often. Many a time we made out we wasn't in when the tally man – or rent man – called. We lived in a three-bedroom flat in Old Ford Road, Bethnal Green. It was here that our last two girls were born, making seven children in all.'

In 1963, a year after retiring from boxing, Albert had his first major brush with the law, which he describes in his memoirs.

'I was at the jump up (jumping in the back of a lorry and stealing parcels), working with a fella from Hoxton named John. We used to follow a van or lorry until it stopped, then while the driver delivered to a shop or factory I would get in the back of his van, nick what I could, throw it in the back of John's van, then we'd have it away.

'John had escaped from prison and had come to my home at 2am asking me to put him up. As I'd known him for quite some time I agreed. We had a van rung up (fitted with false number plates).

'One morning a fella from Hoxton called Joey came to my house. It was common knowledge that John had a van and Joey wanted to borrow it to shift some cigarettes. He said he'd give us £50 when it was all over, so we agreed. About an hour later, there was a knock at the door and the Old Bill (police) rushed in. They turned the place over and found a set of car number plates in the bottom of baby Lesley's pram, and John's prints were all over them. They found a tax disc in the top pocket of one of my suits and a few other odds and sods. They nicked us there and then.

'John got 18 months plus six months for escaping from prison, while I got 12 months for the stolen tax disc plus 12 months for harbouring John, to run concurrent. John went to a YP nick and I went to the Scrubs.'

Prison

'I was a bit apprehensive about going inside because I didn't know what to expect. When we were waiting for induction there was a YP in front of me and when he went in the room he left the door about six inches ajar. The screw asked the boy his name and he told him. "Call me Sir!" the screw said. "Why? You been knighted?" said the boy. I heard such a thump and the boy was dragged away. When it was my turn, I went in and I said, "Albert Carroll, *Sir!*" and I nearly saluted.

'I got to my cell in Wormwood Scrubs about 9pm and everybody was already locked up for the night. I was given a bath in about six inches of water, given shoes, socks, pants, a vest, trousers, a grey army tunic, sheets, a blanket, pot and pillow case. I had to make my bed in the dark because it was after lights out. I laid there and started to think about what I had done with my life. I didn't know what I would do or could do now, or how June would manage. What would she say to the kids? How would they cope when other kids at school started teasing them about their dad? I had a very fitful sleep that first night. Next morning at 7am the door to my cell opened and a screw shouted, "Step out!" I got up, dressed, picked up my pot and walked along to the recess. There were a dozen or so other inmates doing the same as me. Someone shouted, "Albert!", and I looked round and saw Jimmy Walker, who I knew very well. He was a cleaner on the twos.

'Jimmy, whose brother Billy Walker was a very good flyweight boxer from King's Cross, spoke to the screw on the landing and got me a job with him as a landing cleaner. I couldn't believe my luck. The landings were about 100 yards long and all we had to do was mop and dry the landing, which took about three-quarters of an hour, then it was back to Jimmy's cell where we made tea and just laid about talking, cracking jokes and the like.'

After three weeks of cleaning work Albert was transferred to an outside working party, which was tasked with cutting grass and generally tidying up Brompton Cemetery.

'I couldn't wait to tell June,' he recalls. 'As soon as she heard, she suddenly found she had a relative buried there and visited the cemetery once a week. I used to wander over to the catacombs where she gave me tobacco and booze, which I buried there. I always had a two-ounce tin of 'bacco full up when I went back to the Scrubs. We took a chance with the booze, but they only searched about two of the 20 working party inmates, and it was only a rubdown at random.

'This went on till about a fortnight before Christmas when June came up to the cemetery as usual, only this time we had a nosey screw. Most of the screws used to sit in the hut all day, playing cards with the two cons who were supposed to be making tea and sandwiches for us. This one decided to take a walk round the cemetery just as June and I were going round the back of the catacombs. She had a carrier bag full of goodies with her when we were caught.

'I pleaded with them not to nick June, letting them know she had six children and I'd never been in trouble before. The upshot was they let June go with a warning and I was sent back to the Scrubs with a police escort. When I got back I was strip-searched and put in a chokey cell till the morning when I went before the governor, whose punishment was ten days' loss of remission and ten days' loss of privileges. Three days later I was shanghaied to Stafford Prison.

'Once again there were a lot of cons I knew there, so I had a lot of help. Bernie and Peter Hennessee, Micky Holland, Dennis Sullivan, Johnny Lloyd and quite a few others remain my friends to this day. Being an ex-boxer had its advantages: people left me alone and I didn't get into many arguments.

'It was here that I met Mickey Ishmail, who lived near me, in Bow, and we hit it off right away. Mick, Jumbo Lane and myself were all due for release on 6 June 1964 – we were going to have such a party. But Mick had to go back to trial for an assault on the police outside the Pigalle Nightclub in Piccadilly, which had happened before he got his 12 months for receiving. He got another six months on top of his 12, so me and Jumbo travelled home together. We had a party at my house that night and had a real old-fashioned East End knees-up.

'Jumbo lived over the water in Camberwell, so I didn't see much of him during the months that followed. I used to go over Hoxton to see if there was anything going on, but most of the boys I knew over there were either doing bird or working with other people by now.

'I must have borrowed from every publican in Hoxton – you know, £10 here, £20 there – and not paying it back until I had a tickle; then when it was paid back I'd start all over again. I was tempted to make a ring comeback, but I was nearly 30 years old and my weight had ballooned up to 15 and a half stone, so it wasn't on.

'Mick came out in September and we began knocking about over Stratford and Canning Town. I met a lot of new friends and started working with them. Mick and I tried to work together but although we scored once or twice, we never really cracked it. So we decided he should do what he wanted and I should do the same. I went to work with a firm over in Canning Town and we did quite well for a time. I never socialised with them though, and every weekend Mick and I met up and painted the town red with all our mates.'

The Robbery

'About a month before Christmas we were sitting round my house wondering what to do, as we hadn't earned a penny for weeks. Someone said there was a shoe factory in Leicester that collected its wages on a Thursday; it had been looked at weeks before by someone's brother. "It's a big factory so they must pick up at least four or five grand. We could go up there and take a look. If it's still kosher, we could do it next week," they suggested.

'It was Thursday the next day, so we went up to Leicester and watched the two old boys get in their car at the factory. We followed them to the bank at a discreet distance and then back to the factory. As they returned to the factory they drove down a narrow street with little alleyways that separated every fourth house, and we decided that this was where we would do them next week. We spent the rest of the day familiarising ourselves with Leicester and working out our getaway. Then we drove home.

'On the following Monday we had a meet at my house to discuss the plan. It was decided I would go up there with Ruby in a straight motor and the other two guys would go up in a ringer (motor with false plates). We would meet at a certain spot in Leicester, not far from the street where we would stop the factory motor.

'Our driver would drive round to the street, park and wait while Ruby, Bill and I would wait in the alleys either side of the road, opposite our motor. Bill would signal to the driver when the prize was approaching and he would pull out in front of their car, put his car in reverse and slam into their car to shake them up.

'Meanwhile Bill and I would smash their windows, open the doors and grab the money bag. We would all jump into our car and drive off. We would all wear overalls to avoid forensics, take them off and dump them.

'Everything went as sweet as a nut until we went to change cars. When we got there, there were some builders right where we were supposed to park our ringer with all the overalls, weapons and bits and pieces. We didn't want it found until we were back in London, so we had to improvise. We walked across a little park in our overalls, got to the straight car, took our overalls off and put them in a bag. Bill, Fred and I got out to make our own way back home by bus or train when Ruby said, "Give me a hand to dump this gear." I said, "Okay," gave Bill and Fred the money and jumped back into Ruby's car.

'We drove along the motorway, heading for Loughborough and I kept worrying about roadblocks. We had to get rid of this gear a bit lively, so I told Ruby to pull in at a lay-by, which he did. I jumped out the car, grabbed the bundle of clothes and threw them over a hedge. I got back in the car and breathed a sigh of relief. It didn't matter now if we got pulled; we had nothing in the car to incriminate us. Or so I thought.

'We drove for miles and for every mile we drove I felt better, but then we saw a roadblock and had to pull up. I knew something was wrong when as soon as we stopped, both doors were flung open and a copper snatched the ignition key without a word being spoken. I kept shouting, "What's going on? What's this all about?" They shoved us up against the side of the car with our hands against the roof and legs apart.

'They found nothing on me or in the car, but I went cold when they found a white glove in Ruby's pocket. It belonged to one of the four pairs of thin white gloves we'd bought in Woolworths. He'd forgotten to put it in with the other clothes. We were captured!

'They cuffed us up to a copper and put us in separate cars and took us to the police station. On the way there it came over the intercom that a police van had been answering a call about our robbery when it hit an obelisk and turned over. A man working on the obelisk had been killed. "That's it, you bastard," said one of the coppers. "You'll be done for murder now." I didn't answer. I felt sick.

'They took us to the nick, put us in separate cells and CROd (Criminal Records Office checked) us. They found Ruby had a string of convictions and I had only one, so poor Ruby was classed as the ringleader and me the heavy because I was an ex-boxer. They questioned us for hours. They wanted to know who the others were and where the money was. But we couldn't tell them anything because, after all, we were innocent. They had the wrong guys. We had come up to Leicester to visit someone in prison.

'We didn't know what evidence they had until we went on an ID parade. It turned out they had put up a roadblock just outside Leicester after we'd passed the spot. A lorry driver heading into Leicester said he'd seen a man throw a bundle of clothes over a hedge near Loughborough, so they phoned the Leicester constabulary and put up another roadblock at Loughborough Crematorium, which was where they got us.

'The driver picked me out as the man who threw the bundle of clothes over the hedge. When they found the clothes, they found seven white gloves matching the one found in Ruby's pocket. We had no chance. The next morning we went to the magistrates' court and were remanded in custody at Leicester Prison, which housed three of the Great Train Robbers – Tommy Wisbey, Bobby Welch and Jimmy White – in its special wing.

'We were banged up in the remand wing, which was right underneath the special wing. Tommy Wisbey was in the cell right above me and Bobby Welch was right above Ruby. It was funny really because remand prisoners were allowed food parcels sent in, so Tommy and Bobby would have parcels sent in to us. When they arrived, down would come a piece of string, we'd tie a jar of jam or half a pound of butter to it and they'd pull it up to their cells. Anything larger, like a tin of biscuits, would go up to them via the cleaner.

'This went on for a few months, then one day Tommy asked me if a certain bit of food came in the last parcel, and I told him I'd given it to the cleaner to give to Tommy. The upshot was the cleaner had kept it for himself. He was a greedy little jock and was being well paid by Tommy and Bobby. "Don't worry," said Tommy, "we'll see to him when he comes up in the morning." The little jock must have had a warning because that night everyone was turfed out of their cells and we had an almighty turn over by police and screws. Property was smashed, photos were torn off the walls and we were all strip-searched. It was bedlam. It turned out not only had the little bastard been nicking our food but he'd made up a story and told the screws that the train robbers were digging a tunnel to escape. What a way to get shanghaied out of a prison. Ruby and I were sent to Bedford to be tried for armed robbery.

'We were in Bedford jail for about two months before we were taken to court. We were sitting in our cells waiting to go into court when we were told we were going back to Leicester. Apparently the judge, after reading that the crime was committed in Leicester, said, "Why should the taxpayers of Bedford pay for something that happened in Leicester?" So off we went back to Leicester.

'They stopped us having parcels sent in so it was obvious that the little jock cleaner had done the dirty on us. We were not allowed to mix with other prisoners and not allowed to mix with those in the special wing, but their logic being what it is, we were allowed to go to the pictures with those in the special wing.

'One day we were all watching the film *From Here to Eternity*. Montgomery Clift had been stabbed and was on the run because he had killed Ernest Borgnine. He was holed up at his girlfriend's house when the Japs bombed Pearl Harbor. "I've got to go back!" he said. "Don't go back," she said. "What has the army done for you?" "I'm a 30-year man," said Clift. "You ain't on your fucking own mate," said Tommy Wisbey. Everyone fell about laughing, including the screws. Tommy had been sentenced to 30 years for his part in the Great Train Robbery.'

Sent Down

'It was September 1965 when the big day finally arrived. The prosecution had a good case, but on the assumption that there is always a chance, we pleaded not guilty. The trial lasted about a week, and then the jury went out but were back within 30 minutes with guilty verdicts for us both. Ruby, who had quite a few convictions, got nine years, and I got seven years.

'June was in a bit of a state and she couldn't stop crying every time she came to visit me. Although June had her sister Joan living at home with her to help her with the kids, she had all the worry in the world, worrying about me, and was always short of cash.

'One day she didn't turn up for a visit and I wrote her a nasty letter. I got a nasty reply from her sister telling me what a selfish bastard I was and it was about time I stopped thinking about myself and started thinking about June and the kids. It shook me up because everything she said in the letter was true. I looked over the past few years and realised, I was selfish, I was a liberty taker and I was a no-good bastard for what I'd put June through. I wrote to June and we made up as best we could, through letters.'

After a time, Albert was transferred from Leicester Prison to Parkhurst Prison on the Isle of Wight.

'On the way to Parkhurst, I was cuffed up to a bloke who'd been an English teacher in Switzerland and we got talking. He asked me what I'd like to do while I was doing bird, and I told him I'd like to learn French and if possible learn to play the piano. "Well," he replied, "I can teach you French." That's when I found out they speak French in Switzerland.

'I went to the French class once a week and studied for four years. And, although I could read a French book and write a letter in French, I could never speak it or understand it when it was spoken to me by my new friend.

'As for learning the piano, well I tried that too. I found out there was a piano in an empty cell, so I went to the governor to ask if I could learn to play it. He told me they didn't have a music teacher in the prison and if I wanted to learn, I would have to be locked up in the cell with the piano and learn by ear.

'I agreed and so every night – save for the night I went to French lessons – at recreation time, when most of the other cons went to watch television or play snooker, I was locked in a cell with the piano, without music or a teacher, making a hell of a racket. I was tone deaf and didn't know where to start. I gave up after a fortnight and haven't tried it since. I started to write poetry, though, for the prison magazine, and one poem was printed in the *Daily Mirror* by Tom Tullett.

'Every time June came to see me she was getting thinner and thinner, but she wouldn't tell me what was wrong. I began to get extremely worried for her, then one day I got a letter from her sister. June had tried to commit suicide, and the children had been taken and put in foster homes.

'I was broken-hearted. June had tried so hard. She had fed and clothed the children all on her own. She worked part-time in between taking the kids to school and picking them up again. She was going hungry to give the kids that little bit more.

'Apparently it was a close call. June had taken some tablets in a fit of depression, but luckily her sister Joan came round that night and found June unconscious. June was taken to hospital and the kids were taken into care the next day. The kids were away for about six weeks before June was allowed to have them home again.

'Obviously I didn't know any of this was going on at the time, but once I found out I went to pieces. I remember going to the welfare officer to see if he could do anything. I don't think I said a word; I sat down and burst out crying. The next thing I knew I was being taken to the hospital. I had had a nervous breakdown.

'I was in the hospital for I don't know how long, then I was allowed back over to the main wing, and I was given a drug orally every night. I thought it was a sleeping draught but I walked about like a zombie for months. One day the doctor came and told me they wanted to give me electric shock treatment. I had to sign a form and was told I would have to go back into hospital for a couple of days. This I did.

'They put me to sleep with a needle and then put the apparatus on my hand and switched on. They did what they had to do and, I must say, I didn't feel a thing. I don't know if it did any good or not, but my memory wasn't all that good for a while after that. They cut down on my nightly drug and gradually I got better.

'I was still worried about June and the kids, and I got a few extra welfare visits from them. June and I got on a lot better, I wasn't so demanding of her and I began to understand what she had been through while I was in jail. People who go to prison seem to think those outside owe those inside a living. They are very selfish, or at least I was. If I wanted something, all I'd do was write to June and she would send it in to me. I didn't think to ask if she could afford it. I asked for something and expected her to deliver it. That's the way it was before my breakdown.

'After I'd been out of hospital a couple of months, I had a visit from June and we sat holding hands and talking for two hours. She told me what had been happening at home, how she was driven to distraction over money, my demands, the kids and everything else. We talked more that afternoon than we had ever talked together before. I made her a promise that day that I would never thieve again.

'She would never have to go through life without me again once I got home.

'We kissed each other when it was time for her to go and, although we had been married for 15 years, for me at least it seemed that was the start of my married life. I knew that once I was home I would go to work and I would love her for ever. It was hard to keep straight but I kept my promise.'

Ready to Change

'Lots of the cons had hobbies that they did in their cells, and some made models out of matchsticks. They could send money to Bryant & May matches in Bow and they'd send them a reel of about 500,000 matchsticks. They didn't have any heads on them – they were just slivers of wood. I was fascinated by this so I thought I'd give it a try.

'The first thing I made was a lamp stand and shade. It was made out of matches stuck together with glue, rubbed down with sandpaper and varnished. The time just flew by and I became so engrossed in my new hobby that I gave up smoking (you can't roll a cigarette with sticky fingers).

'I found a plan for how to build a dolls' house in a magazine, so I joined the woodwork class and cut out the dividing walls and base. I wrote to Bryant & May for some more matches, then sent off to a model shop for model doors and windows. When everything arrived I started work.

'It took me nearly six months to finish the dolls' house with the matches: it had three upstairs rooms and a living room, a kitchen and downstairs bathroom. I paid a con two ounces of tobacco to make the miniature furniture. I sent away to the model shop for the lights and finished it up a treat. The front of the house opened out and the base was covered with green velvet to represent grass. Ronnie Diamond from Hoxton, who I knew quite well, wrote "To Lesley and Lisa. Love from Daddy" in "ye olde worlde" writing on a strip of wood that I stuck to the front of the house.

'I was so proud of that dolls' house because it was the first thing I'd given any of my children since I'd been away. My brother Roy came down to see me and he took the house home and gave it to June to give to the girls for Christmas. I also made a boat for the boys and for the two older girls I made a panda.

'I started writing poems and sending them to June. You might say I was courting her again, through my letters. I hadn't realised until I had the breakdown how much I loved her and how much she loved me, and I was determined to try to make up for what I'd put her and my family through. I couldn't wait to get home, but I had two more years to do.'

In 1968 Albert was moved to Chelmsford Prison, which was much nearer London and easier for June to get to. He had ten more months to serve and was determined to keep his nose clean. Initially he did washing-up work in the kitchen but was then moved to an easier job in the bakery, where he sat around most afternoons playing chess with the other baker.

'One day I got a letter from young George Happe, who I hadn't seen for years,' Albert recalls. 'He wanted a VO (visiting order) so I sent him one and he and his two brothers came to see me. There was a lot of talk in the papers about people getting parole if they could prove they had a job to go to when they got out. George, Sam and David had opened their own asphalt business and they were willing to give me a job when I was free. They told me not to worry about anything because, even if I didn't get parole, they would still give me a job if I wanted it no matter when I got out.

'I couldn't believe it – I was so pleased. I knew George was one of my best friends from way back, but I hadn't seen him for years: not his fault, mine! I had gone thieving and ended up in jail, and he had gone to work and now had his own business. He had gone out of his way to find me and had now offered me a job that would get me back on my feet. I couldn't wait to tell June the good news. She was delighted.'

In order to start his new life with a clean slate when he left prison, Albert had one more matter to clear up. 'Years ago I'd bought cars, furniture, a telly, clothes and lots of other things that I can't remember for me, June and the kids,' he recalls. 'I used to pay the deposits and then let them take it out on the door knocker. I had court orders and summonses and bailiffs knocking on my door, and someone suggested I should declare myself bankrupt, which I did. I had to pay cash for everything after that. I couldn't get anything on tick or open a business or have any money to speak of.'

Albert had filed for bankruptcy back in 1964, and as things stood he would still be burdened by its restrictions when he was freed. On the advice of another convict, he applied to have his bankruptcy rescinded and to his surprise was granted a court hearing at Kingsway, High Holborn. He was driven there under prison guard.

Albert explained to the court why he wanted his bankruptcy rescinded, telling them the story of how he had wound up in prison and his wife and family's struggle while he was away. To Albert's delight, the court granted his request to take effect on 11 September 1969, a month after the hearing. This was not the only piece of good news, however.

'I don't know whether it was a coincidence or whether someone at the bankruptcy court knew something, but about two weeks later I was called up by the governor. I hated these types of call-up – you always worried that something was wrong at home. But not this time, baby!

'I'd been granted parole. I would be going home on 11 September 1969 and my bankruptcy was rescinded on the same day. A coincidence or what? I was dumbstruck. I had a fortnight to do.'

Free Man

'When the big day arrived, I walked out that big gate and I didn't look back – even the air smelt sweeter. I came home with about a tenner in my pocket, but I was as happy as a millionaire. The kids were all at school but June was there to welcome me. A few of my friends came up and we had a little drink to celebrate. The next day I had to go to the probation officer to register as a parolee, then I was free.

'I got in touch with George Happe about a job and true to his word he started me in work as an asphalter. The work was hard, but I knew it would be after not doing any for the past five or six years. I was being paid a regular wage of £25–£30 a week and I loved it. I was 34 years old, had a good wife who loved me despite what I had put her through, had seven children, a job I liked and I was a discharged bankrupt, so I wasn't in any debt. It was time to make a fresh start.

'When you go to prison you meet people who become friends and some you don't get on with at all. I was lucky because I met three or four blokes who came from my locality, so we looked after each other in there. Every so often one would come home, so we would have a party or a drink in the pub. Many a time I was tempted to go thieving again, but then I thought of what that sort of life had nearly cost me, June and the kids, and I never succumbed to the temptation.'

After a few years, the Happe brothers' asphalting firm hit a bad patch and Albert was laid off. Six months later, however, David Happe, who had started his own business (D.J. Happe Ltd), offered Albert a job and he stayed there for 15 years. In that time Albert was able to take June to Florida four times and once to North Dakota where her sister had moved after marrying an American. 'I can't thank the Happe family enough for giving me the chance,' he says.

After slipping a disc while lifting heavy gas bottles, Albert suffered from recurrent back trouble and was obliged to leave the asphalt trade. He found a job as a delivery driver at a firm called V.M. Thomas, and remained there until he retired, aged 70.

Sadly, in 1996 Albert lost June to cancer. Left alone in a three-bedroom flat, and having previously been strongly reliant on her ('she had done everything for me' he admits) he started drinking heavily and for a while spent much of his time in a drunken haze. But a chance meeting with a lady named Joan – herself a widow – got him back on track. Albert stopped his midweek drinking, learnt to cook and started a courtship with Joan. After a year, they moved in together and have now been a couple for 17 years.

Ring Reflections

Although Albert went through a dark spell in his life, he survived it and turned things around. While professional boxing was just one aspect of his colourful life, it remains perhaps the most outstanding feature.

'If I had me time again I would have been a light-middleweight,' he says, 'because I used to walk around at about 11st. Most of my fights were at 10st 9lb, so I trained down and came in about 10st 8.5lb. But when I boxed for the area championship or the British championship the weight was 10st 7lb, and that last pound or two hurt.

'I used to come home from the gym, have me tea and dry out overnight. Nothing in the morning: no breakfast or tea until one o'clock when I weighed in, then I'd go and have something to eat. It was all right when I was young, but as I got older I found it harder and harder because instead of walking about at 11st, I was walking about at 11st 4lb or 11st 5lb. But in them days they didn't have light-middleweights: it went from welter to middleweight, and there's a stone in between. You had eight weight classes then but now they've got 12.'[10*]

When Albert looks back on his boxing career, which ended over half a century ago, he does so with pride and also in the knowledge that, owing to his poor vision, there's no way the British Boxing Board of Control would have permitted him to box in this day and age.

'You're examined every time you go for a fight, and all the time I was boxing – I had 56 pro fights – not once did a doctor look in my eyes,' Albert reveals. 'All they'd do was look to see if I'd got scar tissue, look at my hands to check they weren't broken and test my heart. Then they'd say, "All right – you're okay."

'It's different today in the game. They have brain scans and everything now. They didn't in them days. Today I wouldn't have been able to box, but I'm glad I done it and I wouldn't change it for the world. There was a lot of heartache, but it was an experience.'

---

10 At the time of writing, there are in fact 15 weight classes recognised by British professional boxing's governing body, the British Boxing Board of Control.

TEDDY LEWIS (DAGENHAM) 1947–51

Londoners believe they have a future star in 18-year-old Teddy Lewis, of Dagenham… When I saw him in his very first contest it was plain to all that here was a youngster well above the average, and, as they say in racing, 'one to watch'… He has a style that promoters like, that of a box-fighter who goes forward all the time and who can punch hard with either hand… don't be surprised if he is a champion two years from now.

– Reg Gutteridge, *Boxing News*, 29 September 1948

% % %

A S I step off the Tube at Mile End Underground Station I am yards from a place that once echoed with the roar of East End fight crowds. For directly behind the station, encircled by corrugated iron fencing and crumbling walls, and sited on a piece of waste ground, once stood the Mile End Arena. Today it lives on in the memories of a dwindling few.

A former 'flea pit' cinema, the Arena opened for boxing in the early 1930s and, unlike so many other London fight arenas, it survived the Nazis' Second World War bombing campaign. In the late 1940s and early 50s the Arena truly came into its own as the only London venue to hold regular summer boxing shows.

On a balmy summer's evening, 2,000 or so fight-goers would file in through its entrance on Eric Street for a modest admittance, while children and thrifty adults climbed on to lampposts and adjoining buildings for a free bird's-eye view of the action. Passing policemen bawled officious warnings at these fare-dodgers only to be rebuked by cries of 'Leave 'em alone!' – and less polite remarks – from the paying customers.

Boxing stars of bygone days such as Sammy McCarthy, Eric Boon, Harry Mason, Al Phillips, Arthur and Alf Danahar and Harry and Lew Lazar all plied their trade here. It was also here that Mickey Duff started his career as a world-renowned matchmaker after he had retired from a short but successful pro career as a lightweight.

After a visit to the Mile End Arena in the early 1950s, Welsh heavyweight boxing legend Tommy Farr enthused:

> The Arena isn't the most comfortable place in the world, but I had a great time because I saw boxing that cracked with all the lusty vigour and spirit of the boxing booths as I used to know them. There was no evening dress at the ringside, no film glamour girls looking for free publicity. The place was filled with people who wanted to see fighting – and did.
>
> How East Enders know their boxing. They don't want to see anyone who should have ribbons in his hair. It's two-fisted gladiators with guts they demand. When a fight is finished, there's no polite, meaningless applause. That has to be earned. The old booth rule of 'Get the next two on quick' applies. With places like this, boxing won't die.

Six decades after its heyday, I am standing near the site of this former East End fight arena for a reason. I am here to meet a fighter who was a big draw at the Arena; a man who in the summer of 1948 scored four straight inside-the-distance wins there to augment an already impressive tally of KOs and stoppages; a man whose ring career was cut frustratingly short. After a ten-minute walk to nearby Bow I reach the home of Teddy Lewis (Dagenham), a talented, crowd-pleasing feather and lightweight of the late 1940s and early 50s.

Ted, as most people know him, stands 5ft 6in tall, is slim-built and, save for some minor scar tissue, his unaltered facial features give no clue of his former profession. He has a calm, friendly demeanour and an eloquent manner of speech. He strikes me at once as a people person, so I am surprised when he tells me he was rather shy and retiring as a youth. Nowadays Ted is regularly called on to give talks to schools and other organisations about his years as a boxer and a porter at Billingsgate Fish Market.

He lives in a neat, tastefully-decorated terraced house with his wife, Betty, whom he met and began dating in the 1940s. Ted tells me she was an invaluable grounding influence during his boxing career. 'I've seen so many good fighters that have spoilt themselves by drink,' he says. 'A lot of it is their ego, where people have praised them up and said, "Come and have a drink with us". But I never mixed with the crowd that got involved in those sort of things. I had Bett all the time – just the two of us going about. She'd have a drink sometimes but I would have an orange squash, and we'd go to see shows.'

After he has introduced me to Betty, Ted shows me to the couple's living room, where I glance through his boxing memorabilia collection before our interview starts. Although the bulk of our conversation is about Ted's life and boxing career, we begin by discussing people and events from before his time.

Fighting Forebears

Ted is the sole surviving member of a London-Italian boxing dynasty that spans three generations. His grandfather, William Lucioni, who was born in Bethnal Green in October 1881, entered the prize ring through sheer necessity.

Bill Lewis – to use the name he boxed under – grew up in abject poverty, his family moving from place to place in the poorest parts of the East End, with occasional spells in workhouses.

He first appeared on the London boxing scene in the late 1890s and in the years that followed established himself as one of Britain's top little men, crossing gloves with some of the best around including Johnny Hughes, Jim Kenrick, Alec Lambert and Buck Shine. Bill boxed with staggering regularity, sometimes three times a week or twice a day. The outbreak of war brought his career to a close in 1914, and on 22 August 1916 he was killed at the Battle of the Somme.

'I didn't meet my grandfather but I'd love to have known him,' Ted tells me. 'I've seen pictures of him and I've heard a lot about him and I was lucky enough to get his record and that was amazing – he'd had 286 fights I think. He was a box-fighter, an aggressive little fighter, and everybody wanted him on their bills because he was a crowd-pleaser. I think I got my style from him. He's on the memorial at the war museum as having died in the First World War – the only Lucioni on there.'[11]*

Ted's father was aged just nine when Ted's grandfather Bill Lewis was killed, and the task of raising him and his two brothers then fell solely to their mother. Naturally, the three lads were obliged to find jobs as soon as they were old enough.

'They all started work early and ended up in Billingsgate Fish Market,' explains Ted, 'where my grandfather had worked before them. And that's how markets were in those days – it was a family thing. They started off as van boys, helping the driver load and unload, and the vans would go into Billingsgate Market and that's how they got jobs there.'

Ted's father (also called Teddy) and his two brothers, Bill and George, all boxed professionally in the 1920s and 30s. 'Amateur boxing wasn't as widespread as it is now,' says Ted, 'and there weren't so many amateur clubs, so I think they turned pro straight away. You had these small boxing shows where they would box maybe for sixpence and a cup of tea; but they boxed at these places because boxing promoters and managers would go to these shows, and if they were any good, and they looked like they'd be a crowd-pleaser, they'd give them a chance to box on bigger shows.'

---

11 His name, along with those of around 72,000 others killed at the Somme who have no known graves, is inscribed on the Thiepval Memorial near Thiepval, Picardy, France.

Teddy, Bill and George Lewis – who boxed out of Bethnal Green like their father – eventually caught the attention of Johnny Sharpe, the East End's leading manager. Sharpe then handled the affairs of all three brothers and installed well-known coach Snowy Buckingham as their trainer. Ted's uncle 'Young' Bill Lewis proved the best of the trio and in 1931 became the first official Southern Area bantamweight champion.

'They had hard fights and they had to be crowd-pleasers,' Ted says of his father and uncles. 'In those days if you didn't put on a good show, the referee could throw you out the ring and you'd get nothing. You had to put on a performance for people, which I think is right. I've always thought that as boxers we were there to entertain people. They were entitled to see us do the best we could and put on the best show we could.'

After his ring career ended, Teddy Lewis senior made his mark as a manager of boxers, handling the likes of Johnny Morkus, Les Carter and Jock Taylor opponents Alf Hines and Vic Phayer. 'Dad had some good fighters and he looked after them well, and they thought a lot of him,' Ted tells me proudly. 'At one time Jim Wicks, who was Henry Cooper's manager, wanted to go into partnership with him. Dad had a couple of heavyweights and he used to take them and Alfie Hines, who was a very fast light-heavyweight, to spar with Henry Cooper. When I mention my father everybody says what a nice man he was. He had a very good name.'

Early Life

Ted himself was born in Bow on 24 August 1929, where he lived with his parents at 5 Ordell Road. His birth name was Edward Charles Lucioni, but the family was by then better known as Lewis because of its boxing endeavours. To make it official, Ted's parents changed the name by deed poll in 1944, whereupon Ted Lucioni became Ted Lewis.

As he casts his mind back to his early years Ted recalls, 'Like most people then we didn't have a house: we had three rooms on the first floor of a house with a toilet and water in the back garden. People talk about it being a hard life in those days, but I only remember it as a happy life. We didn't have a lot I s'pose but nobody else had a lot, and I remember feeling pretty comfortable. Dad was boxing and he also had his job in Billingsgate, so if we had nothing else to eat, we had fish. I think I had quite a decent upbringing.

'I was the eldest of three: I've got a younger sister and brother. We lived in Bow for about six years after I was born, and then it became a slum clearance area so we moved down to Becontree.

'The war started when I was ten, and we was away hop-picking in Kent at the time. That was the only holiday we ever had. I think I was first taken there when I was two weeks old, and I went every year until the weekend war was declared. I was carrying our dinner down to the local bakers to be baked for us. Lovely sunny day, walking along this country lane with our dinner with a cloth over it, then the air raid sirens sounded and war had been declared.

'We stayed there for a while, then we came back to London but nothing happened – it was a false war at first. There was bombing but that was airports and places: no cities. But then they started bombing the cities and they started bombing London and mum decided we should be evacuated.

'I was ten when my sister, brother and I were evacuated to a little village called Uplowman in Devon, and it was wonderful! My brother and I were two of 27 who went. They took us to this little village with this little school hall and all these people came in, all talking a foreign language. "Ooo arrr, 'oo be 'e" and all that. We thought they were Germans at first! They started picking out the children they wanted until in the end there was just me and my younger brother left – he was holding my hand.

'We just stood there and nobody wanted us. But then a woman said, "Mother said I shouldn't bring anybody home, but I'll take you home for the night and maybe they can find somewhere for you tomorrow," which makes you feel wanted. Anyway, she took us home and they looked after us and put us to bed. They was wonderful people, and they never got rid of us – we were there for nearly three years, living on this farm. I still go back there two or three times a year to see all the great nephews and nieces – I've got another family there.

'So I was there till I was 13, and I left school when I was 11 and worked on the farm, and I loved that. But then dad said, "You've gotta come home and get a proper job." And I come home just when the doodlebugs and the V1s and V2s started dropping. We had one drop at the back of the house that we had in Becontree at the time, which blew all the walls out and inside the house it was a bit of a state. But we got over all that and I started work.

'First of all, I was gonna be an apprentice compositor – this is what dad wanted me to be, he wanted me to have a job for life. But I didn't like being shut indoors all day and I kept on at him to let me go to the market because that's where I wanted to be, and the hours were good as well. So in the end he gave in and let me go to Billingsgate.'

At around this time, Ted joined the Campbell Youth Club in Becontree – a decision that would profoundly shape his future. Here he would meet his future wife, Betty, and also lace on boxing gloves for the first time.

Amateur Days

'When I was young, boxing wasn't pushed at me – nobody really talked about boxing to me. I don't think anybody wanted me to box or they didn't think I'd ever be able to box. I think they tried to look after me or thought I was too dozy – this was one thing I was always being told, that I was a dozy little sod when I was a kid,' Ted laughs.

'I was on me own most of the time – I didn't have a lot of friends because I was one of these quiet ones who liked reading, and other kids used to try to take it out on me because of it, and therefore I used to get into fights. I was never beaten in a fight and in the end people never used to bother to wanna fight me. Fighting was just something that came natural to me.

'Dad used to bring other boys in from down the street 'cause parents would ask him to teach their sons to box, and dad would do that, but he would never teach me to box. It just happened that I went to the Campbell Youth Club one night and someone asked me to spar with them, and I did. I'd had a few fights in the street, so I could look after meself. Anyway, the fella who ran the club asked me if I'd box for the club. So I had two or three fights for them and dad said, "If you're really taking it seriously then I'll come with you," and he ended up being the club's instructor.'

Ted soon found he had a natural aptitude for boxing, and with his father's coaching he rapidly progressed. 'Dad always wanted to spar with me, and that's when I first knew how well dad could fight. When we'd get there he'd say, "Put the gloves on," and get in the ring with me, and all the other kids used to say, "Teddy Lewis and his father are fighting again!"

'I think he might have been more aggressive than I was. He would come in throwing punches all the time, and he even used his head sometimes! We used to have a real hard battle. It wasn't until I started punching a bit too hard that he stopped sparring with me. Then he used to make me go in with all the bigger fellas that was there.

'I had about three fights for the club and they entered me for the junior ABA championships. I went right through to the semi-finals and I got beat at the Seymour Hall by someone named White. But I boxed bad – it was my fault I lost the fight. It was 1945 and I was 15 then. Randolph Turpin won the junior ABA championships that year and the senior ABA championships in the same year. I was class A in the juniors because I was under 16, and he was 17 so he was class B. We was sitting there watching him, and as soon as we saw him we said he'd be a world champion. With his physique and the way he boxed, he looked so good – he had everything.'

During Ted's mid-teens his family moved from Becontree to Dagenham and he boxed for several different amateur clubs, including West Ham ABC and Buxton ABC in Walthamstow. He would box for any club that offered him fights, and he even boxed for the Naval Cadets despite not being a member.

So what was amateur boxing like during the war years? 'It was good,' Ted says. 'You got a lot of people coming along because there wasn't much entertainment around. I remember boxing once as an amateur at the Repton, which used to be in Victoria Park Square – it was on the top floor – and halfway through the fight I was having the air raid sirens went. They announced, "If anyone wants to leave, leave now, but the boxing will continue." We just carried on boxing during the air raid. No bombs dropped so it was all right and I'm here today. But that's how it was then – you just carried on as best you could.

'I can only remember being beaten twice as an amateur,' Ted adds. 'Once in the semi-finals of the junior ABA championships and once against someone I knew, and I thought I'd beaten him. I had more of a professional style than an amateur style; I used a lot of body punches, which wasn't all that acceptable in amateur boxing. They was always telling me to keep my punches up, even though they weren't low.

'When I was 17 I was gonna be a senior amateur. You had to win a novices' competition to be able to box in the senior championships. So I entered a novices' competition at Mile End Baths, and I had to have four fights in one night. I won three by knockout and one on points, and I got a silver rose bowl. But after that I decided to turn professional, so I never boxed for any amateur championships as a senior.'

Punching for Pay

Ted's first pro fight took place in Romford on 24 October 1947, exactly two months after his 18th birthday. His opponent was Jim Parsons (Manor Park), a veteran who had been boxing professionally since 1935. Did Ted find adjusting to the pro ring hard?

'Not at all. The only thing was that suddenly I found I was boxing men, and I was still a boy really. The chap I boxed in my first professional fight must have been 28 or 30 and a real man – he was thick set, had plenty of muscle... and he needed a shave. I remember, we got in a clinch and he rubbed his face against me and I could feel it scratching my face, and I don't think I shaved then! But I knocked him out in three rounds, which was a start, and I thought, if I can knock men out as old as him, I can knock anyone out.'

The record shows that Jim Parsons was actually just saved from a knockout by the referee's intervention. But Ted's formidable punching power was strongly in evidence as he had floored Parsons five times.

Ted won his next four fights by knockout, but in his sixth pro fight the wily Tommy Jones (Watford) managed to take him the distance. 'Lewis, a young knockout specialist, had one idea and that was to keep up his short distance record,' wrote *Boxing News*, 'but Jones was too clever… By the third, Jones's punches had raised a swelling under Lewis's right eye, but the Dagenham lad managed to land many good punches to the body. He is a colourful young fighter.'

But Ted out-pointed Jones and beat all bar three of his next 18 opponents inside the distance. Typically they were knocked out, and those who weren't were usually floored several times before being rescued by the referee. For a featherweight, Ted had a tremendous punch and the press duly dubbed him 'the Dagenham knockout specialist'.

'I was an aggressive fighter,' he tells me, 'I went forward all the time. I couldn't dance round the ring, fiddling about. I would go in straight from the beginning, get in distance and land the first punch if possible. A lot of it's psychological: it's how you think and how your opponent thinks. I always went out to land the first punch and let them know how hard I could hit, and that made them a little bit wary. So you was on top then – you'd dictate the fight from the centre of the ring and be the guv'nor. And I still think that's the best way to fight, but you do what you can do.

'One of my pet punches was a right-hand under the heart. I'd throw a left jab, bend my knees and throw a straight right underneath the heart. I knocked a few people out like that. But also I found that after two or three rounds with me really punching hard under the heart, their legs would go. So that was one, and the right cross to the chin and right to the solar plexus as well. I knocked a few people out with my left hand, but it was mainly with my right hand.

'You punch from the feet, turn your ankle when you throw a right hand. I've always said to youngsters, if you throw a right hand, you'll hit them on the chin; if you turn your ankle, you'll go right through their chin. And that seemed to come natural to me and my punching was always hard.

'I started off boxing either four threes or six twos on the bottom of the bill, and I was getting plenty of fights. I was boxing at the start like once a week or once a fortnight, and they weren't going very long so it was more like training for me.

'I was training every day and I never missed a day's work. I used to go to work in the morning, box at night, then be back at work the next morning, in the market. I boxed up in Newcastle twice and in Preston once and travelled back all night to be at work in the morning. The money wasn't a lot then; you couldn't pack up work and be a full-time professional boxer, unless you were right at the top.'

But Ted's job as a market porter was not the hindrance some vocations could have been to a boxer's career. 'It helped me with strength,' he explains. 'I never boxed anyone who I felt was stronger than me. If ever we got into a clinch I could always turn someone and I'd know that I was gonna be stronger than they were. Working in Billingsgate I was lifting 100-weight boxes of fish on to me head and carrying them and pulling big barrow-loads of fish. I'd been working since I was 11 so I was always pretty strong for me size and weight.'

Gyms of the Past

'Dad trained me but not always; I can remember I often trained myself. I would get up at 3.30 every morning, go to Billingsgate, then finish work about 1pm. From there I'd take me bag with me and go straight to the gym. I'd either go to Bill Klein's gym or Jack Solomons's gym. Once there, I would do whatever training I was s'posed to do and ask if anybody wanted to spar with me.

'Bill Klein's gym in Fitzroy Street was down in a basement that had a stone-flag floor. Bill Klein had a little chalet built in the corner that he used to live in and sleep in, and he had some Great Dane dogs, and sometimes they had pups. You'd go down there some mornings and the dogs and pups had been running about and there was mess on the floor and you'd have to sweep it up before you could start training.

'It was only a small room with the ring at one end, enough room for doing a bit of skipping and ground work, and then this little tea bar with a woman serving teas over the back. There'd be fighters going in, having a shower, coming out with nothing on at all and she'd be pouring out tea!

'The changing rooms there were just a little dark bit at the back with a bench that you'd sit on and the showers. I always remember Bill Klein for it, because you'd get in the shower and you'd be in there for a little while when all of a sudden it'd turn *freezing cold* and he'd say, "You've had enough hot water!" and you'd have to come out. He'd been an Olympic wrestler at one time, and he wanted to show you that he was still the guv'nor – "I'm in charge!" sort of thing – and he'd walk about with these dogs behind him.

'That was one type of gym, but when you went to Jack Solomons's it was more open and had plenty of windows in it. One lot of windows overlooked the Windmill Theatre, so you could see the girls through the window and wave to them.[12]* Bruce Woodcock, Freddie Mills and all those people were training there at the same time, and you all got under the showers together.

'I remember one time going there and a couple of friends from Billingsgate came with me to do some training. We've gone and had showers afterwards and we're coming out and we can hear Freddie Mills saying, "Where's my towel? Someone's got my towel!" As we was going down the stairs one of the chaps I was with said, "I picked up his towel by mistake! It's in my bag but I'm frightened to give it back." So I took the towel back for him,' chuckles Ted.

'Jack Solomons's gym used to have a Sunday morning nursery for young people to come along and learn to box. I remember the Kray twins going up there on a Sunday morning and I used to spar with them. They was about 14 and they was very likely doing villainous things then, but you never thought that when you were up there with them. They was just kids, and I was teaching them.

---

12   The Windmill Theatre was famed for its shows that featured glamorous nude females on stage – the legendary 'Windmill Girls'. The theatre's proprietor overcame the strict censorship laws of the day by ensuring the girls were presented as 'living statues' in motionless poses.

'I remember when I was working at Billingsgate Market one time – I had me leather hat on and me white coat – and the Kray twins come down when they was in their prime: all dressed up in black jackets and striped trousers, white shirts and black ties – they looked like bankers. But as they've walked past me they've said, "Ooh hello, Mr Lewis." So they had respect for you then.

'Boxers earned respect in those days, and they still knew me as Mr Lewis because I'd trained them, or showed them how to box, up in Solomons's. A lot of boxers got involved with the Kray twins – a lot of my friends ended up working for them, running pubs and clubs and things like that – but I never got involved with anything like that. I've enjoyed me home life too much.

'Jack Solomons's gym was great because you had all the facilities there, but I trained in a lot of different gyms including one at Islington, near Hoxton Market, that was under a church. A lot of them were Sunday morning gyms over pubs. There was always a lot of people there you knew and you'd stop and have a drink afterwards. Although *I* didn't drink at all then, and I didn't smoke either, but me dad used to go and have a drink with a few of his friends.

'There was nothing special about these gyms but they had a good atmosphere. All we had was a medicine ball, a mat on the floor, skipping ropes, punch bags, a boxing ring and gloves. But I'll go to a gym now and see so many machines and wonder, what d'you do with all these things? Back then it was basic, but you did all you had to do – you didn't need all these other things there.'

Sparring Reminiscences

'In Bill Klein's gym, when the coloured fighters first started coming over there was a lot down there, and they would spar with you for the week for about half a crown. So I used to get plenty of sparring partners that way. But I also used to get jobs sparring with different blokes, like Billy Thompson, the British lightweight champion, Tommy Barnham, George Daly, and the American fighters that came over here, like Dado Marino, the world champion.

'One of the cleverest boxers I ever sparred with was Eddie Miller from Australia. He was featherweight champion of Australia and he'd come over to box Ronnie Clayton for the Empire title. I went up with him to Liverpool when he boxed Clayton. I think it was a 15-round fight and after the tenth round Eddie Miller was just exhausted, he couldn't get up off the floor like, you know – he was about 32 then.[13]

'But I had a great time sparring with him – I really enjoyed it. Whenever he came here I was always his chief sparring partner, and his manager, Jack Warner, asked me to go out and box in Australia. Eddie Miller had his own business out there – he was a bookmaker on the pony racing. Jack Warner offered me a house to live in, a job working for Eddie Miller and guaranteed me £90 for me first fight – and I was getting a fiver a fight here at the time. But in those days Australia seemed such a long way away that I didn't wanna go. I don't regret it either.

'The only fighter that ever really hurt me was Billy Thompson. He hit me with a body punch and I thought he'd left his glove up in me stomach! And I danced round the ring with this silly grin on my face, pretending I'd not been hurt, and wondering if I was ever gonna breathe again. But my breath come back and I was all right.'

The man who had arranged for Ted to spar with British lightweight champion Thompson was a well-known Jewish manager called Benny Huntman. 'He often asked me to spar with different boxers he had,' recalls Ted with a smile. 'It was mainly South Africans that came over and he'd ask me to go to Joe Bloom's gym to spar with them. With Benny Huntman, if he was gonna give me a pound a round or 30 shillings a round, I'd always say to him, "Benny, give me the money first." Because I knew that if I went up and sparred with them, I'd *never* get the money off him. Once you'd done it, you'd done it and he'd avoid you or wouldn't pay you.

---

13 The contest took place at the Liverpool Stadium on 11 August 1949. After building a good points lead, Eddie Miller was floored for the full count in the 12th round by a solar plexus punch. After the fight he announced his retirement from boxing.

'Some of his fighters would go for their money after their fight and he'd say, "Oh, I'm sorry. I'll have to give it you tomorrow. I've lost that on the dogs," or something like that. He loved a gamble and he'd use their money to do his gambling. But he was one of the characters then. He also managed Jimmy Davis of Bethnal Green, and he liked to gamble as well, so they had a bit of a problem between the two of them.'

While in South Africa with former British lightweight champion Eric Boon in 1947, Benny Huntman became acquainted with an up-and-coming Transvaal featherweight named Tony Lombard, who quizzed him repeatedly about boxing in England. A year later, Lombard travelled to London and signed with Huntman, and Ted was hired as one of his sparring partners.

'We didn't get on too well,' Ted laughs, 'me and Tony Lombard. And he gave me the opinion that South Africans are flash and think too much of themselves – that's what I thought of him in the end. He had a couple of dodgy fingers – or a couple of fingers missing – on one hand; on his left hand I think, and we used to train in Joe Bloom's gym, which was just off Tottenham Court Road, opposite Shaftesbury Avenue, on the first floor, upstairs.[14] That's where all the South African fighters trained, and film stars and people like that used to train there. It was very, very clean, and Joe Bloom was someone so fussy, you'd be skipping and he would be going round sprinkling disinfectant on the floor!

'Me and Tony Lombard used to start off sparring but we'd end up having a real fight – one time we ended up on the floor both wrestling each other. What I didn't like about him was when I started hurting him he would say, "Ooh my hand hurts" and he'd stop because he said his hand hurt.

'I remember one time, we'd finished and we went and had a shower. After I'd finished boxing my skin was always dry and it used to get stiff, so once I'd had a shower I would rub surgical spirit on me face, like aftershave lotion. And Tony Lombard said,

---

14 Lombard had reportedly lost the index finger and thumb of one hand and part of the index finger of his other hand in an accident with a circular saw when he was at trade school.

"What's that you're putting on your face?" I said, "It's surgical spirit. It loosens up your skin and it seems to protect your scars a bit" – I had a couple of scars on me eyes then. He said, "Can I have some?" So I said, "Sure."

'I gave him some but I didn't tell him how much it stings. He put it in his hands, rubbed it on his face and screamed. He said, "*You bastard* – you're trying to blind me!" As I say, we didn't get on too well together, me and Tony Lombard.'

A Golden Era of Boxing

When I talk to Ted about the profile boxing enjoyed in the late 1940s – and the culture of British boxing then – his response is revealing. 'It was as popular as football is now,' he says. 'Think of the crowds that go to see football, well boxing was the same.

'Those were the days when you went to box someone and there'd be two or three fighters there with their bags hoping someone didn't turn up, so they could take their place. And there were so many shows on in those days. Almost every night of the week there was a boxing show somewhere. There was always a full house and the atmosphere was fantastic.

'You had all this chipping: the supporters of one fighter on one side and the supporters of the other fighter on the other and they'd be chipping each other, but it was all fun – there was nothing malicious or nasty about it. You didn't hear the things you tend to hear today. There were so many witticisms and Betty used to love it. She used to come along with me and she'd sit with my uncles and the other supporters and they'd have a great time. Everything seems so aggressive today, but it was fantastic to go to boxing then.'

In November 1948 Ted had the first of a series of fights at Walworth's Manor Place Baths, a venue that stands out as his favourite. 'Mile End Arena was great for atmosphere, but I liked the atmosphere in Manor Place. Lennie Cottrell, who was a friend of dad's, was the promoter and I got on well there,' he says.

'I got to know people there and they used to come up and congratulate me. There was one fella who used to always give me a bar of chocolate after a fight. He worked in the market and he used to bring his daughter along. After I'd finished the fight, I'd get out the ring and before I could move two or three steps he'd be beside me giving me a bar of chocolate and introducing me to his daughter!

'You had the domestic baths to change in, so I would be in the baths afterwards, having a bath, and a lot of people would come in – bookmakers especially – and give me something out of their winnings. So I got a few bob on top.'

Apart from being born with a natural punch and an innate aptitude for fighting, Ted was also blessed with a cool temperament and did not suffer pre-fight jitters. 'I can't say I was ever nervous getting into the ring. I treated boxing like a job. People had paid to see me and I was there to entertain them – to show them what I could do. So I used to relax beforehand. I've always read a lot, and very often I would take a book with me and I'd sit in the baths reading Dickens or something like that until they called me out and it was my turn to go on. I never worried about it.'

Curiously, Ted never worried about who he was fighting either. 'My manager would tell me I'd be boxing somewhere on a certain day and I wouldn't even ask who I was boxing. In fact, I used to find out who I was boxing from a tramp – we used to call them that then.

'Billingsgate then was between London Bridge and Tower Bridge – like in a valley – and it's all hills. So when you had a barrow-load of fish to deliver, you had to pull it up these hills. You'd have half a ton, maybe more, on your barrow, and when you got to the bottom of a hill there'd be two or three tramps standing about. You'd shout out, "Up the hill!" and they would run behind you and push your barrow up the hill, and you'd give them tuppence or thruppence. There was one there who always used to come up and say, "Hello Ted, I see you're boxing so and so," and that'd be the first time I'd know who me opponent was. I never used to ask who the opponent was – I wasn't bothered.'

Ted won his first 21 pro fights, 18 of them by stoppage or knockout. In his 14th fight, versus Eddie Giddings (Hammersmith), Ted tasted the canvas for the first time when he was floored twice for short counts in the first round. But, proving that he fought even more fiercely when hurt, he dispatched Giddings with a swift KO at the start of the second. Ted had impetuously risen too soon after the first knockdown, but he would not make this mistake again.

In Ted's 22nd contest, held on 27 January 1949, he faced Glasgow's Gene Caffrey at the East India Hall in Poplar. This would be one of those rare occasions when the fight went the distance.

'It was the first time I'd had to go eight rounds,' he recalls. 'I'd been boxing eight-round fights but I'd won them inside the distance. In the fourth round you begin to wonder, will I be able to get through the eight rounds – I feel tired. But after that you get a second wind, and I found I came out for the last round a lot fitter than he was. I had him down a couple of times in that last round and the papers all reckoned I should have got the decision; but they made it a draw.'

Ted won his next two fights inside the distance, then on 21 April 1949 had a rematch with Caffrey. 'I got beat on points by him,' Ted sighs. 'There are times when it seems as though you don't get the adrenaline going properly and I didn't box good that time.' Ted's impressive unbeaten run as a professional had ended in his 25th fight.

Booth Fights

Typically touring with a travelling fairground, boxing booths were an important part of the fight game in Britain before and for a while after the Second World War. During the summer, as many boxing halls closed or cut back on shows, the booths came into their own. At a time of year when fights on proper bills were harder to come by, the booths offered professional boxers a chance to stay fit, sharpen their skills and earn ready cash.

A booth was a large marquee with a platform erected at one end in front of an ornately decorated facade. A man known as the barker – or spieler – would summon an expectant crowd, often with the blare of a trumpet or beating of a drum. He would then introduce each of the boxers, who were lined up along the platform, and call for challengers from the crowd. When challengers had been found, the crowd were invited to pay an admittance and file inside the marquee, where a temporary ring had been pitched. That set of contests – known as a 'house' – then got underway.

Champions such as Freddie Mills, Benny Lynch, Tommy Farr, Jimmy Wilde, Jim Driscoll and Joe Beckett emerged from the boxing-booth scene, while the booths also attracted ex-fighters who no longer performed in regular boxing halls but needed money.

Some booth fighters travelled with the booth as it moved from town to town, while others, at the request of the booth owner, boxed on the booth when it arrived in their locality.

'There was one booth that I boxed for all the time,' says Ted, 'the only booth I boxed for really – the owner was Tom Woods. He used to come down from Scotland with his boxing booth and he'd phone me up and say, "I'm in London" or "I'm down in Weymouth" or wherever. "Could you box for me?" I would go there from work and he'd pay me £2 a fight, and I'd go round with the hat after. I'd be on the front, taking on all comers, and they'd be offered £1 if they could last three rounds and £5 if they could knock me out.

'There was several of us on the front but I was the smallest one, so nearly everybody who came up wanted to fight me. But if nobody came up to challenge anyone, you'd have to close down, which wouldn't be any good. So you always had two or three people in the crowd, and if no one come up and challenged, *they* would come up and challenge. So then you'd put on what was called a gee fight – and they were better than the real fights really, because we'd really be able to let ourselves go.

'One fella, Bill Brown – who used to live round this way – he'd get in a clinch and he'd say, "Hit me on the chin." Then I'd step back and hit him with the inside of the glove, but just beneath the chin, it'd make a real loud noise and his head would go back. He'd very likely dive right through the ropes, in amongst the crowd, and they'd have to help him back.

'If ever I wanted to go on the floor, I'd say, "Hit me up the stomach," and I'd go down slowly and see where I was going. You'd get to know each other and you could put on a really good fight like that. It was like all-in wrestling – it's amazing what people see. I've gone round afterwards and people have put as much as a pound into me hat. "Great fight!" they'd say. "That was a lovely right hand you caught him with," and I've not hit him with a lovely right hand. But they see what they wanna see in the end, as long as you can put it on for them.'

What about legitimate challengers from the crowd?

'You got plenty of those,' says Ted. 'You'd get crowds of youngsters, like you have now. They might be tearaways, but getting in the ring with a pair of gloves on and rules to follow, it makes a load of difference.

'I remember boxing at Tottenham and at first no one come up so we had to put on a gee fight. When we're in a clinch I'm saying to the bloke, "Hit me up the stomach," and I've gone on the floor a few times. Round the corner I was in there's this group of young fellas and I could hear them saying, "Go on, you can have him. Hit him up the belly – he can't take it up the belly." So, anyhow, after the fight had finished one of them's jumped up and said, "I'll challenge. I'll fight *him*!"

'In the first round I walked out towards him, held me arms up and let him hit me up the stomach. He hit me up the stomach and I didn't move. Then I hit him on the chin about twice and he went on the floor and didn't get up.

'I had one come up and challenge me in Kent somewhere, and he looked so big – he had a big overcoat on and looked like a light-heavyweight. But he said he only weighed ten stone seven pounds and I was nine stone, and I would box anyone up to that sort of weight, so I said I'd box him.

'When he strips off and gets in the ring he weren't any fatter than that,' says Ted as he holds up an index finger. 'I walked out for the first round, hit him on the chin and he shook like a leaf. So I grabbed hold of him, because people have all paid their two shillings to come in and you can't knock 'em out in one round. I've held him up, walked him round and they've all clapped me for being a sport.

'It went on for about three rounds, and in the end I have hit him and he's gone down and stayed down. When we got back in the changing rooms I said to him, "What *d'you* come up for? You must know that we know something about fighting." He said, "I've never been beaten before. I was a schoolboy champion, but I haven't done boxing for a while – I've been weightlifting." And he didn't have a muscle on his body!

'I used to go to Epsom every year for derby day: they had a big fair on the downs there. I used to get four or five fights in the afternoon with people who'd lost all their money on the races and were trying to get a few bob for their fare home. Some of them could fight a bit but most of them weren't all that. One time I'm in the corner and one of the chaps in my corner says to me, "Have you heard about this fella? He's just come out of prison for GBH." And I thought, oh what's he about, like? But he couldn't fight anyhow and I knocked him out.

'They're fine when they're in the streets and they can kick and do things like that, but when it comes to standing up and having a fight they crumble.

'Sometimes you got someone who'd done a bit of boxing come up and they were usually the ones that went the distance. But not many did go the distance because you couldn't afford to let them do that. If the booth owner was paying you £2 to fight, you had to save him as much money as you could. I boxed someone in Gloucester once who was the featherweight champion of Wales. That was on a booth and he come up and challenged me. I didn't knock him out, but we had a decent fight.

'After the fight we used to go round the crowd with the hat and collect nobbings – you shared it out with the fella you were boxing. I used to come home with socks full of coppers, thruppenny bits and half crowns. We used to pour 'em out on the table, me and Bett, and sort them all out.'

In 1947 the British Boxing Board of Control introduced a rule that barred licensed professional boxers from boxing on booths. Eventually this led to the demise of the booths, but at first many licence-holders, including Ted, defied the Board.

'You weren't really allowed to do it but everybody did, and I'm sure the Board of Control knew that,' reveals Ted. 'When you boxed on the booths you boxed under a different name and I used to fight under the name of Teddy Bartlett. Tom Woods said that James Cagney had used that name in a film.[15] I remember [fellow professionals] Laurie and Alex Buxton boxed on the same booth at times and Georgie Last, the heavyweight, he came with me once. There was a lot of them doing it.'

National Service

After his first professional defeat – at the hands of Gene Caffrey in April 1949 – Ted's next fight was an eight-round points win over Brighton's Les Turner. Two months later, Ted took on Jackie Lucraft (Islington) but was stopped because of a badly cut eye. Three weeks later, Ted lost a return fight with Les Turner, although *Boxing News* suggests the Brighton man was lucky to get the verdict. Then, frustratingly, in January 1950 Ted's eye injury reoccurred as he was stopped against Welshman Benny Rees with blood severely impairing his vision. There follows an 11-month gap in Ted's fight record.

'I had to go in the army for a while, but I was late going in,' he admits. 'I was boxing at the time so I didn't register to go and do national service. It wasn't until I was 20 or 21 that they caught up with me and wrote to me, so I had to go in then.

'Going in later like that, I was older than a lot of them. They was kids of 18 and 19 and to me they *were* kids, 'cause I'd had quite a life really: professional boxing and working in Billingsgate – I had all me tailor-made suits when I went in the army.

'Once I got in there, I started going to the gym to do a bit of training and people got interested in watching, then I became a PT instructor. But I had to make myself train – I had no one pushing me: no trainer or manager around. I would train of an evening or afternoon – any time when I wasn't working as a PT instructor. I used to take all the troops on their nine-mile marches

---

15 James Cagney played the gangster Eddie Bartlett in *The Roaring Twenties*, Warner Bros., 1939.

and three-mile runs, so I got really very fit then, and I had plenty of sparring partners. People were always asking if I'd spar with them, especially officers.'

Step Up to Lightweight

Ted returned to the ring, as a lightweight, on 8 December 1950, when he avenged his previous controversial points loss to Les Turner with a first-round stoppage of the same man. 'Lewis formerly fought as a featherweight, but with an extra eight or nine pounds poured into his fine frame he showed no signs of surplus ounces and after seeing him dispose of Les Turner in one round it would appear that the new division might suit him even better,' wrote *Boxing News*.

This was the first of four consecutive bouts Ted had at Hoxton Baths and he won all four. In his next two fights, however, he was again stopped on cut eyes. 'Dad always worried about me,' he says, 'and when I started getting my eyes cut he used to say, "I'm unlucky to you – I won't come in your corner." And he would stand at the doorway, half in and half out of the place because he was worried I was going to get my eyes cut again. I think you'll find if you check the newspaper reports – in all the fights that I lost with a cut eye, I was in front at the time I got the eye cut.'

After four months out of action, Ted returned to the ring at New St James' Hall, Newcastle where he dropped a decision to Jimmy Ford (New Brancepeth). Three weeks later Ted won a return with Ford, then on 23 October 1951 he fought at the Royal Albert Hall for the first time. Unbeknown to him, this was to be his final fight.

Boxing News wrote of the contest:

> There was a sensational finish to the last contest of the evening, when Johnny Lewis (Blackfriars) beat Teddy Lewis (Dagenham), the referee stopping the fight at the end of the third. Near the bell, Teddy, ahead on points, drove his opponent against the ropes, but was caught by a right hook to the side of the head, which must have landed on an optic nerve.

His eyes closed but he went into a clinch, and fighting by sheer instinct, followed his opponent into the opposite corner, whipping punches to the body. As the bell signalled the end of the round, he dropped his hands, turned, took two steps forwards towards his own corner and fell flat on his face.

It became obvious that he was seriously hurt. The referee stopped the bout and a doctor was called into the ring. Several minutes later he was assisted from the ring, still in a semi-conscious condition, and taken to hospital, where he made good progress.

Reports of Ted's sudden collapse made the next day's national papers. When I ask him about the fight, he tells me, 'I just don't know what happened. I was boxing Johnny Lewis down the Albert Hall, the fight was going well and I was sure I was gonna beat him. He's told me since that he didn't wanna fight me because I punched too hard. I walked back to my corner at the end of the third round and I just blacked out.

'I was still in the army at the time and I'd been playing basketball and I'd cut me head open. They put some boracic powder on it and said it was all right, so I just went away and trained. But after the fight I ended up in Queen Mary's Hospital and they said a blood clot had shifted. I think there must have been a clot there and when you start fighting your adrenalin's going, your blood flows faster and it moved and I just blacked out.

'I had to pass a medical afterwards and they gave me my boxing licence back. But Bett was worried so I never went back to it, although I carried on boxing in the booths now and again to earn a few bob. I did that for a little while but after that I never boxed again, and I regret that. I wish that I'd gone on. I'm sure I could have done better, but it's one of those things.'

Life After Boxing

After hanging up his gloves Ted continued to work at Billingsgate Fish Market. At age 25 he married Betty, and the couple moved to Bow and had children.

For a while Ted served as a trainer at the Fisher Amateur Boxing Club where he coached, among others, ABA champions Phil Lundgren and Johnny Ould, who both boxed at the 1960 Rome Olympics. But family duties curtailed his coaching career. 'I found that I was spending more time with other people's children than I was with me own,' Ted explains. 'So I stopped doing it and I didn't get involved with boxing so much. But I started doing other things.

'I was working in Billingsgate and someone came down from the radio. They was doing a programme called *I Know What I Like*: it was giving the ordinary man in the street's opinion of museums and things like that. A friend of mine had done some broadcasting and they wanted him, but he suggested I go along as well. So we did this radio programme and it went over very well. We got a write-up in the *Sunday Times* and letters from people saying how good the programme was.

'Talking to the producer of the programme, I started telling him about my life, boxing, being evacuated and things like that, and he said, "Would you do a programme just talking about yourself?" So I said yes, and I did this programme, and Lee Crutchley was the compere who spoke to me and asked me questions. It was only about 20 minutes long – and it was in the interval of a classical concert on Radio 3, so I thought nobody's gonna listen to this.

'But I had letters come from all over the country: people who'd heard it telling me I should have been a school teacher and I should have done this and should have done that. I even had someone offering me and the family a holiday up in Wensleydale. So that went off quite well.

'After that, I became a local councillor for a while with the Liberal Party. I was never a Liberal really, but they were the only ones doing anything in this area. We had a complaint about something where we were living and we went to the Town Hall, and I got up and I spoke about it. Then they came to me and said, "Would you like to become one of our councillors?" So I did that for a couple of years, but that got to be too much pressure in the end. I was worrying about other people's problems more than they were, so I gave it up.'

Today Ted still leads an active life and regularly gives talks at schools, youth clubs and social clubs. He has written poetry, enjoys gardening and has a passion for photography. Another interest is reading. 'I read all sorts of books. I love classics, but I also like modern detective stories and things like that.'

Referring to his favourite author, he says, 'I love Dickens. Every now and then I'll feel like reading another Dickens, and as I've already read them all I have to read one again. But I always find something more in it each time I read it.'

'I don't do anything athletic now, but I'm finding a great thing in life is meeting other people: meeting people and talking with people. I just wish people would talk to each other more.'

Reflections

'It's great for your ego,' Ted says of boxing, 'it did me the world of good. I was always a little bit self-conscious and a bit shy – I would have a job getting up and talking in front of people and doing anything in front of people. But put a pair of shorts on me and a pair of boxing gloves and put me in a ring and I felt I could do anything. You begin to walk down the street and people know you and say, "Hello Ted," and people ask for your autograph. Suddenly you feel you're someone, you find that you can talk to people and your ego becomes good.'

Reflecting on his ring career, Ted says, 'I started off earning £5 for doing four threes or six twos. Then I think it went up to about £12 or £16 for doing six twos and then it was around about £60 for doing eight threes. The most money I ever got was £100 for boxing at the Royal Albert Hall. Television had come along then and it was just starting to make the purse money go up. I was billed to box Jackie Turpin at Bermondsey Baths on television, but I boxed the week before and got me eye cut, and I couldn't have that one. So I missed out on the TV break.

'If you wanted to box at the big places, you boxed for Jack Solomons. But my manager, George Morris, didn't get on with

Jack Solomons and so I could never get on Solomons's bills. The only time I boxed for Solomons, until I boxed at the Albert Hall, was at Bermondsey Baths where he used to run a charity show every year. I was selling a lot of tickets in that area because I boxed at Manor Place Baths a lot, and so I managed to get on the bill for that.

'George Morris was a friend of dad's who worked in the market and managed a few fighters, so I went with him. I often wish I'd had another manager. Jarvis Astaire asked to manage me – he wanted to buy me contract – and I said no. But since then, when I think about it, things could have been a lot different if I'd gone with him.'

As we discuss boxing from recent times, I ask Ted how modern boxing compares with the fight game of the 1940s and 50s. 'I s'pose it compares in as far as there's two people boxing, but I think the media and money has spoilt what boxing was and it's spoilt boxers the way they were,' he says.

'I would have boxed for nothing because I enjoyed it and it made you feel like you were someone. But now it's all money-orientated and they have two or three fights a year. It's ridiculous. How can you be a good professional boxer when you're having just a couple of fights a year?

'I don't like all this slagging off and staring people in the eye and calling them names. You respect the people you're boxing with. If they've got the guts to come up and fight you, then they need respect, don't they? These are the sort of things that upset me now and what's done it is television and the media.'

When I ask Ted about the quality of modern boxers he smiles and tells me, 'All old footballers and old boxers think they were better in their days, but I think they were. I watch boxing now and I think, why are they missing with so many punches? Why are they throwing them when they're out of distance? And I wonder who's teaching them now.

'People try to copy other people much more now than they did then. I think Muhammad Ali was a great fighter for what he did and for what he could do, but he did so many things wrong. He would punch with his feet off the ground and was moving in all sorts of ways, and dancing round all the time. There's too many young people trying to copy that, and they can't do it, and in fact it spoils fighters.

'If I was telling youngsters who to watch to learn boxing, I would say watch films of Joe Louis. I see so many young fighters now that dance round and round the ring, out of distance all the time, and miss with so many punches. But Joe Louis was so correct in the way he boxed. He never danced around, he was always in distance, and he could knock someone out with a six-inch punch. He's always been my hero and always will be. I don't think I've ever seen anyone that could match him.'

When asked what advice he would give to an aspiring fighter Ted says firmly, 'If you start professional boxing, for those years you're doing it you've got to live it. You've got to do everything that's right – make sure you're going training all the time, make sure you're really fit – because you can spoil it so easily.'

SAMMY McCARTHY (STEPNEY) 1951–57

After 30 years in the fight game, there isn't much sentiment left in a man, but when I think of young McCarthy I dare admit that I can get a catch in my throat... For this London boy is the straightest and most lovable champion of them all. The smiling kid from Stepney has rightly been called 'every mother's angel'. To me, young Sammy is a fighter in a million.

– Snowy Buckingham, boxing trainer, *The People*,
17 October 1954

IN the early 1950s an exciting young featherweight from Stepney burst on to the London fight scene and took British boxing by storm. Sammy McCarthy had a beautiful boxing style centred round a flashing straight left, fast and nimble footwork, clinical body-punching and skilful defence. But Sammy had an extra, indefinable star quality that turns a boxer into a box-office hit. The people of London took Sammy into their hearts, not just for his colourful boxing style but for his straightforward, sportsmanlike and unpretentious manner. This shy Cockney lad did not seek stardom, yet a star he became.

The press nicknamed him 'Smilin' Sammy' for his face seemed to be always lit by a beaming smile. As the late boxing writer and historian Gilbert Odd noted, 'Even when fighting his face was wreathed in smiles; he even smiled when taking a punch which was most disconcerting to his opponents.'

Sammy lived a clean, modest life outside the ring, was always neatly turned out, and noted for being exceptionally courteous to everyone he encountered, irrespective of who they were. Although by his own statement wealth meant nothing to him, he earned enough fight money to live comfortably for the rest of his life.

It is surprising – almost unbelievable when you meet him – to learn that some time after his boxing career ended Sammy became an armed robber and served three long prison sentences, which broke up his otherwise happy marriage. Such is the enigma of Smilin' Sammy.

%. %. %.

I visit the former British featherweight champion at his home: a small, tidy flat in Wanstead, where I am greeted by a short, slim, sprightly bald-headed man, smartly turned out in a green roll-neck jumper. He extends a warm handshake and flashes the famous McCarthy smile, as bright and infectious as ever 60 years after his fighting prime. I am at once made to feel welcome by Sammy and his daughter Jackie – who stays with her father for several days each week – and the three of us have a long chat before the interview starts.

I find Sammy McCarthy kind, polite, exceedingly humble, self-analytical and at times unduly self-critical. He has an optimistic, philosophical outlook on life and is not the type of man to harbour bitterness or bear grudges. But nevertheless I sense his smile hides a fair amount of sadness and pain that he carries with him from the past.

He speaks eloquently in a formal tone more befitting a former bank manager than a former bank robber; yet he is open and frank about every topic we discuss, including his legal transgressions.

At one point I hesitate over how to word an awkward question, but he quickly assures me, 'Ask me whatever you want, however embarrassing you might think it will be to me. You've come a long way and I want to help you.'

Although he has earned the right to speak with pride about his boxing achievements, he instead plays down his success with a refreshing modesty that would serve as an object lesson to certain self-aggrandising sports stars of the modern age. I doubt boxing has ever produced another character quite like Sammy.

※ ※ ※

He was born Samuel Daniel McCarthy at 48 Winterton Street, off Commercial Road, in Stepney on 5 November 1931. There were ten McCarthy children (six girls and four boys) of whom Sammy was born sixth.

His parents were both from Stepney but his heritage is part Jewish and Irish. 'If you saw my father you'd swear blind he was a yiddisher man, 'cause he looked like a yiddisher man,' says Sammy. 'We were brought up amongst Jewish people; my brother's married to a Jewish girl so theoretically my nephews are both Jewish, 'cause as you know they take their mother's religion. I'm a Roman Catholic, I think in all probability because it was the closest school to where we lived.

'Prior to the war I went to St Mary's and St Michael's School, and then a day before war was declared I was evacuated with three of my sisters to Egham in Surrey, which isn't all that far away, but it seemed miles away then. I loved it down there but obviously I was pleased when the war was over to come home.

'After the war we lived at 705 Commercial Road – again in Stepney. It's still there and I never go by there without taking a look. It was quite a big house 'cause there was ten children but it was so bloody old and almost falling down, I was almost ashamed to say I lived there. I remember then we couldn't even afford the rent and it was probably only about 25 shillings a week; but now the house is worth about £1m.'

The gentrification of formerly run-down working-class streets to provide conveniently located homes for well-off City workers is a peculiarity that lifelong East Enders like Sammy have witnessed first-hand. 'I go through Stepney and I see houses which would seem very poor years ago, but some of them look so nice because people have money to spend on them, and now these houses are worth so much.

'Life was different then,' says Sammy as he casts his mind back to Stepney in the 1930s and 40s. 'People there could look after themselves, it was a hardy area, like Poplar and Bethnal Green and all the surrounding districts – they were all pretty hard. Stepney was a great place to be, but also a great place to move from, don't misunderstand me.'

Reflecting on the prevailing culture in the East End at the time, Sammy says, 'A woman in those days had no say; the man was always the guv'nor. Whatever the man said went. Your mum was just a housewife and a mum, but nowadays things are reversed, and rightly so. I didn't take too much notice of it then, I probably thought all the rest of the world was like this. The only difference I saw was when I went to the cinema and things were different there.'

Though Sammy was born and raised in this harsh masculine environment, he was not a typical East End lad. Clean, tidy, shy, sensitive and polite, he could have easily been a target for local thugs had he not learnt to defend himself. Fortunately, learning to box was inevitable for any boy in the McCarthy household.

Introduction to Boxing

'I can remember just before the war, when we lived in Winterton Street, hiding under the table. My parents knew I was there obviously – my dad was there, my mum and my dad's pals, probably just come from the pub, and they were listening to the Joe Louis versus Tommy Farr contest for the heavyweight championship of the world, and Joe Louis won on points as you probably know.

'They always spoke about boxing and boxers in my house – my father and his pals – and they always spoke about my brother Freddie, who was an excellent boxer. His club was the same club

I went to, Stepney and St George's, and he won the Federation of Boys' Clubs Championships, which was a big thing in those days; they used to hold the finals at the Albert Hall and places like that. And then he won the junior ABAs. I don't know whether he would have turned professional because I'm not sure whether my brother Freddie had the discipline that I had, but he probably had more ability than I did. But the war ruined his chances anyway. My two younger brothers, Jackie and Charlie, both boxed as amateurs as well.

'In those days if you won the ABAs it was like being champion of the world. There was a boxing club on the corner of almost every other street, and every street had a couple of amateur boxers. I remember going to the amateur fights when I was 14 or 15 and you couldn't even get in the door. I knew all the amateur boxers – I don't mean I knew them personally but I knew the competitions they'd won, who they'd beaten, who they'd lost to, and I used to be absolutely positively thrilled to go there.

'Anything to do with boxing, amateur or professional, I knew all about the history of the fighters; I've probably forgotten about them now but when people mention their names certain things come to mind.

'I always thought as a little boy that the more you could fight the more masculine you were; and of course you realise when you get a little older how ridiculous that is. I thought if you could fight, you were a real man. And I always wanted to box but I was always very frightened, very nervous, you know. But I was also frightened of being frightened. I thought it wasn't masculine to be frightened so I overcame it the way you overcome things – I started doing it.'

Sammy began boxing shortly after he returned from evacuation in 1945 when he joined the Stepney and St George's club. 'It was a great club and they were wonderful days. When I first went to it, it was in Cable Street and then afterwards it moved to The Highway, which runs parallel with Cable Street and goes right through the centre of east London. The staff at the Stepney and St George's Club were all working men – they worked in the docks most of them – and they gave up their time to be there two, three or four times a week; and they all did a wonderful job.

'When I joined the club I used to go four times a week: Monday, Tuesday, Thursday and Friday and I absolutely loved going. Although having said that, every time I went to the gymnasium I was very very nervous – almost petrified – but on coming home I was so elated that I'd been and done what I had to do. I got such a high out of it – it was like a drug.

'My first trainer was a lovely guy called Johnny Mann. I think a lot of trainers can get you fit but they can't always teach you all that much: maybe they haven't been boxers themselves. But Johnny Mann had been a great amateur and professional boxer way before my time, so he could get in the ring with you and spar with you and he was absolutely wonderful.

'My very first contest I lost. I didn't tell my father but of course he knew and he told me off for not telling him. But then I started to win, although I lost now and then.'

Sammy's first contest, a defeat to E. Stannard (Eton Manor), he later avenged with a win over that boxer. In 1947 Sammy won the North-East London Divisional Junior title at 7st and a year later went one better when he captured the London title at 7st 7lb. But he really came into his own when he entered the senior ranks.

Amateur Boxing's Golden Boy

On 17 January 1949 Sammy took to the ring in a pair of his brother Freddie's cast-off shorts for his first senior contest. 'I boxed a guy by the name of Norman Watts, who came from south-east London,' recalls Sammy, 'and he was the reigning English representative [at the weight]. It was unknown at the time, that a man in his first amateur senior contest would box someone of such a high calibre. I boxed him over south-east London, I out-pointed him and it caused a minor sensation.'

'Little 17-year-old Sammy McCarthy (Stepney and St George's), boxing his first senior contest, gave me my biggest thrill of the season last week by out-pointing Norman Watts (Fitzroy Lodge) tipped by many for this season's ABA title,' enthused the

Boxing News amateur correspondent. 'On his showing against Watts he looks a champion of the future.'

The fight had been held at Camberwell Baths and in his second senior contest (held at Mile End Baths three weeks later) Sammy fought a return with Watts and cemented his superiority by again earning the decision with a beautiful display of upright boxing.

In the ensuing months Sammy went from victory to victory, often against top-class opposition, and his popularity soared. In June 1949 *Boxing News* described him as a 'shining star', its amateur columnist remarking, 'Every season my job takes me to see many hundreds of special amateur contests… But of all the bouts I sat through in 1948/49, none gave me greater pleasure than those featuring Sammy McCarthy.'

By now Sammy's popularity was soaring. Each time he fought, a dozen coaches were laid on to ensure his fans could get to the arena. Outside the Crown and Anchor in Watney Street they only had to put up a board saying 'McCarthy Fights Tonight' to guarantee a full coach. There was even a Sammy McCarthy fan club.

With characteristic modesty, Sammy does not attribute his popularity to his exceptional talent, but rather he insists, 'I had a great following because my two uncles used to sell tickets on my behalf in the markets and they set up the coaches to go to see me box. Of course, when you sell that many tickets whether you fight well or not is immaterial, people want you on their bill. The bottom line is always pounds, shillings and pence. And also, living in the East End and going round the streets all my life with my father, I knew almost everyone. Even if I didn't know them by name, I knew them, so they used to follow me.'

Despite Sammy's newfound fame there was no danger of him becoming egotistical. For one thing this was utterly against his nature, and for another his day job, helping his father, kept him grounded, as he explains:

> My father was a greengrocer, only had a barrow. He used to go
> round the streets and I used to go round with him, but I didn't
> like it to tell you the truth. Not because I didn't want to help

my father but because I thought it was so bloody common, walking round the street with a barrow. I think subconsciously I wanted to be posh.

I started early and I always finished about one o'clock in the day, but it used to be bloody freezing in the winter. When you're pushing the barrow, you're knocking on doors and the wind's getting you from every angle. In those days boys always wore short trousers until they started work, which was at 14, but I never started wearing long trousers until I was 15 or 16. My father used to say to me, 'No, son, wear short trousers – let the air get to your legs.' That was his excuse, but I think probably it was because he couldn't afford to buy them.

But working with his father brought Sammy into contact with a wide mix of local people and the vibrancy of market life became a source of fascination to him.

'We bought all our produce at Spitalfields Market,' Sammy recalls. 'It was always very colourful there. I used to hear the men all shouting and swearing at each other and I couldn't quite comprehend it at the time; I used to think they were gonna have a fight. They were shouting and swearing but it was just their conversation, "Get out the f-ing way" or whatever, and everyone accepted it, they didn't take a blind bit of notice of it.

'In those days you used to get a hell of a lot of fighters down Spitalfields, Covent Garden, Billingsgate, all the markets. That's where a lot of the fighters used to work. They worked there because it allowed them to work in the morning and go to the gym in the afternoon or evening.'

※ ※ ※

Just as Sammy's amateur boxing career was gathering momentum he was liable to be called up to complete his national service, but his family had prepared for this. 'I think I actually wanted to go into the army,' Sammy reveals, 'because I hated working with the barrow. But my father got one of my brothers to write letters to the Board beforehand, saying that I was needed. They started that a year or two before I was due to be called up, when I was 16 or 17, so I wasn't called up.'

With the potential obstacle of national service avoided, Sammy's amateur career continued apace. He boxed for England several times but was destined to go down as one of the finest amateurs never to win a senior ABA title. Twice injury robbed him of the chance of competing in the preliminary rounds, then in his final season as an amateur he was beaten on a razor-thin decision by the eventual champion, Ron Hinson, whom Sammy had defeated on another occasion.

'I never won any major championships funnily enough, but I still had a great, great following,' says Sammy. 'So I think it was almost taken for granted that I would turn professional 'cause I had such a great following.'

I ask why Sammy turned professional when he did and he reveals, 'It was probably my father, my brother and people suggesting to me that I should turn professional. They said, "You'd beat this one and that one, and be getting this amount of money." Although the money didn't make any difference to me really; I just wanted to fight and I wanted to win. The money meant nothing to me, I'm sorry to say.'

On paper Sammy's professional manager was the experienced Jack King, who at various times had stewarded such champions and near-champions as Al Phillips, Dave McCleave, Phineas John and George Davis, but in reality there was another man who made decisions for Sammy behind the scenes. 'Jack King was a sort of frontman, for want of a better word,' Sammy explains. 'Jarvis Astaire was involved in the background – Jarvis and Benny Schmidt, but mostly Jarvis, though Jack was a good manager anyway.'

Sammy then explains how his association with Jarvis and Schmidt came about:

> Benny Schmidt or Ben Schmidt-Bodner, or Benny Smith
> as they knew him, was in the schmutter business – in the

clothes business – in a big way in Margaret Street in the West End. His firm was called Green & Co and they had a lovely showroom and shops, and my brother worked for him as a presser.

Benny Schmidt used to promote boxing shows at the Seymour Hall [in Marylebone] and obviously Benny spoke to my brother, with Jarvis Astaire – him and Jarvis were partners – and I went to see them and it was taken for granted that I was going to go with them when I turned professional. But they were excellent managers, Jarvis and Benny. I had a great team around me – I was very lucky in that respect. Some people complain about their managers or trainers but mine were absolutely first-class.

Today Jarvis Astaire is well known for his business endeavours in banking and property investment as well as his activities as a boxing manager and promoter (he was instrumental in bringing Muhammad Ali to Britain to defend his world title against Henry Cooper), while the late Benny Schmidt-Bodner in later years was well known as a racehorse owner. Intrigued, I ask Sammy why this duo elected to stay behind the scenes.

'I'm not quite sure,' he admits. 'I imagine they were looking forward – they probably saw in front of them much more than I would have done at that stage in my life. If they got a number of fighters behind them, they could start promoting shows like Jack Solomons. He was the only big promoter in the country then, pretty much. I still see Jarvis very occasionally and he still looks well. The last time I saw him, a couple of years ago, he was still very straight and upright. I suppose he'd be about 90 now. Benny died some years ago.'

To complete the team, Sammy went under the care of renowned trainer Snowy Buckingham, who worked in tandem with Jack King. Snowy (real name Sydney), a 5ft 2in East Ender named for his ultra-light blonde hair, was oddly enough never a boxer.

In 1915 Snowy had quit a job as a warehouseman to learn the business of a boxing instructor and eventually he found a job as an assistant to one of Britain's finest pre-war trainers, Jack Goodwin. In 1932 Goodwin died at the ringside of a heart attack at the Royal Albert Hall while seconding Canada's Larry Gains in his Empire heavyweight title fight with South Africa's Don McCorkindale. Thereafter Snowy took over training duties for Goodwin's impressive stable of boxers, and using what he had learnt from Goodwin he went from success to success.

Before training Sammy, Snowy had worked with such top-notchers as Bob Olin, Larry Gains, Walter Neusel, Eddie Phillips, George Cook, Dick Corbett, Eric Boon, Charley Belanger, Archie Sexton and Jack Hyams.

'He lived by himself and he had problems, Snowy; he wasn't the happiest of people,' Sammy recalls dolefully. 'He was only small and his eyesight was extremely bad and a lot of people used to knock him for this. But he was an excellent trainer, knew his business, and I had him all through my professional career. If anyone tried to tell you something or interfere or try to make themselves busy, he would cut them off short.

'But he was a good man to have on your side – he knew me to a tee. He knew when I was doing too much or not quite enough and when I was taking liberties with eating and drinking. When I say drinking, I don't mean beer; I mean when I'd been over-enthusiastic with the liquids, like tea or whatever.'

Snowy Buckingham would fondly tell the story of when he first met Sammy, after Jack King had sent the youngster along to prepare for his first professional fight. 'When this McCarthy turns up I don't believe he can be a fighter,' Snowy would say. 'He looks so smart, acts like a little gentleman. He opens his bag of kit – and there I get a shock. I have never seen a bag more neatly, cleanly and carefully packed – so unlike the jumbled mess of soiled kit you usually see. I showed him where to change and a few minutes later he came out dressed all in white. He was incredibly clean, and with his shy smile and boyish face he looked about 15.'

Snowy was pleasantly surprised to discover that, despite his clean-cut appearance and modest manner, Sammy was a first-class boxer. Snowy had been instructed to prepare the lad for his first pro fight and thereafter a fight-a-month campaign until he could get a title bout.

Sammy the Professional

Sammy's first paid fight took place on 30 April 1951 at London's Empress Hall, where he faced Hector McCrow from East Harling in Norfolk. McCrow was the type of opponent likely to go the distance with most but against whom a gifted debutant would shine. For this scheduled six-rounder Sammy was paid the then unheard-of sum for a debutant of £150. '£150 to me was like an untold fortune,' he smiles. 'When I worked with my dad, on the barrow, my first week's wages were £1 and 25 shillings, and I'd felt wealthy at the time earning that!'

Was Sammy nervous before the fight? 'I was absolutely petrified, but I won in the first round so it wasn't all bad. It was over almost before it started because I happened to catch Hector,' he says modestly.

Sammy caught McCrow with a clinically placed left hook to the liver and the Norfolk man dropped to his knees in agony and was counted out. The bout had lasted just 57 seconds.

The crowd had been denied the chance of seeing Sammy's full range of silky skills, but he was back in the ring a fortnight later to despatch Roy Groome (Clapham) with a third-round KO, this time with a left hook followed by a fast, finishing right. For a fighter who was not a noted puncher Sammy showed he was an excellent finisher and ended 12 of his first 16 fights inside the distance.

In his tenth fight he inflicted the first stoppage defeat on tough Guyanese fighter Hugh Mackie, who had never previously lost inside time in the 34 contests he'd had since arriving in Britain. 'McCarthy's display of box-fighting, and the manner of his victory, rates him as one of Britain's finest prospects,' wrote *Boxing News* after the win.

Boxing at the Royal Albert Hall, Empress Hall, Seymour Hall Baths, Manor Place Baths and the Mile End Arena, Sammy's fervent following grew and grew. He was voted 'Best British Prospect of 1951' by the readers of *Boxing News* and presented with a silver cup

by the legendary former three-weight British champion Len Harvey
at the trade paper's annual awards ceremony at the Savoy Hotel.

London Derby

> The East End of London has a new idol – a shy, 20-year-old
> barrow-boy named Sammy McCarthy, who can touch off a
> fight-frenzy there equal to those aroused by the giants of the
> past – 'Kid' Lewis, Teddy Baldock, 'Kid' Berg... Sammy has
> 'caught on' because he brings a breath of freshness, simplicity
> and youthful sportsmanship to the oft-unkind blasts of the
> fight game. He boxes the classical way – plenty of brain work,
> plenty of fast, repetitive straight lefts, the more occasional
> right cross and the sudden switch to a body blow. His defence
> is part evasion, part the dying art of picking off punches with
> glove or elbow... Wherever he boxes in London, it is a sell-out.
> He shows his watchers good boxing and good entertainment.
> And always that mischievous smile remains.
>
> – *Boxing News*, 11 June 1952

By early 1952 it was obvious that sooner or later Sammy and
Freddie King (Wandsworth) – Britain's two brightest featherweight
prospects – would have to meet in the ring. When they met on 20
May 1952, Sammy was unbeaten with 14 pro fights to his name.
King had turned pro ten months before Sammy, had suffered five
defeats in 33 pro fights, but had avenged two of these in return
matches. Although he lacked the assurance of an unbeaten record,
he clearly had the edge in experience.

'This is another Boon–Danahar, Lazar–Silver, Walley–Bostock
scrap for those who remember those epic encounters of the past,'
wrote *Boxing News*. 'Two young London lads, each with brilliant
records, equally ambitious and popular performers.' The bout was
staged by Jack Solomons at Harringay Arena for a purse of £1,000,
a stunning figure for an eight-round non-title fight, of which the
winner earned 60 per cent.

Boxing News said the McCarthy–King contest produced
'a splendid bout of box-fighting with Smilin' Sammy just that

much more scientific to enable him to prove his superiority'. After five hard-fought rounds, Sammy began to dominate and in the sixth sent King reeling. In the seventh Sammy continued his bombardment before the referee decided his game opponent had taken enough and wisely stepped in.

'Freddie King was an excellent fighter,' says Sammy. 'He'd beaten them all in this country and he looked like being the next champion, but I beat Freddie in the seventh round. I got a lot of publicity for it – probably more than I deserved – but it was great anyway.'

The victory made Sammy a hot favourite to capture the British featherweight crown. But ironically, at 20, he was too young to challenge for a title. British Boxing Board of Control rules then required title contestants to be 21 or older, so he would have to bide his time.

A Hard Night at Mile End Arena

Although Sammy boxed at the crème de la crème of Britain's boxing arenas – Harringay Arena, White City Stadium, Empress Hall, the Royal Albert Hall – the unglamorous Mile End Arena is the venue he holds most dear.

'It was a great place,' Sammy informs me. 'All it was was a bomb ruin with a ring and a dressing room, but the atmosphere was fantastic in the 1950s. You'd get throngs of people there. The dressing rooms were shabby: it was like walking into a toilet and much, much worse. As far as I remember you couldn't even have a wash there. There may have been a tap but that was it. If you went there with a suit on, you'd come out smothered in dust and white because the walls were whitewashed. But it was great there. It was just behind Mile End station. I always look whenever I go by – I have a lot of memories from there.'

Three weeks after winning the crunch match against Freddie King, Sammy was at White City in his first scheduled ten-rounder, which pitted him against Jackie Turpin, a brother of the famous world middleweight champion Randolph Turpin. Sammy stopped Turpin in four rounds then the following month (July) was back in the ring at a packed Mile End Arena to take on a dangerous opponent.

'The guy's name was Johnny Molloy and he was a tough fighter, an excellent fighter,' says Sammy, with good reason. Liverpudlian Molloy, a former amateur star, had beaten ABA and professional lightweight champion Billy Thompson in the unpaid ranks and as a pro had defeated British champions Al Phillips and Ronnie Clayton in non-title affairs. In 1949 he challenged Clayton for the British featherweight crown but lost on points that time. By 1952 Molloy was past his peak but nonetheless vastly more experienced than Sammy.

'He must have been one of the hardest punchers I faced 'cause afterwards I couldn't even remember the fight,' reveals Sammy. 'I couldn't even remember getting into the ring with him. All I could remember was sitting in my corner before the fight and then hanging over the ropes when he caught me with a punch, and then the next thing I remembered I was in the Turkish Bath afterwards. Obviously I thought I'd been knocked out, but I'd won the fight on points!'

Sammy had apologised to his brother Freddie for losing the fight before being told that he'd actually won. When he studied press reports of the contest, Sammy had the surreal experience of reading about a fight held days earlier that he had practically no recollection of taking part in. So what actually happened?

It transpired that he'd been clipped several times by his opponent's hard right hand, and had blood streaming from his nose and left eye, when he was sent crashing to the canvas by a thundering right in the sixth round. Instinctively Sammy rose at nine but was overwhelmed by a fierce two-fisted attack and forced to take another count.

'It looked all over bar the shouting,' wrote *Boxing News*, 'but McCarthy now showed his natural fighting instinct. When he got up he hit back at Johnny, now desperately trying to finish it off. He failed because Sammy boxed coolly and cleverly to keep out of further trouble to the bell.'

In the remaining two rounds *Boxing News* reported, 'McCarthy made no more mistakes… he was content to frustrate all Molloy's efforts to land another of those devastating right hooks. Not by blocking or running away, but by boxing his man off. He did this successfully, using the ring and sticking in an accurate left hand that rarely missed Molloy's nose. Try as he might Johnny could not get within striking distance of his clever rival and the final gong found him behind on points...'

If there had been any doubts over Sammy's all-round fighting capabilities, they were now surely allayed. He had proved, not only did he have brilliant boxing skills but tenacity and a great fighting heart too – even if Molloy's concussive punches had robbed him of his memory of the fight.

Uncrowned Champion

> The London lad has terrific drawing power. His speed, punching power and general ring demeanour have made him a great box-office attraction, while he is a wonderful ticket seller... those who follow Smilin' Sammy so assiduously view him as a definite featherweight title-holder of the future.
>
> – *Boxing News*, 5 November 1952

After the Johnny Molloy battle, Sammy scored four more straight wins, squeezing the fights into a two-month time frame. The last of these, on 11 November, saw Sammy complete his first ten-rounder when he went up against the teak-tough Scotsman Jim Kenny, a fighter in championship class. Two years earlier Kenny had gone 15 rounds with Ronnie Clayton in a British featherweight title challenge, and two months prior to fighting Sammy, Kenny had actually beaten Clayton in a non-title fight. The winner therefore would have a strong case for gaining a shot at Clayton's title.

The Kenny–McCarthy fight was action-packed and closely contested throughout. Both men finished the ten rounds bloodied and bruised, but Sammy was a clear points winner. 'Sammy McCarthy may not have scored a spectacular knockout win over Jim Kenny,' wrote *Boxing News*, 'but he gained a brilliant victory, perhaps the best of his short professional career.'

A month after Sammy's war with Kenny, the fight that all London had clamoured for was finally staged. Sammy was matched with the reigning British featherweight champion, Ronnie Clayton (Blackpool), in a ten-round non-title affair. His chance to definitively prove that he was Britain's number-one featherweight had arrived.

Since winning the title in 1947 (when he beat the Aldgate Tiger, Al Phillips), Clayton had proven a very fine champion. To his credit were wins over many of Europe's finest bantams and feathers and his most notable victory, back in October 1949, saw him out-point the reigning world bantamweight champion (and International Boxing Hall of Fame inductee), Manuel Ortiz.

But boxing – and Mother Nature – stand still for no one. By late 1952, at age 29 and with over 100 pro fights to his name, Clayton's time at the top was drawing to a close.

Sammy had the natural speed and stamina of youth on his side, but with just 21 paid bouts to his name, and having gone a full ten rounds only once, he was conceding a mountain of experience to the champion. It was difficult to confidently pick a winner, although Sammy's loyal fans were adamant his unbeaten record would remain.

The fight, held at a packed Harringay Arena, saw Clayton constantly on the attack, while Sammy boxed more defensively than usual. 'Sammy gave further evidence in this bout that he uses his brains in combination with his artistic boxing,' observed *Boxing News*. 'He adopted the right tactics in using the ring and scoring with the left on the advancing champion. He refused to indulge in infighting at which Clayton was his obvious superior.'

Sammy boxed on the back foot throughout and continually caught Clayton with snappy lefts. Whenever the champion got inside, Sammy tied him up and then got away to resume his long-range boxing. In the fifth, Clayton connected with a short right and Sammy crashed to the boards. But the youngster wisely stayed on one knee, rose at eight and fought back fiercely to spoil the momentum of the champion's attack. After ten intelligently boxed rounds, Sammy was a close but conclusive winner.

On hearing the decision, Sammy was glad but above all relieved. His supporters, meanwhile, were ecstatic. Their boy had beaten the reigning champion, and it seemed London finally had a potential world-beater who, with a little more experience, could pick up the mantle from those pre-war greats Lewis, Baldock and Berg.

On his way back to his dressing room, Sammy was stopped by a well-spoken man in evening dress and told that somebody important wanted to meet him. He was ushered towards a tall, dignified-looking man with an aristocratic air. This gentleman was none other than Prince Philip, Duke of Edinburgh and husband of the recently-crowned Queen Elizabeth II. As the former barrow boy from Stepney stood shyly before him, the Duke smiled and said, 'Mr McCarthy, I've read and heard a lot about you, and I've enjoyed every minute of the fight. You two will have to meet again – but for the title.'

In its next edition *Boxing News* carried a picture of Sammy with the Duke on its cover with the headline 'Uncrowned Champion: Duke of Edinburgh Congratulates Smilin' Sammy'. In its editorial the paper substantiated this bold statement by explaining, 'Sammy McCarthy stands out today as the uncrowned featherweight champion, seeing that he has now beaten both the titleholder and his official challenger, Freddie King.'

Having recently celebrated his 21st birthday, Sammy was now eligible to contest the British title, but it was Freddie King, who'd won a qualifying final eliminator fight against Glasgow's Tommy Miller, who got the opportunity first (Sammy had been left out of the title eliminator fights because he was then under 21). King challenged Clayton for the championship in May 1953 but lost by fourth-round KO. Sammy meanwhile would continue to take on all comers and patiently wait for his own shot at the title.

In the interim the press and the majority of London fight fans continued to trumpet Sammy's cause. In a letter to *Boxing News*, reader F. Silver (citing the case of lightweight champion Frank Johnson) suggested Sammy could and should be given a title fight without having to box eliminators. 'McCarthy has given boxing a "shot in the arm" and has done all that's been asked of him... He is the "Uncrowned Feathers Champion" in everyone's eyes,' asserted the disgruntled Mr Silver.

I ask Sammy whether, back in 1952 and 53, he had felt frustrated about the situation, but he assures me, 'No, I was quite happy. Once I left the gymnasium I never had too much on my mind – other than what was on at the cinema that week!'

Great Windmill Street and the Thomas a' Becket

By now Sammy's training routine was well established, and having left his job assisting his father after turning professional, he was able to devote all his time and energy to boxing. 'My whole life revolved around boxing,' he says. 'I used to run in the morning at about 6am or 7am, go to the gymnasium about 12pm and train in the afternoon. And I was talking about it, going to the fights, et cetera.

'I used to think the harder you trained, the fitter you would get, but it never works out that way. Everything I did, I did wholeheartedly and I think sometimes I trained too hard and left too much in the gym – I think a lot of fighters do that. I was a very clean-living guy and I used to come to peak fitness very quickly, but I did enjoy the training so in some respects I was my own worst enemy. I trained at Solomons's gymnasium, which was right opposite the Windmill Theatre. It was a good gymnasium and the atmosphere was great.'

Jack Solomons, who (as mentioned in the section on Sid Nathan) began promoting before the war at the Devonshire Club, in the immediate post-war era established himself as Britain's number one boxing promoter. While his domination was doubtlessly to the detriment of other promoters and he was also criticised for pitting the likes of light-heavyweight Freddie Mills against world-class full-blown heavyweights, there was no denying his excellence at putting on a show. A Solomons promotion was a brilliantly orchestrated, grand affair, which took boxing promotion in Britain to new heights in style and ambition.

Solomons's gym (also his HQ) was sited in the middle of London's brightly-lit show-business district, in Great Windmill

Street. Next door to a delicatessen, up a murky stairway and past a first-floor billiard hall, lay this gem of a gym.

'You used to get so many characters there,' says Sammy, 'and you got champions from all over Europe and the world training there so it was always interesting. People could go in from the street to watch – I think they used to charge about two shillings or half a crown to go in and watch the boxers. You always had an audience so you always within reason wanted to look your best.

'When there was a weigh-in there for one of the big fights you'd see all the film stars come down to watch it. I can see now Jean Simmons, John Mills, Stewart Granger and all the actors and actresses being there to see the weigh-ins. Remember around that time people were deprived of entertainment in London because of the war years, so when things were back to normal they all flocked to the West End.

'When I trained at Solomons's gym always there was Ted Kid Lewis. He was a great fighter, Ted. I always used to speak to him and he was a lovely, charming man. He was welterweight champion of the world, and when he was fighting, in the 20s and thereabouts, it must have been so very hard.

'Whenever I go to the West End now – I take my daughter sometimes – I always stand outside the Windmill Theatre and look across the road 'cause I have so many memories there.'

In 1954 rising costs and taxes caused Solomons to shut his gym and at that point Sammy moved his training south of the river to the famous Thomas a' Becket. 'The Becket was a great gym as well, excellent gymnasium,' says Sammy. 'Joe Lucy had it at one time and also Alex Buxton, or one of the Buxtons, had it for a time.

'I enjoyed going to the gymnasium, but having said that, when I had a few fights on the turn – especially if they were hard fights – and it came towards the end of the season, which invariably was in the summer, I always looked forward to having a month or two off, just to be able to relax.'

Gym Mates and Sparring Partners

'I had so many sparring partners that I can't even think of them all,' says Sammy. 'But the ones who stand out in my mind most are an Irish guy called Pat McCoy – lovely fella, typical Irish fella – and another one by the name of Terry Murphy, who came from Hoxton. They were both great sparring partners but more importantly they were both nice people.'

Under Snowy Buckingham's supervision at the same time as Sammy were some excellent fighters including Lew Lazar (brother of the brilliant Harry Lazar), Albert Finch (Jock Taylor's old adversary) and Yolande Pompey, a Trinidadian who challenged the legendary Archie Moore for the world light-heavyweight crown.

'Yolande Pompey was a lovely man,' recalls Sammy. 'I remember like yesterday he came to this country about 1951, with a heavyweight by the name of Ansell Adams and a featherweight named Rolly Blyce. They were excellent fighters and Snowy trained all three.

'Albert Finch, the middleweight champion, and I went away a few times to Brighton to train when Albert was boxing for the championship or I had an important contest. Snowy was training both of us so we went away together. We used to stop at a place called the Crown and Anchor, a big pub with a nice gym.

'The governor and missus were very nice, and the food was absolutely excellent. We only had two meals a day. We used to eat a late breakfast at about ten or 11 o'clock, and we'd have dinner about six o'clock in the evening. There was a park [Preston Park] right opposite, where we used to run. And the gymnasium was underneath us virtually. It was a good experience.'

I ask Sammy whether he preferred training in a more tranquil seaside setting to training in London and his answer surprises me. 'Strangely enough I didn't. I liked training at home because I think subconsciously when you were away you knew you were away for a reason. Although you don't train any harder, you're not at home, you're not doing the things you'd normally do, you know. With a routine you feel safer – somehow or other – or at least I did.'

Later Sammy was joined by another British champion who, like him, was managed by Jarvis Astaire: Peter Waterman. 'I always think of Peter when I see his brother Dennis Waterman, the actor, on TV,' says Sammy. 'I've never met Dennis but I've met his other brothers.

'Peter was a good fighter. He wasn't the friendliest of people – he had an aloof air about him – but what I admired, or envied, about Peter was his quiet confidence. No matter who you put him in with he would think he was going to beat them, and usually he did. He beat some good fighters, and whenever he boxed in the gym his sparring partners never had an easy time. He was like Dave Charnley – he couldn't hold back. I sparred with Peter quite a bit – he used to sort of chase me round for speed. But I had to keep out of his way anyway 'cause he was a bloody solid puncher!'

On the Championship Trail

In early 1953, at the second annual dinner of the Boxing Writers' Club (held at the Criterion Restaurant in Piccadilly), the writers voted Sammy the 'Best Young Boxer of 1952' and he was presented with a commemorative watch by the famous former British heavyweight champion Bombardier Billy Wells.

Shortly afterwards, at the seventh annual *Boxing News* luncheon, Sammy was presented with an inscribed silver belt after being voted 'the boxer who did the most for British boxing in 1952'. It was not quite a Lord Lonsdale belt but it was certainly a fitting acknowledgement of his achievements so far.

After fighting 14 times in 1952, Sammy was rightly given a less hectic schedule in 1953, with eight ring appearances. After beating several continental fighters, Sammy defeated Scotsman Gene Caffrey and former ABA bantamweight champion (and future Southern Area featherweight title-holder) Ken Lawrence.

In September the BBB of C officially named Sammy as the next challenger to Ronnie Clayton's British featherweight title, and Jack Solomons planned to stage the bout on his first bill of the season on 3 November. But the fight was postponed until January 1954 to allow Clayton to fulfil an engagement with Vic Toweel in South Africa. As a substitute, Solomons pulled an ace from his sleeve. He managed to draft in the reigning European featherweight champion, Ray Famechon (France), who was actually a tougher proposition than Clayton.

A month prior to fighting Sammy, Famechon was set to defend his European title against the Belgian Jean Sneyers. Should he beat Sneyers and retain his crown, he promised to defend it against Sammy. Meanwhile the Stepney stylist had a big fight of his own to come through. In what was undoubtedly his toughest test to date, he was matched with a dangerous up-and-coming Nigerian named Hogan Kid Bassey.

Bassey (real name Okon Bassey Asuquo) hailed from Calabar, south-east Nigeria, and was still at school when he became a professional boxer. By his late teens he had won Nigerian and West African titles, but in a bid to earn a living from boxing he decided to move to England. In late 1951 he took a boat from Lagos to Liverpool, where he found himself digs and a place in the Liverpool boxing stable run by former fighter Peter Banasko. Under the same trainer-manager were fellow Nigerians Sandy Manuel, Bola Lawal and Israel Boyle. They trained in a converted basement of a Liverpool community centre which, although it had gloves, punch balls and punch bags, lacked a boxing ring.

In a whirlwind fight campaign Hogan Bassey boxed 19 times in 1952 and in February 1953 shot to prominence when he defeated former European bantamweight champion Luis Romero. Later that year he moved up to featherweight, deposited a £1,000 side-stake (comprising £500 of his own money) with the BBB of C and issued a challenge to Britain's leading feathers, specifically naming Sammy McCarthy as a wanted opponent. Sammy (or rather Jarvis Astaire) accepted the challenge. The pair met over ten rounds at the Royal Albert Hall on 6 October 1953.

'It was first-class stuff,' wrote *Boxing News*, 'so good and entertaining to the connoisseur of boxing, that the rounds sped by and the last was coming up before we realised it.' The fight was nail-bitingly close throughout and per the reckoning of *Boxing News*, with three rounds to each fighter and one round even, its outcome rested on the final round. In this, 'Keeping up the pressure, Hogan had Sammy tiring and was able to keep him more on the defensive. They had another terrific rally in mid-ring, but Bassey was slightly the more effective and won the round and the contest.'

Sydney Hulls of the *Daily Express* called it 'the most brilliant fight of the season and probably of many more seasons to come… this fight will be talked about in the pubs and clubs of Britain for months to come, and referee Tommy Little's verdict will be disputed a thousand times. My scorecard says Bassey won the fight by the narrowest margin permitted under British boxing rules – a quarter of a point. But he *did* win.'

Sammy's tremendous unbeaten run as a professional had ended in his 29th fight. Not only had he lost his unbeaten record but a whopping £1,000 side-stake as well. 'I was disappointed,' he recalls, 'but I knew it was gonna happen some time, and maybe it could have happened beforehand. It was disappointing that I disappointed my family and the people who followed me. The fight had frightened the life out of me 'cause there was so much talk about it; I was petrified of letting everyone down, and myself. I lost on points but it was a very close contest and it was a good contest, and everybody seemed to enjoy it.'

Sammy of course had let nobody down and he had put on yet another wonderful display. The man who had only just beaten him went on to become Nigeria's first boxing world champion when he won the world featherweight title in 1957. He held the world crown for two years and even beat the legendary Willie Pep. For Sammy to narrowly lose to such a boxer was no disgrace.

Fighters with long unbeaten runs are often deeply unsettled by their first defeat, which can impact their future fights. I ask Sammy whether the Bassey defeat gave him a confidence knock and he replies with admirable frankness, 'Not really. I was never too confident in any fight I had – irrespective of who I was boxing I always doubted myself. Going into a fight I don't think anybody could have been more nervous than I. It's a lack of confidence, which is what I have. I'm not putting that down as an excuse, but you are as you are.'

Ray Famechon

On 17 October 1953 Sammy and Snowy Buckingham flew to Brussels to watch Sammy's next opponent, Ray Famechon, put his European featherweight title on the line against Jean Sneyers. The idea was to get a preview of Famechon's style and plan Sammy's fight strategy accordingly. They watched from ringside as Famechon lost the title on a close decision to Sneyers, but he managed to look extremely good in defeat.

When asked by Sydney Hulls of the *Daily Express* how his opponent-to-be had shaped up, Sammy for once wasn't smiling as he said gravely, 'Famechon was tough and strong. Superbly fit. He was at his best when he fought inside. Once he beat his way past Sneyers's guard he never let up, and he was fighting as fiercely at the finish as when he started. I'll have to be prepared to fight at top speed all the time.'

The day after watching the fight, Sammy and his trainer flew back to England and with no time to waste set up a training camp at Brighton. Although his chance to win the European featherweight crown had evaporated with Famechon's loss to Sneyers, the fight was still a huge event and a chance to prove his worth for a crack at the European title.

In Hogan Kid Bassey, Sammy had faced a talented up-and-coming fighter who, like himself, was still a work-in-progress. But in Famechon he would, for the first time, be facing an exceptionally experienced world-class boxer at the height of his powers, who in *The Ring* magazine's last annual ratings had been ranked the number-one contender to world featherweight champion Sandy Saddler.

Famechon, aged 28 and part of a famous French fighting family, started boxing professionally when Sammy was just 13 years old. For five years Famechon had ruled the European featherweight roost as champion and his recent defeat to Sneyers was truly a rare blip in an outstanding fight record. He had beaten and drawn with Sneyers prior to their last meeting, and in 11 months' time he would win back the European crown with a third-round stoppage of Sneyers. His other scalps included the cream of Europe's 9st men, boxers of the calibre of Ronnie Clayton, Al Phillips, Joseph Preys, Kid Dussart and Roy Ankrah.

Famechon had fought ten times in America, topped the bill at Madison Square Garden and gone the distance with the great Willie Pep for the featherweight championship of the world. At this stage Sammy had only gone the ten-round distance on five occasions, whereas Famechon had completed ten-rounders at least 46 times and had boxed six full 15-rounders as well.

There was no doubt about it: this was Sammy's greatest challenge to date. Should he defeat Famechon, Sammy was promised an 8 December 'super fight' with the aforementioned former world featherweight champion (and all-time great) Willie Pep. Once more, the pressure was on.

Going into the fight, Sammy McCarthy fans were bucked by reports from across the Channel. Rumour had it Famechon – who was famed for his brilliant straight left – had lost his snap in the punch after wounding his left shoulder in a shotgun accident back in March. His fight with Sneyers, which of course he had lost, had been his first since suffering the injury. The boxing world was therefore wondering if the rumours of lasting damage were true.

As the fight got underway, however, the rumours were quickly dispelled. Peter Wilson of the *Daily Mirror* observed that Sammy had finally met 'a man who could use a left as well as he could – with the advantage of a longer reach'. And as the fight progressed the Stepney youngster had the disheartening experience of finding his veteran opponent was just that bit better than he was at practically every aspect of the game.

There was no mistake: Sammy was up against a master boxer; an opponent he could not fathom out. But to the Stepney fighter's credit, as *Boxing News* put it, 'it could never be said that Sammy was outclassed'. He stuck to his task doggedly, made some of the rounds very close, and never stopped trying to turn the fight around.

Sportingly, at the end of many of the rounds Sammy acknowledged his opponent's wonderful work by appreciatively patting him on the head or back. There was no blood or brutality, just round after round of first-class boxing. Peter Wilson called it 'one of the cleanest, most sporting and utterly gentlemanly professional boxing matches I have ever watched… for anyone who regards boxing as a sweet science and who enjoys the arts and crafts of the sport this was never anything but enthralling.'

'McCarthy was left with little but his winning smile and his untarnished badge of high courage,' wrote Desmond Hackett of the *Daily Express*. 'But this McCarthy has courage in every ounce of his make-up. When Famechon had completed his lesson he embraced this so-brave boy and brought him to the centre of the ring to take the salute of a slightly saddened fight crowd. Here was McCarthy, the bright shining young hope, who after 28 fights without defeat now loses the last two – this one so clearly.'

When we discuss the fight, Sammy is reverential about Famechon and tells me there is no question that the Frenchman had deserved the verdict. 'I had a good left hand – so they tell me – but he had a great left hand and was a great boxer all round, and very experienced.'

But although he had dwarfed him in knowledge and experience, Ray Famechon was very impressed by the young Englishman as well. After the verdict was announced a bemused crowd saw the Frenchman grab hold of Sammy's left arm and attempt to illustrate a point to him. Then, back in his dressing room, Sammy heard a polite tap at the door. In walked Famechon who, before a small crowd of newspapermen, proceeded to give Sammy some further boxing tips.

The Frenchman then turned to the pressmen and said, 'Sammy will be a champion in two or three years' time… He's a great fighter and boxer and I hold it a great compliment to be able to, in some small way, help him along with his boxing career.'

Famechon also invited Sammy to train with him in Paris so he could share more of his wisdom, but Sammy's management declined the offer.

Jean Sneyers

After losing to Famechon, Sammy consoled himself with a ritual he enjoyed straight after every fight; an experience he looked forward to and had certainly earned after weeks of training and dieting followed by ten tough three-minute rounds.

'Snowy Buckingham and I always used to go to a Turkish Bath afterwards in Jermyn Street in the West End,' he recalls. 'And I love a Turkish Bath; I love any type of heat. We used to stay there all night long – not in the bath all night long: we used to sleep there, have breakfast there, and it was always great 'cause you'd get rid of all your aches and pains and the bruises came out a little easier. I used to be able to take a hell of a lot of heat. I always looked forward to it 'cause you could eat and drink what you wanted down there [without gaining weight] 'cause it came out automatically.'

Sammy's next fight should have been his already deferred British title challenge against Ronnie Clayton, but when Clayton was obliged to withdraw through illness Jack Solomons pulled from his hat an even bigger substitute fight. Sammy would now take on the reigning European featherweight champion, Jean Sneyers (Belgium), for the championship of Europe.

Sneyers was the first boxer in history to win European titles at three different weights. In 1950 he had beaten England's Terry Allen for the European flyweight title, in 1952 he defeated Scotland's Peter Keenan for the bantamweight crown and, as previously mentioned, he beat Ray Famechon in 1953 to win his current European featherweight title.

Naturally, after Sammy's conclusive defeat to Famechon, some press critics questioned the wisdom of pitting him against a man who had recently beaten Famechon, and pondered how the Stepney prospect could possibly overcome the gulf in experience. This would be the third consecutive world-class opponent Sammy had faced. Like Famechon, 26-year-old Sneyers had fought at a consistently higher level than Sammy, had many more rounds under his belt and had lost only five of 58 pro bouts.

Sammy, for his part, simply accepted the challenge with his customary smile, but again experience proved an insurmountable obstacle. Although Sammy made a promising start to the bout, from the mid rounds onwards his masterful opponent dominated the exchanges. To Sammy's credit, though bloodied and bruised, as *Boxing News* noted, 'He stuck it out to the final bell with great courage.' But the referee's verdict could only conceivably go to the champion. 'He was a great box-fighter,' says Sammy of Sneyers. 'Whatever I may have done, he did a little bit better – at the time.'

I ask whether Sammy feels his European title challenge arrived too early and he says, 'I think the fight proved it came too early, but having said that when you get an opportunity you don't refuse it.' Considering the question further he then adds modestly, 'He was the better man. I boxed him later on in my career and the fight was much, much closer – but he still won on points.'

As well as being Sammy's first professional title challenge, this bout was also his first 15-rounder. Today the maximum period any boxer can spend in the ring is 12 three-minute rounds, and only in a championship fight. It is a rare privilege to speak to a man who has experienced boxing 15 three-minute rounds. Seizing the opportunity, I ask Sammy how he found travelling this daunting distance in the ring.

'I was always apprehensive of it, but I was always fit so it shouldn't have bothered me, but it did – up here,' he says, touching his temple. 'But if it was 20 rounds I would have managed it. You always found something there.'

He then explains the importance of pacing a long-distance fight. 'If someone tells you to go out and run 100 yards as fast as you can and you come back and they say, "Now run a mile as fast as you can," automatically you don't start off as fast. And automatically the crowd goes with you in that respect. They know you're boxing 15 rounds or six rounds or whatever it might be. You pace yourself accordingly. I really, really loved boxing but I was always pleased when the last bell went. I thought, that's nice, I can relax for a few days now.'

British Championship Challenge

Sammy had lost three fights on the spin, but it had to be acknowledged that all three were against world-class men, and what's more he was still unbeaten against British opponents. After three tricky and demoralising defeats Sammy's handlers could have been excused for picking a soft touch for his next opponent, but this did not happen.

He was instead matched with the hard-hitting danger man Teddy Peckham (Bournemouth), one of the best crowd-pleasers of the 1940s and 50s. 'He was a good fighter and a good puncher,' recalls Sammy. 'He could knock out anyone if he hit them on the chin. He had a lot of fights and he beat some excellent men.' Boxing between 1944 and 1959, Peckham won 94 of 162 professional contests and 49 of his wins came by stoppage or knockout.

True to form, Peckham gave Sammy a tough night when they met over eight rounds at Walworth's Manor Place Baths, but at the same time it proved a perfect warm-up match for Sammy's imminent British title challenge. The Peckham fight was fought at a blistering pace and bitterly contested by the Bournemouth man in every round. Sammy had to work hard to keep on top, and from the third round till the final bell his mouth bled incessantly. He finished the fight, though, a clear winner.

Sammy now turned his full attention to his forthcoming title fight with Ronnie Clayton, which would take place two months hence. In the run-up to the fight, Clayton left his native Blackpool and set up a training camp at Brighton, while Sammy elected to stay in London and trained at the familiar Great Windmill Street gym.

The Clayton–McCarthy rematch was among the most eagerly awaited British fights of the 1950s. When an unbeaten Sammy McCarthy had won a ten-round decision over Clayton in December 1952, many felt that if the pair met for the title – over 15 rounds – Sammy would again prove victorious. But through various postponements 18 months had elapsed since then and Sammy's professional record had been tarnished by three successive defeats. Clayton, meanwhile, had shown no decline in form, and word from Brighton had it he was in tip-top shape.

Now a McCarthy victory seemed far less certain, and *Boxing News* boldly predicted that Clayton would keep his crown. Sammy's loyal army of fans, however, were as confident as before that their boy would win the title. 'Everyone was expecting me to win because I'd beaten him before, but I wasn't as sure as they were,' confesses Sammy.

The fight was yet another Jack Solomons extravaganza, staged at the suitably enormous and prestigious White City Stadium, a venue built for the 1908 London Olympic Games. As Sammy left his dressing room and walked out before a huge crowd at Britain's finest boxing arena on possibly the biggest night of his career, doubtless there were more than a few butterflies tickling his stomach, and the wait in the ring before the first bell must have felt like an eternity.

But when the bell rang Sammy got straight to business in a composed, workmanlike manner. From the outset it was clear he had decided to box on the retreat and let the champion advance onto his shots as in their first encounter. This time the plan worked even more effectively than before, and it was evident Sammy had improved after facing Sneyers and Famechon.

Throughout the fight Sammy caught Clayton repeatedly with perfectly-timed lefts, and showed great versatility in his work. The champion looked bewildered by his younger rival's hand-speed, as Sammy continually caught him with one-two combinations, double-lefts and several times a left hook to the body followed in the same motion by a jolting left hook to the chin. 'McCarthy was boxing with all his old joy, moving beautifully and smiling with sheer enjoyment,' observed the *Daily Express*.

At long range Sammy was the complete master, and when the champion got in close to launch vicious body blows, Sammy's defence proved more than equal to the assault.

Towards the end of the fifth, Sammy connected with a left-right followed by another left to the head and the champion rocked back on his heels. Suddenly Clayton retreated, raised his glove to his right eye with a worried expression and blinked repeatedly. He kept away from Sammy for the rest of the round and when the bell sounded seemed to have trouble finding his corner.

Clayton battled on through the sixth and seventh but as the seconds ticked by, Sammy, who was almost unmarked, dominated the fight all the more. A crashing right to the face had the champion bleeding from the nose and mouth at the start of the eighth, and the Blackpool man made a valiant but vain last stand in that round. But, as *Boxing News* observed, 'McCarthy made him miss with all the ease in the world and scored almost at will with either hand to the head. Ramrod lefts jolted back Clayton's head, his jaw was screwed round from well-placed rights and we could tell that the end was not far off.'

At the bell Clayton walked to his corner grimly shaking his head. As Sammy was about to spring from his stool for the start of the ninth, Clayton's manager, George Dingley, called referee Andrew Smythe over, pointed to his fighter's swollen-shut left eye and explained that his vision was badly impaired. Smythe asked the champion if he wanted to retire, and he nodded dejectedly. There was no sense in going on.

It took Sammy a few seconds to comprehend what had happened. Nine years of sweat and sacrifice had finally come to fruition: he had just won the featherweight championship of Great Britain.

As the crowd cheered him to the echo, Sammy grinned with a mixture of shyness and pride and wiped a tear from his eye. BBB of C president Mr J. Onslow Fane, then climbed through the ropes and draped a gleaming Lonsdale belt around his waist. There were great bursts of light as the ringside photographers snapped away and Sammy politely posed and acquiesced to their requests.

A new featherweight king had been crowned. Sammy had brought back to London a nine-stone title that was lost as long ago as May 1929, when Sheffield's Johnny Cuthbert took the championship from Harry Corbett of Bethnal Green. The Smiler from Stepney had done himself and all London proud.

The New Champion

The fight game thrives on changes and the crowning of a new champion puts zest into the business. From the time of James Figg it has been the aim of promoters to find someone to beat the titleholder; the risk of a championship changing hands has

always stimulated the interest of the followers of the Noble
Art.

– Gilbert Odd, *Boxing News*, 11 June 1954

Three days after the fight, Sammy was invited to Pinewood studios
where comedian and screen star Norman Wisdom was filming
boxing scenes for his new film *One Good Turn*. As a film buff,
Sammy jumped at the chance of seeing the inside of a film studio
for the first time and meeting one of his favourite comedians.

'I remember being at the cinema when he made his very first film,'
says Sammy, 'but I hadn't met him then. The film was called *Trouble
in Store*. He was a very nice guy and supposedly he did a bit of boxing
when he was young. I've seen photographs of him shaping up.'

Sammy's arrival at the studio created a hubbub and he was kept
busy chatting to doormen, electricians, carpenters, scene-shifters
and extras who were boxing fans and wanted to ask him questions.
Norman Wisdom was thrilled to see Sammy and congratulated
him on winning his title, before the pair posed for photos together.

Unlike some champions whose fights become few and far
between after they win a title, Sammy's handlers had a busy
schedule lined up for him. Two months after his title win, the
Stepney stylist was back in action on 24 August 1954 in a ten-
rounder against Enrico Macale (Italy) at Clapton Greyhound
Stadium. It was obvious from the start that the Italian was out
of his depth and could not match Sammy for skill or punching
power. Macale looked appealingly to his corner throughout the
third, fourth and fifth rounds before the referee halted this uneven
contest halfway through the fifth.

On 14 September Sammy took on the top Belgian Joe Woussem,
who had recently caused a minor sensation by out-pointing
Hogan Kid Bassey. Woussem was 'convincingly outpointed and
outpunched by British featherweight champion Sammy McCarthy
over ten sizzling rounds', reported *Boxing News*.[16]*

---

16 Further down the bill, future household name Henry Cooper and his twin brother
    George – who boxed as Jim Cooper – made successful pro debuts, George winning on
    points and Henry scoring a one-round knockout.

Then, on 12 October, Sammy chopped down the lanky 5ft 9in Frenchman Pierre Richaud in six rounds despite big height and reach disadvantages – referee Tommy Little coming to Richaud's rescue.

These regular fights helped keep the new champion fighting fit and revealed an improved Sammy McCarthy, whom the fight scribes felt was boxing in a more relaxed and confident manner since winning his title.

The Black Flash

After three one-sided wins, promoter Jack Solomons promised London fight-goers to match Sammy with a top American, and the US-based Mexican featherweight champion Baby Ortiz was picked as an opponent. But when Baby Ortiz cried off two weeks before the fight, a replacement opponent was drafted in. As soon as he got word of the Mexican's withdrawal, Roy Ankrah telephoned Solomons and told the promoter he would happily take Ortiz's place. Solomons took him at his word and quickly got to work to make the match. As substitute fights go this was a sizzler – an even better match than the original.

Ankrah – nicknamed the Black Flash for his furious fighting style – was born in the Gold Coast (now Ghana) on Christmas Day in 1925. He started boxing at ten, turned pro at 16 and won the Gold Coast national title at five weights. It was British and world light-heavyweight champion Freddie Mills who first saw Ankrah's potential when the pair met in Calcutta during the Second World War. Mills was then in the RAF and Ankrah the Royal West African Expeditionary Force, in which he served as a sergeant motor mechanic.

Mills, who was touring India with a party of boxers, was so impressed by young Ankrah that he invited him to join the troupe. After the tour, Mills tried to persuade Ankrah to come to Britain when the war ended, but the homesick West African instead returned to his home city of Accra, resumed his peacetime job as a garage mechanic and continued to box purely in the Gold Coast.

Eventually the lure of unbelievable wealth (by Gold Coast standards) proved too great for Ankrah, and at the invitation of manager Joe McKean he arrived in Glasgow in early 1950. It's said by that time that Ankrah had 100 or so African fights to his name, but the majority go unrecorded, so it's impossible to produce a reliable record of his ring activity prior to boxing in Britain. What is certain is that he was already very experienced and brought an unconventional but exciting fighting style to British rings.

British fight fans were either mesmerised or appalled by Ankrah's unorthodox, swarming, non-stop, jack-in-the-box style, which showed scant regard for boxing fundamentals but proved highly effective and earned him the appellation the Fighting Octopus. Barring a disqualification, Ankrah was unbeaten in his first 25 fights after arriving in Britain and beat the likes of reigning European bantamweight champion Luis Romero and reigning British lightweight champion Tommy McGovern.

In April 1951 Ankrah became the first Gold Coast fighter to contest an Empire title when he took on the British and Empire champ, Ronnie Clayton, over 15 rounds. Not only did he challenge Clayton but he out-pointed him and won the title, and then ten months later he stopped the Blackpool man in a return title fight. After winning the title Ankrah told the press, 'I could have kept my pace up for 20, 30, as many rounds as you like. I had no worries at all about becoming tired.' And this boundless energy seemed to be the key to Ankrah's success.

By the time Ankrah fought Sammy, he had won 33 of 37 fights since arriving in Britain. The only men to beat him were the superb Ray Famechon, European champ Luis Romero (in a return) and the clever Ulsterman Spider Kelly, although Ankrah had won two out of three fights with Kelly.

Boldly Ankrah laid down a £500 side-stake on himself to beat Sammy McCarthy, while the music hall star Bud Flanagan took up the challenge and gave Jack Solomons a £500 cheque to cover Ankrah's money. Cheques from both men were deposited with a newspaper; the winner to collect them after the fight. Flanagan was a great admirer of Sammy's and Sammy was a big fan of his. 'Bud Flanagan used to come to the gym quite a lot 'cause he was friends with Jack Solomons,' he recalls. 'I used to go and watch

Bud and Chesney Allen quite often – I enjoyed watching the music hall shows.'

The McCarthy–Ankrah contest lived up to expectations as the Gold Coast warrior pressed the champion through every minute of every round. Sammy, meanwhile, boxed on the back foot and counter-punched with well-timed blows, mixing straight lefts to the head with full-blooded rights to the heart and lefts to the liver.

Although Ankrah strove to fight inside, McCarthy kept the battle at long range. The pace had been relentless and many rounds had been close, but Sammy won the majority in what *Boxing News* called 'one of the best performances of his brilliant career'. At the final bell referee Jack Hart had no hesitation in raising the Stepney man's arm.

'When I had my first professional contest Roy Ankrah had topped the bill against Ronnie Clayton for the British Empire featherweight title,' Sammy recalls. 'He was non-stop for ten rounds, 15 rounds, but I out-pointed him at Harringay. I was pleased with that win – he was an excellent fighter.'

In addition to Sammy's superb boxing skill, it was his outstanding fitness that allowed him to stay on top of the Gold Coast fighting fury. 'I was always very fit irrespective of who I boxed,' explains Sammy. 'I loved the training and I had a great trainer in Snowy Buckingham. I never abused myself, I never smoked or drank and I was never out late – I think I was too frightened apart from anything else. My father would have bashed me up,' he laughs before adding, 'I don't mean that literally. But I always played the game. I was always, always fit.'

With such a stringent training regime, and without the temptation of London nightlife and all that goes with it, Sammy pursued a gentler pastime when he wasn't boxing. Like many Brits in the days before TV sets were widespread, he was a big cinema fan.

'In those days I was very much a film buff and I still am today, although I don't go to the cinema much now. I love watching films,' he says, 'new films, old films, but more so the old films. I think the films were better years ago but maybe it's my imagination.

'I remember the very first time my friends, my cousins and I went to the West End to see a film and we thought it was so plush, because the seats were so soft and rounded and comfortable. They were probably no better than they were in the East End of London but we thought they were better anyway.'

By now Sammy McCarthy fans had an added incentive to visit the cinema. In the 1950s, newsreel footage of recent news and events was shown before the start of a film, and Sammy was now a big enough star for footage of some of his fights to appear on the big screen. Newsreel footage of Sammy's next ring encounter – one of the most pivotal fights of his career – would be shown to crowds of cinema-goers across the country.

Into the Spider's Parlour

Sammy's first British title defence was against the trickiest, most skilful title aspirant around. Billy 'Spider' Kelly, in terms of ability and credentials, stood head and shoulders above all other would-be challengers.

After the BBB of C selected the Spider as Sammy's official challenger, there had been some wrangling over who would stage the fight. The usually all-powerful Jack Solomons had wanted to hold it in London, but surprisingly the Northern Irish promoter Bob Gardiner won the right to stage the contest in Belfast. Sammy's end of the purse would be the highest of his career, and since Kelly had recently won the Empire featherweight crown from Roy Ankrah, the winner would take home both the British and Empire 9st titles. It would be Sammy's first fight outside London.

In challenging Sammy, Derry-born Kelly was truly following in his father's footsteps. Aged six, in front of 8,000 jubilant fans, he had been hoisted into the ring at the King's Hall, Belfast, as his father, Jim 'Spider' Kelly, was presented with the Lord Lonsdale belt after beating London's Benny Caplan for the vacant British and Empire featherweight titles.

Young Kelly had been brought up on boxing and, wanting to emulate his dad, had joined his local amateur club. In 1948 he won the Ulster Youths' flyweight title and in 1949 the bantamweight title before turning pro in 1950 and adopting the same Spider moniker as his father. It fitted both men perfectly for each had a clever, cagey style that was apt to lure opponents into traps.

There were uncanny similarities between the McCarthy–Kelly fight and the one in which Spider Kelly snr. had won the British and Empire 9st titles 16 years earlier. The venue, the weight, the titles at stake and the place of origin of the boxers involved were identical. Not only were Benny Caplan (St George's) and Sammy from the same London district, but they had both learnt their trade at the same Stepney and St George's amateur club. Was this a bad omen for Sammy?

⁊⁊ ⁊⁊ ⁊⁊

Kelly trained for the fight in Northern Ireland under his father's supervision. He enlisted the 1952 Olympic silver medallist John McNally (Belfast) and British bantamweight champion Peter Keenan as his chief sparring partners, as both had a similar style to Sammy. Sammy meanwhile trained in Brighton and hired former opponent Teddy Peckham as his main sparring partner. The choice of Peckham, however, raised some eyebrows among newspaper critics, as the Bournemouth man's battling, come-forward methods were the stylistic opposite of Kelly's evasive, counter-punching approach.

The morning after he wound up his training at Brighton, Sammy was due to fly to Belfast and arrive on the afternoon before the fight. But when he, Snowy Buckingham and Jack King arrived at London Airport they found all the planes had been grounded due to severe fog. A dash by taxi from the airport got Sammy and his party to Euston Station just in time to catch the London to Belfast rail and sea service, which was scheduled to arrive at 7am on the morning of the fight.

'The weather was absolutely atrocious and there was speculation that the fight may even be postponed because the weather was so bad. But we decided to get a boat over there,' he recalls. 'The crossing was very bad and it was awkward sleeping on the boat because the sea was so rough that the boat was up and down – and the boats then were small compared to today.' The journey took 14 hours and Sammy got no sleep at all.

After catching a taxi to their hotel and checking in, a jaded Sammy and company set off for the 1pm weigh-in before Sammy gained what rest he could before the fight.

Within 24 hours of the match being announced over 1,000 seats had been booked at the King's Hall, Belfast, and the remaining tickets had long since sold, which meant that 15,000 cheering fans – the majority rooting for Kelly – had crowded into the venue come fight time on 22 January 1955.

Kelly, as challenger for the British title, entered the ring first wearing a faded, pink-patterned dressing-gown that his father had used in his ring days, and received a thunderous ovation. Sammy appeared next, smiling shyly and wearing his usual crimson gown. He received a surprisingly warm welcome from the overseas crowd.

Sammy forced the pace throughout the 15-round fight while Kelly repeatedly evaded his blows with adroit head movement while scoring with snappy counters. Sammy won some of the rounds through sheer persistence, but his elusive opponent always seemed in control.

'Billy made his rival do all the leading,' wrote *Boxing News*, 'made him miss with ridiculous ease and then countered him with the greatest discourtesy. Or he drew a half lead from Sammy, sometimes even only a feint, and then beat him to the punch… Whenever the Smiler struck, the Spider wasn't there; when Kelly employed a stroke, Sammy managed to get his face in the way.

'The great shame of it all,' opined the newspaper, 'was that McCarthy was so much below his usual par. Perhaps the fact that he had a somewhat hazardous and lengthy journey to Belfast, owing to the adverse weather conditions, accounted for some of his lethargy. Perhaps it was fighting out of London for the first time in his life that made all the difference. Whatever it was, the Belfast folk saw a McCarthy strangely different from the immaculate boxer we know him to be.'

After 15 largely one-sided and unexciting rounds, to the delight of the Belfast crowd Kelly was declared the winner. Ever the good sportsman, though his pride and feelings were hurt dearly, Sammy enthusiastically congratulated Kelly and looked on with a warm smile as the Lonsdale belt that an hour ago had been his own special possession was strapped round the Derry man's waist.

Kelly's father, Jim, had the moving experience of standing with his son in the exact same ring as he had 16 years previously for the presentation of the British featherweight belt. This time he was watching his son with pride, whereas before it had been his young son looking up at him. It was the first time a father and son had won the same boxing titles.

Whether it was Kelly's clever boxing and masterfully executed strategy or Sammy's 14-hour journey without sleep that proved the most telling factor in the fight is debatable, but the latter no doubt affected Sammy's performance to some degree. In addition, it was revealed in the press two days later that Sammy had injured his right hand on Kelly's elbow in the third, and thereafter was scarcely able to use it in the fight.

Initially he had injured the hand the previous month in his fight with Roy Ankrah. Both Sammy and his trainer had thought the fist was fine again after treatment, but it had evidently not healed. In light of the second injury, Sammy would visit a bone specialist and take several months out of the ring.

Sammy is a man who hates to make excuses and is reluctant to blame his injured hand or the chaotic journey to Belfast for his defeat. 'The crossing was bad but it didn't affect me too much,' he says dismissively. I tell him that I've read his injured right hand was practically useless from the third round on in the fight and he replies, 'That's right, yeah. But Billy was an excellent boxer. He was very hard to hit; he was a very elusive boxer and I didn't like elusive boxers. I preferred someone to come to me, but he was quite the reverse.'

I remind Sammy that he'd said in the press after the fight that he felt he could have beaten Kelly if he'd been at his best. 'I did say that, yeah; I did feel that,' he admits. 'Whether it was so or not is another thing entirely. I'd love to think I would have won but it's not necessarily the case. Billy Kelly was a great boxer, much better than he was credited with being.'

Kelly was warm in his praise of Sammy after the fight. 'It was the cleanest fight I ever took part in,' he told *Boxing News*. 'Even when he knew he was well behind Sammy never changed to anything remotely approaching doubtful tactics. I enjoyed the fight. I hope Sammy feels I was as sporting as he was.'

Sammy and Kelly would remain on friendly terms in years to come, and Sammy even managed Kelly's younger brother, Paddy Kelly, when he moved from Derry to London to further his own pro career in the late 1950s and early 60s.

'I phoned Billy a couple of times in Ireland,' Sammy recalls. 'He died a little while ago: he died tragically from a fall. I phoned up and spoke to his wife – I've never met the lady, but I felt I had to ring up just to say I was thinking of her. You feel you must send your condolences... you want to, but when someone dies words are inadequate.'

Weight Revelations

After the Kelly fight Sammy was obliged to take a five-month rest from boxing to allow his injured right hand to heal. He returned to the ring on 14 June 1955 and showed devastating form when he stopped Teddy Peckham in a return fight in three rounds and looked a class above the Bournemouth man. Sammy then fought twice in September, once in October and three times in November, beating boxers from Spain, France, Belgium and Austria with dazzling ease.

Boxing News felt Sammy was boxing better than ever, and in a departure from his previous policy of only boxing in London, fight fans from as far afield as Newcastle, Liverpool and Glasgow had the privilege of seeing the famous Stepney Smiler in action. 'Sammy's judgement of distance and fast, accurate punching were a joy to behold,' wrote one Scottish fight-goer in a letter to *Boxing News*. 'I think I am speaking for all Scots boxing fans when I say I should like to see more of him.'

In his final fight of the year, on 29 November, Sammy took on his old adversary Jean Sneyers at Streatham Ice Rink in a ten-rounder. Sammy had improved markedly in the 21 months since his first fight with the Belgian, and many felt this time he would come out on top. As expected, the fight was much closer and both men put up a 'fast, clever and highly entertaining' display (*Boxing News*). But Sneyers was still a shade too good for Sammy, and again the brilliant Belgian got the verdict.

One surprise on the day of the fight was that Sammy had failed to make the 9st 3lb stipulated weight – a poundage set by himself – and had to pay a £75 forfeit. Shortly after the fight Jarvis Astaire notified the BBB of C that in future his charge would box as a lightweight.

The announcement was a bolt out the blue for the British boxing fraternity, as Sammy had been odds-on favourite to be the first challenger for Billy 'Spider' Kelly's featherweight titles. In addition, the Stepney boxer had a 9st 3lb bout with Mohamed Omari (Algiers) scheduled for 16 December, but in light of the weight revelation the fight was called off.

Unbeknown to the boxing public, since the start of his career Sammy had gone through hell to make weight and staying a featherweight was no longer an option. 'I always had a job doing nine stone,' he explains. 'It wasn't so much the food that put on the weight – or at least that's what we were led to believe – it was the liquid. Between fights I could go up to almost 11 stone, but it was only liquid weight. When I say liquid weight, I don't mean booze; just tea. I would never refuse a cup of tea when I wasn't boxing because I knew that when I started training I'd start to dry out immediately – from the very first day.

'I could talk to you all day long about drying out but I could never really get through to you what it was like. It was horrendous; it was absolute agony. When you dry out your throat quarterises – it closes up and you can't swallow – and you don't want to eat anything because you can't swallow and because your throat is so dry. I used to walk along the street weeks before a fight and all I could think about was drinking lemonade or drinking Tizer, or milk or tea or whatever. And sometimes it was a pleasure to go to sleep at night just to get away from the agony.

'It got to the point where I used to go and drink a whole bottle of Tizer and then right away, just before my dinner, go to the toilet and vomit everything up. It's a funny thing: it allowed me to control my stomach. Even today, I could eat or drink anything and go right away to the toilet and bring it up if I want to. I don't do that now, but I'm just saying.

'I had weight trouble all the way through my career. Even when I was an amateur my trainer used to give me a button to suck. I used to walk around the streets quite often sucking a button just to lubricate my mouth.

'The reason for it all was I seemed to be very small for the weight I was boxing at. I could have gone up a weight and made things a little easier but the guys who I would have been boxing there would have been so much larger than I, and they'd probably come down from a higher weight and within the weight stipulation they were physically all round bigger than I was. They used to say to me, "Sam, you're too small to fight any heavier – you must have heavy bones." At lightweight it wasn't so bad but even then I used to go up to 11 stone.

'It's a funny thing, it's controlled my life in many respects – even now I don't eat too much and I'm lighter now than when I was boxing. I love my food but I don't eat unnecessarily. I never eat between meals and the most I have is about four meals a week. I never have a sandwich or cake or biscuit or whatever. I think most people eat far, far too much. I think nowadays, in the West, more people die from over-eating than not eating enough.'

Lightweight Contender

The withdrawal of Sammy McCarthy from the featherweight ranks and his entry into the lightweight division will put more pep into a class that hasn't had a really colourful performer since the days of the redoubtable Eric Boon.

– *Boxing News*, 9 December 1955

In finding Sammy an opponent for his first contest at lightweight, his handlers went straight to the top and secured him an overweight 9st 11lb non-title fight with the reigning British lightweight champion, Frank Johnson. Although at first sight this may seem a foolish move, there was logic behind the decision. A win over the lightweight champion would immediately establish Sammy as a leading contender for the title and save him the trouble of a long fight campaign to prove his worth at the weight.

Sammy's opponent, Johnson, was born at Withington, Manchester in 1928. His real last name was Williamson but he adopted the ring name Johnson in tribute to the pre-war Manchester middleweight Len Johnson. And he wore the name well: he was a skilful performer in the tradition of Len Johnson and those other pre-war Manchester greats Jackie Brown and Johnny King.

Going into his fight with Sammy, Johnson had a splendid record of 42 wins and only six losses. He had beaten such notables as Tommy McGovern, Joe Lucy, Tommy Barnham and Guy Gracia, and although now a little past his best, he was still a force to be reckoned with.

The fight, held over ten rounds at the Royal Albert Hall on 24 January 1956, was another action-packed affair (Sammy was seldom involved in a dull fight). Johnson took the first two rounds and looked on the way to victory, but in the third Sammy sent the champion reeling into a neutral corner with a crashing right followed by a swift left to the jaw. Johnson fought back fiercely, his mouth oozing blood, but Sammy pinned him to the ropes and unleashed a lightning bombardment of blows.

There were more punches exchanged in that third round than in many entire fights, and Johnson was not the same thereafter. He fought on gamely but could not match his nimble-footed opponent's speed or stamina. As Sammy took round after round, and opened a cut over Johnson's left eye, that side of the champion's face was masked by a curtain of blood. At the final bell the Stepney Smiler was the only possible winner.

So the gamble of pitting Sammy against the champion had paid off. 'It was an excellent fight and a good win for me because he was probably the second-best lightweight in the country. I think the best was Joe Lucy,' Sammy says.

Sammy's statement is borne out by the fact that three months later Johnson lost his title to Lucy. Even so, by virtue of his win over Johnson, Sammy was matched with Lucy in Lucy's first title defence on 26 June. In the interim, on 3 April, Sammy took on a fearsome up-and-coming young Dartford southpaw called Dave Charnley in a £500 side-stake match.

Sammy entered the fight a firm favourite against Charnley, who was then an 18-fight novice; the Stepney Smiler could not have possibly known he was taking on one of Britain's best-ever lightweights.

Drama came quickly as Sammy was dropped for a count of nine in the second round from a hook to the chin. Then in the third an almighty right – which would have spelt the end for most fighters – caught Sammy flush in the body.

He says, 'I remember he hit me and as I went to move away, the pain came on me, and I've never been so hurt in all my life. I could have cried – it was so painful. I think it was the equivalent of a left hook to the liver but with him being a southpaw it was a right hook. I was in so much pain that I had to go down on one knee. I got up though, that's the main thing.'

Sammy showed great heart in rising to his feet and battling on in a bid to turn the fight around. In the fifth he had Charnley gasping from his own crisp body blows, and by the seventh some felt the Stepney man had gained a narrow lead through his superior long-range boxing. But late in the fight Sammy was drawn into a close-quarter brawl, despite screams from his corner imploring him to 'Box! Box! Box!'

Frank McGhee of the *Daily Mirror* called it the fight of the year, writing, 'It was close, desperately close… The fight had everything – action, crisp punching, knockdowns. The lot.' The decision in favour of Charnley caused a huge upset, but, taking the knockdowns into account, the Dartford man had just done enough to clinch it.

Some felt, in view of the result, that Charnley should be given a shot at Lucy's title ahead of Sammy. But the Dartford youngster was impeded by the fact he was still some months short of his 21st birthday. The officious BBB of C age-cap of 21 for British championship contestants, which had hindered Sammy as a 20-year-old featherweight, now worked in his favour.

Former Repton amateur and Billingsgate fish porter Joe Lucy (who was now the licensee of the Thomas a' Becket pub and gym), was the same man who had out-pointed Ted Berry in the North-East London Divisional lightweight final back in 1948. The speedy, awkward, fleet-footed Mile End southpaw proved an unsolvable puzzle to most of the men who stepped in the ring with him, and trying to get to grips with his slippery style would be one of Sammy's toughest challenges yet.

The pair met at Wembley's 10,000-seater Empire Pool on 26 June 1956. A BBC camera crew would be present to film the 15-round McCarthy–Lucy fight along with the other top-liner, which featured Kitione Lave and Joe Bygraves in a British Empire heavyweight clash. For the first time on British television, highlights of two championship fights would be broadcast within 24 hours of their taking place.

TV viewers and ringside spectators alike were in for a disappointment, though, as Sammy's fight proved a monotonous affair. After taking a count of seven in the opening round, Sammy suffered a slow, methodical beating from the champion, whose elusive style he could not fathom out. Just before the end of the 13th, with Sammy hopelessly behind on points, referee Ike Powell stopped the bout in Lucy's favour. In doing so, he deprived Sammy of his record of never losing inside the distance.

'Joe Lucy was a very under-rated fighter,' says Sammy. 'He was an excellent boxer but very defensive. He wasn't the most exciting boxer to watch but hardly anyone beat him. I could never really handle southpaws anyway, especially people like Joe who used to box on the back foot. If someone was aggressive and they came to me, I was far better than if I had to chase them.'

Sammy finished 1956 with four consecutive wins, beating Johnny Miller (North Shields), Frenchman Jacques Dumesnil and Birmingham's Johnny Mann (no relation to Sammy's amateur trainer) twice. On 22 January 1957 Sammy lost on points to France's Guy Gracia at the Royal Albert Hall, but this loss was no disgrace.

'Guy was a good fighter,' recalls Sammy. 'He had beaten almost everyone in this country; he'd beaten Charnley twice. The only British guy who beat him at that time was an excellent fighter named Ronnie Hinson – he was a lightweight. Ronnie and I boxed as amateurs, he beat me and I beat him and he beat me in the championships. He wasn't champion as a professional but he was an excellent box-fighter, and he beat Guy Gracia twice. But isn't it funny, Ronnie lost to Dave Charnley on points and Dave Charnley lost to Gracia, but that's the way it goes. Some styles suit you far better than others.'

Sammy did not know it then but he had just fought his final fight.

This Is Your Life

On 4 March 1957 Sammy was unwittingly led into the King's Theatre in Hammersmith on the pretext of a meeting to discuss the possibility of publishing a book on his career.

'They said they wanted to take me to see the people who were going to put the book together, and once again I believed everything I heard,' grins Sammy. 'I didn't realise it but I was in a TV studio 'cause we went in through a back door. And when I walked into the office to see the people writing the book I was on the stage but I didn't realise that until I saw Eamonn Andrews [the *This Is Your Life* presenter]. I was surprised. Most people watched the TV show *This Is Your Life*, I used to watch it myself; I enjoyed watching it.'

Sammy was the first boxer to be honoured by *This Is Your Life* and, at 25, he was also the youngest subject at the time.

Sammy was further surprised when he was prompted to announce his retirement from boxing on the live TV broadcast. 'I had no idea I was going to retire,' he admits. 'I was pretty easily led and I wanted things to be happy with no arguments, but I suppose I was quite happy with the situation. I think I must have been past my best and others must have seen things that I never saw.'

Guests on the show included Sammy's parents, his six sisters and three brothers, Snowy Buckingham and former opponents Jean Sneyers, Ronnie Clayton, Hector McCrow and Norman Watts. Another highlight was the 1956 Olympic flyweight gold medallist, Terry Spinks, who idolised Sammy and was about to turn pro, asking him live on air if he'd manage him. Sammy agreed and the success that Spinks achieved in the pro game kept Sammy in the limelight for years to come.

'I'm only sorry Johnny Mann, who trained me as an amateur, wasn't on the show,' says Sammy. 'I was very disappointed and I thought it was very unfair 'cause he should have been on it. But these things happen and it was nice to be on there.'

Search for a New Buzz

In 1956 Sammy had married his sweetheart, Sylvia Clancy, so with new domestic responsibilities and having made a great deal of money from his many high-profile fights, it made sense for him to leave boxing at this point. But having dedicated his teenage and young adult life to the squared ring, he was now left with a void. What he would do to replace the buzz of boxing was a dilemma he would find difficult to solve.

He says, 'My wife and I were living in Upton Park at the time and we went on a cruise – the first cruise I'd been on – with some neighbours of ours, and they met some friends of theirs on the cruise who ran a public house called the Hero of Waterloo on Waterloo Bridge. We was talking and they said, "Come over, Sam, one day and you'll see how it is." My wife and I used to go over and help them out and I sort of liked it: I quite enjoyed serving people.

'They managed the pub. Well when you're managing big pubs – I didn't realise at the time – you can have as many helpers as you want as long as the figures are all right. But when you have a pub of your own it's so difficult 'cause you're there 24 hours a day. I didn't know the difference really, but I should have done.'

Sammy bought a pub called The Prince of Wales – known as Kate Hodder's – in Duckett Street, Stepney, but quickly found the life of a pub landlord was not for him.

'You'd get a lot of people saying, "Can you change a cheque for me, Sam?" And quite often they'd bounce,' he recalls. 'They're not friends of yours but customers and they give you a cheque knowing very well it's going to bounce, and then you don't see them. I don't mind the hard work – I wouldn't mind working from six in the morning to six at night continuously – as long as once I'd got home I'd finished.

'But in the middle of the night you'd get phone calls, "Sam, can you open up? We've got a party; we've run out of beer." It could be two o'clock in the morning, and you can't refuse them. Even now I think it must be the worst job in the world. Although I did have two or three other pubs at different times, I put managers in them.'

Another potential replacement for actual boxing that Sammy tried was the management of other boxers. This began with Terry Spinks who, with Sammy as his manager and Ted Berry's old friend Jimmy Davis (Bethnal Green) as his trainer, became British featherweight champion and a household name.

'I managed Terry Spinks with Jarvis Astaire,' Sammy reveals, 'and I managed a few other fighters on my own. I had Brian Bissmire, he boxed out of Plaistow, Terry Gill of West Ham (they were both pretty good eight-rounders) and Terry Brown of West Ham. I also managed Spider Kelly's younger brother, Paddy Kelly – he wasn't a bad little fighter – and Terry Lawless trained him.

'Although I managed fighters it wasn't something I really enjoyed, again because I like home life. I love going out in the evening: going to the cinema, going to the pub, having a meal, but then coming home. But when it's to do with work: you've gotta go to see certain fighters or go to fights, go here or go there, and I'm sort of a nine-to-five man.'

I ask whether Sammy ever considered becoming a trainer and he tells me, 'I think some people, apart from being good boxers themselves, have it in their ability to impart their knowledge and others can do it less well. I think I could have done it, but I'm not sure whether I'd have liked to have gone to the gym every day and been there at the weigh-ins and the fights. It's not from nine to five and finish. From nine to five I'll work as hard as anyone, but I like to go home and just watch the television or whatever. Laziness doesn't come into it; it's the way you're built.'

Crime and Punishment

> They used to let my friend Sammy McCarthy down to see me from the wing. Sammy was the gym orderly for years. He used to be a brilliant boxer – he was British featherweight champion years ago. I love the guy. He was serving 18 years for robbery. He never complained; he just got on with it... I'd rate Sammy as one of the greatest men I've ever met. He would come down and see me on one of my bad days and leave me feeling happy again. A story from Sammy was like a breath of fresh air. Thanks, Sammy!
>
> – Charles Bronson, Britain's most famous convict,
> writing in his autobiography, *Bronson*

After Sammy failed to forge a new vocation in either pub ownership or boxing management, his life took a turn which for a man of his nature would seem an unlikely transition. He became immersed in the criminal underworld and involved in armed robberies.

I ask Sammy whether he is willing to speak about this dark time in his life and he generously agrees to do so but prefaces his recollections by telling me, 'I'm not speaking openly about this because I'm proud of it; I'm quite ashamed of it. But it's something that happened and I want to tell you the truth.

'You worked with different people. You get a reputation for one thing or another and they get in touch with you, and obviously you wouldn't work with somebody you didn't know, and invariably, it's like boxing, you all get to know each other. They'd get to know what sort of work you do, what you're capable of, whether you're game, whether you can be trusted. Most of the guys know each other or know the people they work with.

'It was either banks or payrolls or lorries we robbed. It could be money going to a bank, money coming out of a bank. You could stop a security motor on the road or you could stop a lorry going north, south, east or west that may have a hell of a lot of either spirits or cigarettes on – and obviously these were all sold before you'd even attempted to get them. You had people buying them in advance.

'A couple of you might have guns but quite often, believe it or not, all you shot was Uncle Ben's Rice – 'cause it made just as loud a noise and it also drew blood, and if nothing else it would bloody frighten the life out of you, which is bad enough.

'If you was going on a very heavy robbery, though, like you were stopping a security van, you couldn't shoot Uncle Ben's Rice into it 'cause nothing would happen. You had to let them know inside that you had the real McCoy. But you wanted someone to get hurt like you wanted a hole in your head, because you knew if somebody got hurt the police were gonna come down even heavier than they would do normally, 'cause pressure would be put on them.

'I done three years in prison, I done six years, I done 15 years and people say to me, "Sam, they went very heavy on you," but everything I got, believe me I deserved.'

Sammy makes no complaint about his prison time and when I ask if he found it hard, he insists that, aside from missing his family, he did not. 'I had three good jobs: I was always in the gymnasium, which is really a good job. But even if it was a bad job, I'd have still got on with it because I'd been caught, been captured, and you're not gonna talk your way out of it, you're gonna have to do what you have to do.'

While serving time at Albany Prison on the Isle of Wight, Sammy became acquainted with Britain's most infamous inmate, Charles Bronson, who's since been the subject of numerous books and the 2008 film *Bronson*, in which he was played by the actor Tom Hardy.

'I knew about Charlie Bronson before I'd met him,' Sammy recalls. 'He wrote to me and I answered him and we corresponded occasionally. Then he was moved to Albany, where I'd been for some time, but he was segregated from everybody. After he'd been there a little while he started performing, as he did in most prisons. I think he broke a couple of records there for press-ups and one-armed press-ups, and they got the whole prison together to cheer him on – it's good PR for the prison.

'They used to take me down to his quarters, where he was segregated from everyone – a prison within a prison – to sit and talk to him, and he was as nice as pie. We'd talk continuously for hours about everything. He was always easy to talk to and it was always very interesting 'cause you never knew what he was gonna come out with.

'Quite often he'd get the prison officers into his cell and he'd kidnap them. He never hurt them – he was as gentle as can be with them – he probably just wanted company. He'd tie them up and make them pots of tea all day. Then they used to get me down from where I was working in the gym, down to his cell, to be with him for a couple of hours, talking to him – not calming him down, because he was calm anyway. I still keep in contact with him: he writes to me occasionally and I write back and I've been to see him.'

Talking in general about prison life, Sammy reflects, 'You get some very nice people there but at the same time you get the dregs of humanity. But having said that, although they're the dregs of humanity, in all probability they never had the chances in life that I had in the past. I'm not saying it makes them right, but understandable in some respects.

'I regret it now, not for the time I did but for what I did to my wife and family, my mother, father, brothers, sisters and my friends. It helped break up my marriage and I've suffered for it ever since, and bloody rightly so. My daughter, my son and my wife, they all suffered. They used to come to visit me every week, every month or whenever they could. No matter where I was, whether I was here or on the Isle of Wight, they were always there.'

When I ask Sammy why he turned to crime he jokes that the hours and money were good, before revealing what was probably the real root cause. 'When I started doing it I found it exciting and

I was always frightened of getting caught. It became almost like a drug. The bigger a thing was, the more frightening it was – it was like training for a bigger fight. I got a great high out of it. I'm not proud to say that but it's a fact.'

After serving a lengthy sentence at Albany, Sammy last left prison two decades ago and has remained on the straight and narrow ever since. 'Things happen in life,' he sighs, 'next time around I'll do it differently. I'd love to talk to young guys now about it and say how foolish I was, but whether this would help them or not, I don't know.'

Sammy Now

By 1950s standards Sammy earned a great deal of money with his talented fists. Boxing writer Gilbert Odd once estimated he had made around £50,000 through boxing, and while Sammy does not know the exact figure he says this is a reasonable guess.

'I must say all my purses were absolutely first-class,' he explains. 'I can't remember the exact figure but I think the most I got for a fight was about £4,000 or £4,500, which in 1955 when I defended my title in Belfast was a hell of a lot of money: you could probably buy a couple of houses with that or maybe even more.

'I earned a hell of a lot of money but where it went to I don't know. I never went out with girls unfortunately, I was never a boozer and I never went to clubs, but for some reason or other I didn't look after it, I used to knock it out right, left and centre. But never mind, you live and learn – you can't put an old head on young shoulders.'

Despite being a naturally shy and modest person who never courted publicity, Sammy admits he enjoyed fame. 'It's nice to be recognised,' he tells me, 'it doesn't do you any harm. Probably some people need it more than others. I think you get treated with a little more respect, which is always nice 'cause it's nice when people generally treat each other with respect. You treat someone with respect and they reciprocate.'

Today Sammy lives a calm existence but stays busy and as a member of the London Ex-Boxers Association regularly attends meetings and functions, always immaculately turned out on these occasions in a smart suit, shirt and tie. 'The people who used to follow me years ago, like all my cousins, I still see them now,' he says, 'and we still speak about boxing. And all my friends as boys, who followed me in boxing, we still see each other now and we talk about years ago as though it was yesterday.'

He also remains something of a fitness fanatic. 'I love going out, I love having a walk, going down the market and seeing old friends,' he says. 'I can walk for miles, although I'm having trouble with my knees at the moment, but that don't bother me. I still like keeping fit. Even right up until a little while ago, I used to run every day or go to the gymnasium and work out, and when my legs started to go I started to go swimming every morning. I don't mean some mornings; I was there every morning. But now all I do is walk. It's a great exercise because you're not pulling your guts out and yet you're moving all your joints and muscles.'

When we talk about modern boxing Sammy tells me, 'I watch the fights now and some of the fighters today are pretty good. I'm impressed with some of them but with others I'm not. I'll see a world title fight with two like six- or eight-round fighters. I'll think, "They're boxing for a world title," I can't comprehend this. But that's the way things are – good luck to them. Having said that, in defence of them I'll say, everything you look at years ago always seems to be better. I think the films were better years ago, but I don't know whether they were or not. Maybe it's my imagination.'

Despite the break-up of their marriage, Sammy and his former wife Sylvia remained firm friends. Sadly today she suffers from Alzheimer's and is in a nursing home, but Sammy, daughter Jackie and son Nicholas each visit her several times a week. 'I always say to people, "If you've got your health – on my life – you're a multi, multi millionaire",' Sammy tells me earnestly.[17*]

After three long prison sentences Sammy has more than re-paid whatever debt some may feel he owed society. The pleasure

---

17 Sadly, Sylvia passed away in October 2013, several months after my interview with Sammy.

he gave thousands of fight fans and the excitement and colour he brought to British boxing outweigh the mistakes he made in life.

When I ask Sammy how he earned his nickname, Smilin' Sammy, he reveals, 'I used to smile a lot, the reason being, I was so nervous and it was a defence thing.' When asked why he smiles just as brightly today he tells me, 'Even on my lowest day I think it's wonderful to be alive. I'm just happy being here.'

Today Sammy is regularly stopped in the street by Londoners (both men and women) of a certain age who remember his 1950s heyday with affection. Some are strangers to him while others are old friends, but all are cheered by meeting him. For he reminds them of a time when the East End was one big community: a time when dockers, market porters, costermongers, hawkers, pawnbrokers, rag and bone men, bus conductors, street bookmakers, pie and mash, jellied eels, trams, trolley buses, greyhound tracks and atmospheric, smoke-filled fight halls were part of London life.